Makunschan, Meeanjan, Miganchan, Meanjan, Magandjin

Every tribe ... has its own dialect, if not language ... stamps their locality much, know every acre of land belonging to their 'home'... each plant, flower, tree, shrub, grass, bird, beast, insect ... every mile of a river or watercourse its own appellation, from the highest source to the mouth or junction always had a name of its own.[1]

—Henry Stuart Russell

Gaja
Kerry
Charlton

Gaja Kerry Charlton is a Yagarabul person, an Elder and traditional owner in three native title claims—Yuggera Ugarapul Peoples, Quandamooka and Kabi Kabi—with Gulf ties to Walangama Country.

Edited by **Melissa Lucashenko**, an award-winning novelist, essayist, short story writer and editor of Goorie and European heritage.

The invitation to write for the *Meanjin* magazine is welcomed in the spirit of Reconciliation and Truth-telling. I share from my *Goori doogal* (Aboriginal heart) about my family and tribes, culture and history with colonisation; our *Wularanguru* historical language mapping project; and of matters still to be resolved, including the original language placenames. 'Brisbane, port, the capital of Queensland, Australia and the country's third largest city. It lies astride the Brisbane River on the southern slopes of the Taylor Range, 12 miles (19 km) above the river's mouth at Moreton Bay.'[2]

Our 500-year strategic plans

Our Elders' words echo always—language is culture, culture is language—but what does this mean with a history of being forcibly removed, shredded by disconnection? Goori-ness hinges on connection to Country. Unpacking original placenames and their meaning is paramount for Truth-telling, and healing People and Country in the

1
Henry Stuart Russell, *Genesis of Queensland*, 1888, p. 315.

2
'Brisbane', Britannica Online.

3
UN Declaration of the
Rights of Indigenous
Peoples.

4
*Industrial and
Reformatory Schools
Act 1865; Native
Labourers' Protection
Act of 1884; Protection
of Aboriginals and
Restriction of the Sale
of Opium Act 1897.*

5
K. Charlton and
B. Brown, 'Languages
of Moreton Bay ... '
transcription by
K. Charlton from taped
interview of *Winyuba*
(Mary Jane Sunflower
Morton), by Elwyn
Flint, c. 1960. 2019,
p. 1.

6
Commonly used
term that refers to
our languages.

7
Uncle Steven Coghill
and Moreton family
Elders.

8
Yagara Djarra and its
nearest neighbours
with approximate
boundaries.
Wularanguru map of
languages of Moreton
Bay, 2019–2023.

9
Kate Ballard, *Brisbane,
the Beginning: Being a
story of 18th Century
Miganchan ...*, 2007,
p. 5.

light of *Story of Place*. Self-determined language repatriation is a fundamental right of First Nations peoples.[3] Several acts of government implemented in Queensland exerted increasing levels of control over the lives of its First Peoples.[4] The *Protection of Aboriginals and Restriction of the Sale of Opium Act 1897 (The Act)* increased institutionalised racism and assimilation through forced removals of First Nations peoples, firstly the vulnerable and sick, then all, from family, tribe, Country. Our Moreton Tribe was impacted for six generations by 'the Act'—a time of attempted assimilation, destruction and terrible losses. Siblings *Mookin* and *Winyuba* secured exemptions after decades under its rule. Back on Country they were concerned to find their languages being inaccurately published, including placenames.[5] The mandate from our Elders was to 'get it right, do it our way'—'protocols proper way' to repair and protect our culture and lingo.[6] Now we are Elders. Our *Yagara—Magandjin* Aboriginal Corporation continues their Vision. We talk in terms of 500-year strategic plans; of cultural custodianship, and sustainability, for our grandchildren's grandchildren.[7]

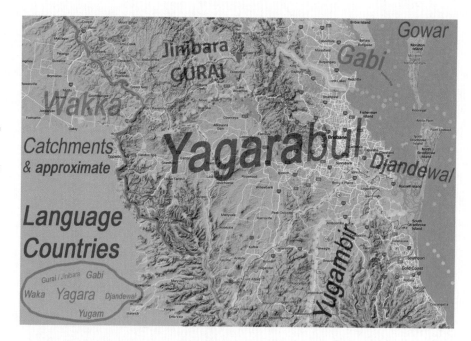

Ancient Cultural Connections

The above coastal map shows *Yagara* country and bordering language neighbours in this section of Moreton Bay.[8] Their names *Gabi (Kabi), Wakka, Yugam* and *Jinibara's Gurai* are derived from the negator word in each of their languages for no, not, nothing, never, nowhere, etc.[9] Suffixes *-bul, -wal, -bir* denote 'is, is of'; *-bara*: people or group; *-uba*: uses first word as a name.

Who am I? Firstly, I am *Yagarabul and Gabi Gabi* with ties to *Walangama* in North Queensland. *Goori way*, I am a senior cultural custodian. *Dugai way* I hold formal teacher, trainer and counsellor qualifications. I'm also a researcher and writer.

We have tribal ties across the southeast and are recognised as traditional owners in three registered native title claims: 1. *Quandamooka*, 2. *Yuggera Ugarapul* Peoples (YUP), and 3. *Kabi Kabi* (*Gabi Gabi*).

Quandamooka, the name chosen for the first native title claim, means 'Spirit of the Dolphin'[10] or 'the Spirit of Moreton Bay'[11] based on a creation story about the culturally significant relationship between Goori and dolphins in Moreton Bay. The *Yagara* name for Moreton Bay is *Boroogar*.

Our Moreton family's completed connection report shows our intangible cultural heritage—family oral history—confirmed in records. Tangible connection to *Djerrangerri*, our original name for Stradbroke Islands, verifies these old ties through *Mookin*'s father. It states:

> The Moreton descent group is said to have descended from Charlie Moreton, *Dandruba*. The documentary records are consistent with the oral history regarding the existence of *Dandruba* at North Stradbroke Island at or around the time of settlement.[12]

Mookin, son of *Dandruba*, was our great grandfather and grandson of *Kerwalli*, King Sandy of Brisbane. Born in 1871 at Amity Point on *Djerrangerri*, his remarkable athletic and linguistic abilities earmarked him to be a message-stick bearer, and holder of knowledges across Queensland. Naturally, *Mookin* received training and knowledge from his renowned grandfather. *Kerwalli* provided names and story of place including Mt. Kut-ha. In 1905, a journalist interviewed his daughter *Dinaba*, *Mookin*'s mother, on the meaning of the name Wynnum (*winnam*).

When *Ngugi* author Paul Tripcony asked *Mookin* about any known letters on any 'Aboriginal Letter Sticks', he replied, 'What we classed as letters were signs that the sender of the letter stick, and the person who received the same, and their close associates, understood the symbols engraved on the letter sticks as containing news of past events, or heralded the prediction of future important tribal ceremonies,

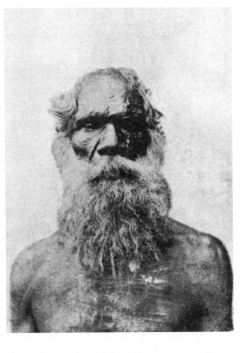

Kerwalli, grandfather of Mookin, told naturalist James Craig that he was 'King of the tribe' of the land where Brisbane now stands. In James W. Craig, Australian Joint Copying Project, National Library of Australia, and State Library of New South Wales: Papers of James Whitelaw Craig [microform]: [M978] 1873–1877; entries 5 and 23 December 1875.

10
Donna Ruska, personal communications, 2000–17.

11
Christine Peacock, *History, Life and Times of Robert Anderson, Gheebelum, Ngugi, Mulgumpin*, 2001, p. 64.

12
Quandamooka native title claim, summary of Moreton family connection report, 2007.

13
Paul Tripcony
(1901–1975),
Manuscript
Moongalba: Birthplace
of a Great Chief,
Stradbroke Island.

14
'A completed warrior'
who had achieved all
feats of initiation and
ceremony.

15
Moreton Family
Cultural Oral History,
Indigenous Cultural
Intellectual Property.

and also the sealing and ratification of a previous sacred ceremonial agreement on the subject of peace and friendship. The person delivering a Message Stick was given safe conduct throughout the territory of his travels.'[13]

Mookin was a renowned *Malara*[14] remembered by others as a visitor to their Country, who travelled long distances and spoke many languages. Most Goori spoke more than one language. Such cultural roles brought resistance to taking 'exemption', a key tool of assimilation, with the condition requiring applicants agree they were no longer an Aborigine; didn't associate with Aborigines which limited culture and speaking ones' lingo. *Mookin* and *Winyuba* were among a group of old knowledge holders on the reserves working to preserve Goori knowledges, language and culture to protect it from 'extinction', an intention of the Act! Both were recorded by academics. The tapes and written materials are vital to resourcing our language repatriation and maintenance for future generations.

Healing the past brings a healed future

Table 1. The below *Goori Nharul-Milen* (family/kin group) table illustrates the Moreton Tribe's ancestral affiliations, languages and territories based on Country, flora and fauna. Read across the table to learn about the names of Moreton family members, their clans/tribes, and where they were based. *NB This work is my Indigenous Cultural Intellectual Property. It is not to be used without my written permission. This is our Goori Milpulbul (living Goori).*[15] © *Kerry Charlton*

Family Members		Clans / Tribes		Place or Area	
Names	**Translation**	**Clan / Tribe Names**	**Translation**	**Place Names**	**Translation**
Mookin / Mugin Yagara (son of Dinaba and Dander-uba) 1871–1949	Big, strong Uses Country as a name -uba: suffix	Koenpal / Goenpul Janderwal / Jandai Kirkham / Gergum Ngunda (Ngoonda) Joondabari/Undanbi	Pearl oyster shellfish Narrow leaf Ironbark tree Brisbane – Yagara tribe He / she is, very coastal -bari: group; -gal: 'is of'	ɡerraŋeri Goompi, ɡerraŋeri Magan-djin Gabi Gabi	Stradbroke Island Dunwich, Strad.Is. Tulipwood trees Negator word
Winyuba, Janie (1883–1964)	Dugong bird -yuba (same as -uba suffix)	Janderwal / Jandai Kirkham / Gergum Ngunda (Ngoonda)	Narrow leaf Ironbark tree Brisbane – Yagara tribe He / she is, very coastal	Goompi, ɡerraŋeri Magan-djin Gabi Gabi	Dunwich, Strad.Is. Tulipwood trees Negator word
Di:naba / Sarah (mother of Mookin and Winyuba, 1845–1907)	Clan name	Gergum/Kercoom Gorbenpan Ngunda (Ngoonda)	Brisbane – Yagara tribe Brisbane – Yagara tribe He / she is, very coastal	Magan-djin Benarrawa Gabi Gabi	Tulipwood tree Oxley, Oxley Ck. Negator word
Danderuba Charlie Moreton (c. 1840–1873)	Ironbark tree -uba: suffix	Danderr / Tanderoo Koenpul / Goenpal	Ironbark tree, thin leaf Pearl oyster shellfish	Goompi ɡerraŋeri	Dunwich area Stradbroke Is.
Nawin / Sarah (c. 1825–1880)	Dugong bird	Ngunda (Ngoonda) Darabul / Turrbal	She / he is, very coastal Oyster, clan / tribe name	Nambor – Pine River Ngooyeera	Ti (tea) tree Toorbal Point
Kaerwalli / Gairballie King Sandy (c. 1820–1900)	Split, spilt Yandee	Gergum / Kercoom Gorbenpan Ninge Ninge	Brisbane – Yagara tribe Brisbane – Yagara tribe Oyster, Redcliffe group	Magan-djin Benarrawa Gabi Gabi	Brisbane district Oxley Creek Negator word

The *Wulara-Nguru* historical language mapping project

Wulara-Nguru is a historical language mapping and repatriation project mandated by the Moreton Elders. The term 'repatriation' points to our history of colonial conflicts, resistance and dispossession.[16] The definition 'to return one to their Country' accurately describes our situation. We didn't 'just stop' using our languages. It was forcibly removed from daily use under the Act instituted to 'smooth the dying pillow' for survivors of colonial terrorism.[17] Begun in 2007, after a decade or so of initial community-based language revival efforts, it consists of myself and *Dugai* colleague Barry Brown and a Language Support Group. *Wulara* means speak, talk, language, while *Nguru* is shadow, spirit or breath. We're a work in progress. As a Language Fellow at the University of Queensland in the School of Languages and Cultures, I'm involved in transcribing the tapes for reconstruction of our language and community-based programs. We have achieved a substantial database of the languages of *Yagara* country and south-east Queensland. The years of data compilation, evolving methodology and cautious surveying led to our 2019 lexical handbook, *An Introduction to the Languages of Moreton Bay: Yagarabul and its dialect Djandewal and Moreton Island's Gowar.* It's a major step towards our vision of 'healed' language; community-based language programs and growing language fluency. This field periodically emerges waves of vicarious trauma from what eminent *Yagara* Elder Dr Aileen Moreton-Robinson describes as 'ontological disturbances from encounters with the white western paradigm, racial blindness and cultural bias.'[18] We work to heal *Budjang dja*, Mother earth, too.

It's important to highlight that many language words were historically recorded with multiple spelling demonstrating the challenges for early writers with foreign ears attempting to phoneticise an ancient language. Versions of *Yagara* include *Yuggera*, *Yuggara, Yugara, Jagera, Jagara, Ugara* and *Ugarapul.* Margaret Sharpe, a linguist of Australian Aboriginal languages who specialised in *Yugambeh – Bundjalung*, with special regard to *Yugambir*, explained this comes from linguists trained in Europe, using the International Phonetic Alphabet (IPA), which writes the small 'j' for the 'y' sound in 'yes'. 'In German, "j" is used for the "y" sound, but some Germans who kindly wrote down Australian languages did use "y" because they were writing for an English reading audience. "Y"s should always be read as "Y"s.'[19] In his consonant sounds list, Nils Holmer wrote: '"j" is a palatal semivowel, like "y" in English "yes"'.[20] We knew the *Yagara* word early as a name for great grandfather *Mookin.* His sister *Winyuba* (Janie Sunflower) confirms its pronunciation on tape recordings by academics from the University of Queensland.[21] *Yagara* is said correctly with a 'y' sound.

In our research *Wulara-Nguru* works to a four-level ratings scale with sources of language, which include original Goori speakers of south-east Queensland languages, and colonial collectors (c.1825–1900). These elderly language speakers born around and after the 1870s, whose languages and knowledges remained intact despite incarceration under the Act, were recorded on tapes between 1950-60. *Wulara-Nguru*'s four-level scale starts at 0: the native speaker; 1: you're at the source, speaking with, listening to and learning from a native speaker; 2: you're reading records of primary

16
Rod Fisher (ed.), *Brisbane: The Aboriginal Presence 1824–1860*, Brisbane History Group, 1992.

17
Rural Health Training Unit, *Cairns: Introduction to Recent Aboriginal and Torres Strait Islander History in Queensland*, 1997, p. 8.

18
Aileen Moreton-Robinson, *Talkin' Up to the White Woman: Indigenous Women and Feminism*, p. xi, 20th anniversary edition, preface, p. xi, 2020

19
Margaret Sharpe, Report to FAIRA on the Linguistic Literature of the Brisbane Region, July 2000, p. 6.

20
Nils Holmer, 1983, *Linguistic Survey of south Eastern Queensland*, p. 390

21
Janie Sunflower (Moreton) to Lindsay Winterbotham, 1940s to 1963.

22
F.J. Watson,
'Vocabularies of Four
Representative Tribes
of Southeastern
Queensland'.
Supplement to
*Journal of the
Royal Geographical
Society of Australasia*
(Queensland), p. 9.

23
Edmund Lockyer,
Esquire, 'Journal of
an Excursion up the
River Brisbane in the
Year 1825', *Australian
Quarterly Journal*,
vol. 1 (1828), p. 590.

24
Thomas Petrie, 'Letter
to Editor: Native Name
of the Brisbane River'
in *Science of Man*,
22 Jan, 1902, p. 203.

25
Constance Campbell-
Petrie, *Tom Petrie's
Reminiscences of
Queensland* (Brisbane:
Watson, Ferguson &
Co., 1904).

26
Niel Gunson,
'A Missionary
Expedition from
Zion Hill (Nundah)
to Toorbul, Moreton
Bay District', in
1842–43: The Journal
of the Reverend
K.W.E. Schmidt, from
Aboriginal History,
vol. 2, 1–2, 1978,
p. 120.

source who spoke with, learnt from the source, a native speaker; 3: you're hearing from or reading a secondary source who was informed by primary sources. Therefore, the higher the score, the further away from the original Goori speaker the material is. In the early days of colonial presence, First Nations language speakers taught their few *Dugai* friends and allies their languages. These became fluent speakers, primary sources and some recognised 'experts'. Prevailing racial attitudes or ignorant assumptions led to excluding original speakers from providing correct information. Watson wrote: 'For many years, there have been no full-blooded *Yugarabul* who could speak the language.'[22] At the same time native speakers like *Mookin*, *Winyuba* and others were locked away on reserves continuing to speak their languages with each other. The incomplete or mixed-up vocabulary continued be regurgitated.

Magandjin the district; Darabul (Turrabul) Tribe; Yagara the country

> Several natives were seen on the side of river opposite to the settlement
> [Edenglassie] ... Natives upwards of 30 men, women and children; seemed
> desirous to cross the river had swam across higher up ... couldn't be persuaded
> into the settlement nearer than 2 or 3 hundred yards; where they remained
> looking at (for about an hour) the buildings and the cattle for about an hour,
> then went off and weren't seen again ...[23]

This group witnessed incomprehensible changes: destruction of the village, renamed river and site. Some original names have persisted since, albeit with distortions, *Meanjin* being one. Popular use, however, does not make it accurate. It is the right of First Nations peoples to address historical errors. The desire to support some reinstatement of the right language on Country is influenced by Reconciliation, Truth-telling and Healing; the UN's Declaration on the Rights of Indigenous People of 2007 and International Decade of the World's Indigenous Languages, as well as Queensland's *Human Rights Act*; Many Voices Indigenous Languages Policy and Tracks to Treaty.

Reports show early collections of vocabularies recorded between 1836 and 1878. These informed each other and later collectors, some of whom appear in this article. Thomas (Tom) Petrie was six years old when he and his family arrived in Brisbane in 1837 and began learning the languages of his Goori playmates. Eventually he excelled in what he called the '*Turrubul*' language and tribe.[24] Tom's understanding of and friendships with Goori people proved providential during an era of colonial influx. He became a primary source who provided vocabularies to many, including Reverend Ridley and Archibald Meston, who became secondary sources. Each generated substantial public interest and greatly influenced all the following writers, shaping knowledge, and errors, about Goori language, clan, tribe and Country.

In 1841 Reverend Eipper wrote: 'The Aborigines of the district were subdivided into small tribes, each of which has a certain territory allotted to it, from which they generally derive their names; may number from 50 to 60. Tribal areas could span up to 60 miles, each with a recognised leader.'[26] Reverend Schmidt related about a trip to

Map of Brisbane Town in 1839 from Tom Petrie's *Reminiscences of Queensland*.[25]

Toorbul and Wide Bay, Moreton Bay District in 1842–43, that Aboriginal guides refused to go beyond *Durundur*, then the limit of settlement.[27] In fact they were observing Goori lore-law protocols with territorial boundaries.

In 1851, Tom Petrie supplied Ridley with *Turrubul* vocabulary for his collection projects.[28] The Melbourne Exhibition 1868 procured a survey of vocabulary in 1866 from Petrie and his co-author *Nununga*, a *Kabi* man.[29] Two newspapers reported on the two 'dialects' used around Murrumba and the Pine Rivers catchment, describing 'Thurwell' as additional to the better-known Brisbane 'dialect'. Ridley wrote 'we see

27
Rev. Niel Gunson, 'Journal of K.W.E. Schmidt to Toorbul, Moreton Bay District, in 1842–43'. p. 115.

28
Rev. Ridley, *Moreton Bay Courier*, Saturday 1 December 1855, p. 2.

29
Sydney Mail (Guardian), 14 July 1866, p. 6.

30
Sydney Morning
Herald, 10 July 1866,
p. 2; R.H. Mathews,
'L.S. Aborigines of the
Northern Ter., W. Aus
and Q'Land', p. 11.

31
Marcel Aurousseau,
ed. The Letters of
F.W. Ludwig Leichhardt,
(Farnham: Ashgate
Publishing, 2010).

32
Nils Holmer, Other
Languages of South-
Eastern Queensland,
p. 402.

33
Dennis Bannister,
MS2171, IAIAS Folder
7, Njula The Aboriginal
Language of Bribie
Island. p. 4.

34
Edward Harper.
The Queenslander:
'The Early Days on
the Tweed. Some
Errors about the
Blacks'. Saturday
1 September 1894,
p. 410. National Library
of Australia <http://
nla.gov.au/nla.news-
article20719678>.

35
'The Old Brisbane
Blacks', Brisbane Courier,
Saturday 31 August
1901, p. 15 National
Library of Australia.

36
Brisbane Courier,
Saturday 31 August
1901, p. 15.

37
Gaiarbau cited in John
Gladstone Steele,
Aboriginal Pathways: in
Southeast Queensland
and the Richmond
River, University of
Queensland Press,
1984, figure 81, p. 161.

38
Brisbane Courier, 10
September 1901, p. 7.

39
Malcolm D. Prentis,
'Research and
friendship: John
Mathew and his
Aboriginal Informants',
Aboriginal History,
vol. 22, 1998, p. 64.

40
Dennis Bannister
(1986) Manuscript
#2171, Archibald
Meston's words and
placenames collected
1870s – 1900s, AIATSIS.

Turrbul, Durubul and Turrbal as the same dialect name pronounced with a softened "b" and an aspirated (breathy) initial consonant, 1866's Thur-well for Turr-bal ... the native Brisbane dialect and the Thurwell dialect ...'[30] Ludwig Leichhardt described his visit with the Nynga-Nynga (Ningy Ningy) tribe, at Turrabool Point, in September 1843, describing the Turrabool and Bribie tribes as 'a fine race of men, tall and well made'. Archibald Meston in 1923 called them and their language Churrabool'[31] the 'Darabul' mentioned by Yagara speakers to Holmer in 1970.[32] Turbal / Durbal is a Kabi word for oyster.[33] Turrubal is the name of a clan or tribe, not the Country.

Reverend Eipper wrote about the Brisbane language, describing it as 'very meagre as their words go no farther than their wants or employments'; an unsupported view. In contrast, in 1875, Ridley wrote of the grammatical structure that 'the inflections of verbs and nouns, the derivation and composition of words, the arrangement of sentences, and the methods of imparting emphasis, indicate an accuracy of thought, and a force of expression, surpassing all that is commonly supposed to be attainable by a savage race'.

Ned Harper, well-known timber-getter and intimate friend of Aborigines, and therefore a primary source, stated: 'the whole of the blacks on the southside of Moreton Bay and all along its shores to Amity Point use the word Yug-ger-a-bool to signify their respective dialects. The Lytton and South Brisbane blacks used the same word.'[34] Meston correctly identified distinct languages existed in southeast Queensland. His public attention to the 'Turrubul' vocabulary, given by Petrie to Ridley in 1851 and consisting of four languages ignited debates between them. Meston's access to native speakers at Deebing Creek mission,[35] where Mookin was also, generated new information; Meston was remiss in naming the speakers. He too caused confusion, writing both that Wakka was the language and tribute of Brisbane and Wakka one of the negator words spoken on Fraser Island.[36]

Confusion would later reign when colonial reporters mixed ethnonyms (tribal names) with glottonyms (the names of languages). The whole of Moreton Bay between Deception Bay and the Jumpinpin area is in the eastern part of the Yagara language group. This includes the river mouth regions of the Pine, Brisbane and Logan. Hay's Inlet (Redcliffe) forms the coastal boundary that runs northwest. This is Yagara-speaking country to the southwest and Kabi-speaking country to the northeast.[37]

In 1901 Meston and Petrie again debated Yagara or Turrubul, despite the Yagara speakers now at Purga mission outside Ipswich. Meston's son Leo, like Watson, later helped explain how decades of analysis were needed before the confusion could be properly dealt with, writing: 'Ridley and my father acquired their first knowledge of the Brisbane River and Moreton Bay dialects from Tom Petrie, and verified and extended it through their own observations among the aborigines.'[38]

Reverend John Mathew, Kabi specialist and author, considered that apart from native speakers, Tom Petrie was most knowledgeable with Kabi Kabi languages,[39] Archibald Meston foremost with Yagara language.[40] Jinibara Elder Gaiarbau related that he knew and talked with both men; that both mixed up words of one tribe with those of another; Petrie, who chiefly spoke the *Undumbi* tongue very fluently, but did not know the *Jinibara* tribe and its dialect, had affirmed both as one tribe. *Gaiarbau*—also fluent in *Undumbi*—gave him the correct details.[41]

Leo Meston commented on the confusion of dialects on the Brisbane River in Petrie's time and the influx of native speakers from other areas.[42] Watson identified that learning a local language often involved becoming familiar with any neighbouring dialects, and that 'Tom Petrie was most familiar with the blacks who lived near his father's property on the north of the Pine River, and near to the boundary of the territories of the Toorbal and Kabi tribes, and he could speak their languages, the local one fluently.'[43] Norman Tindale's interview in 1938 with original *Yagara* speakers at Cherbourg and inclusion of *Dugai* writers brought both clarity and confusion when he wrote of the *Jagara* (*Jagarabal*), 'their language was *Turubul*, also *Ninghe*.'[44]

Watson analyses the linguistic diversity in southeast Queensland, in particular the border country where he worked for many years. He specifies 'lingual division' in the title of his 1940 pamphlet, *A vocabulary of the language of the Yuggerabul lingual division of Australian aborigines and, incidentally, of the Turrbul sub-tribe at Brisbane.* Watson rightly distinguished the non-linguistic term and the broader, overarching 'lingual' name *Yugarabul*. He wrongly used a *Yugam* word, speculating on the *Turrbul* name meaning of the word as 'People of the Stones'.[45] Perhaps he was inspired by an article about the Toara (To'-a-ra) Ceremony.[46] Leo Meston rightly corrected a suggested meaning behind 'tar'au-bul': '*Darra* does not mean "stones", as stated by Mr Watson.'[47] It's 'stone' or 'stoney' in *Yugam*.[48] The next major linguistic survey was Holmer in 1970–72 but his key material was based on Watson, who based his work on Ridley and Petrie. Anyone using Holmer will continue this cycle of sourcing incomplete and inaccurate material.

This demonstrates why early wordlists and languages spoken must be carefully cross-referenced before inferences are made about tribes, their district and territorial boundaries.

Original names of Brisbane: Magandjin, Miganchan, Meeanjan

> Where Brisbane stands today, was covered mostly by scrub, very thick on the site of the Botanic Gardens, where the tulip trees, *Maginnchin*, gave the 'aboriginal' name to the Brisbane River.[49]

The original name of Brisbane can be traced back to just two phonetic versions of the one name. The table below shows the history associated with them. An examination of the Original Speakers who passed their information to primary sources is crucial in determining which is the likely name. Also critical is correct cultural information based on ancient oral history, some of which appears in the *Goori Nharul-Milen* table. There are possibly three explanations of the same word for spike (*migan*): the shape of the point, ground being dug up, and weaponry.

41
Gaiarbau, in L.P. Winterbotham, *Gaiarbau's Story of the Jinibara Tribe of South East Queensland, 1950–1957* Manuscript. University of Queensland.

42
L.A. Meston, 'Letter to the Editor: Wooloowin and Wonga', *Brisbane Courier*, Fri 5 Jun 1931. p. 15.

43
Brisbane Courier, 9 June 1931, p. 5.

44
Norman B. Tindale, *Aboriginal Tribes of Australia*, Australian National University Press, Canberra. 1974, p. 169.

45
F.J. Watson, *Turrubul or Turrbul: a sub-division of the lingual division of Yugarabul aborigines which occupied the territory about what is now the City of Brisbane*, 1940.

46
R.H. Mathews, 'The Toara Ceremony of the Dippil Tribes of Queensland', *American Anthropologist (N.S.)*, vol. 2, January 1900.

47
Courier-Mail, 2 September 1933, p. 7.

48
F.J. Watson, F. R. G. S. A. *Vocabularies of Four Representative Tribes of South Eastern Queensland*. University of Queensland. p. 62.

49
Daily Mail, 1 December 1923, p. 9; Trove at NLA, <https://trove.nla.gov.au/newspaper/article/218970350>.

Table 2. Table shows historical distortions of Yagara name for Brisbane

Name	Meaning	Sources
Magoo'jan Magan Magandjin / Maganchin	Tulipwood Tree Tulipwood district	Yagara speakers to Meston
Makandschin Megandsin	Region from the mission to Breakfast Cree	Yagara speaker Kabi Kabi speaker to Leichhardt
Magenchen Magenjie / Meeanchin Mi-an-jin (Me-an-jin) Meeannjin / Meegannchin	Brisbane, Brisbane River Name of the Garden Point from the bridge round to Creek Street, taking in the settlement	Petrie
Miantjun, Mientjin	Town	Ridley
Magandjin Meeanchin Meeanjin / Meeannjin Meegannchin	Brisbane River Brisbane Brisbane River Brisbane River	Meston
Migan Dhagun (chargun) Djarra / char / dja' etc.	Spike (Yagara word) Yugam word for earth, ground, soil Yagara for ground, soil, country	Petrie Watson Charlton and Brown
Migan Chagum / Migan Chagun Miganchan / Mianchan Meginchin, Meginchen	Name for early Brisbane from Migan chagun 'place or land shaped like a spike' for land where Botanical Gardens and Domain form the point	Watson and versions Ballard collected from newspapers
Miguntyun Megendjen (-djin) Megenden /Migindjin Megendjin)	Brisbane Tribe Name of a tribe on lower Brisbane River (Toorbal tribe), later the native name of Brisbane	Bunjoey in Bell Holmer via Tripcony via Watson

Leichhardt offers the earliest written source of the name for Brisbane, which includes the Gardens Point area as shown in Petrie's map. In 1843, he was given two names: *Makandschin* from an original Brisbane man and *Megandsin* from an original speaker from a different country.[50] Ridley via Petrie wrote *Miantjun* and *Mientjin*. Meston listed *Magoo-jin* then *Magandjin*, based on *Magan*, the name of the Tulipwood tree, from elderly Goori speakers who asserted they were 'Brisbane natives'. Their knowledge is based on *Goori Nharul-Milen*.

From a Goori knowledge base the names based on the Tulipwood tree fits best for the original Goori name. The suffix -djin indicates plural, e.g. people, district, river. The *Migan-dar-gu-n* (*Mi'andjan*) version describes the use of a sharp tool, possibly ground being dug up, likely the first convict garden, which the Petrie map shows multiplied across the whole of the promontory. Another explanation of this name is 'land shaped like a spike'. Both these are based on *Dugai* activity and *Dugai* lens. Dredging of the river for navigation purposes further defined the shape. The secondary names are the result of the arrival of newcomers, not from Goori customs.

50
Darragh and Fensham, 'Memoirs of the Queensland Museum' *Culture* vol. 7 pt. 1, 2013; The Leichhardt diaries: Early travels in Australia during 1842–1844' Edited by Thomas A. Darragh and Roderick J. Fensham, Queensland Museum 30 June 2013.

Spike is a foreign word. Goori technology of agriculture based on cultural beliefs and spirituality differed greatly to the European practice of rendering all the ground bare due to our spiritual connections to ground, flora and fauna. For example, my family history connects my totem *Cabool*, carpet snake, to the grasstree as brothers, which determined our practice. Our Creation Stories give us specific spiritual connections to sites and aspects of language regarded sacred; sign language; gendered language—words that belonged to the women which men could not use and vice versa. *Mookin*'s custodial role prevented him being recorded on tapes although he guided the stories and language that could be shared. He gave permission for *Winyuba* and *Gaiabau* to be recorded, specifying content that could be discussed. This is based on our traditions and customs. It can't be freely shared. Therefore, harming or eradicating trees on a massive scale breaks Goori lore/law. These traditions and customs live on through family oral history, intangible and tangible cultural heritage. *Magandjin* fits as the original word for an area of what is now called Brisbane. *Migandjan* refers to digging the ground—either gardens or buildings. However, the term *Migandjan* spread.

As demonstrated, language repatriation is a work in progress. Because of the extremely close connections between languages, wider First Nations cultures and ways of relating to and belonging on Country, it is of the utmost importance that First Nations languages be recorded and transmitted accurately. It's also imperative that historical mistakes be acknowledged and rectified. Goori wisdom guides us to the future. As Pat Dodson said, 'Nothing about us without us.'

Wirrepi: Return to us.

• • •

Gaja Kerry Charlton is an Elder and traditional owner from south-east Queensland, with ties to the Gulf. Her Tribes are recognised in three native title claims: *Quandamooka*, *Yuggera Ugarapul* (YUP), and *Kabi Kabi* Peoples, and she was taught by elderly speakers while growing up. Gaja Kerry is a trained teacher, counsellor, community worker, cultural educator and consultant, and an experienced member of boards, committees and working groups. With colleague Barry Brown, Gaja Kerry co-founded the Wulara-Nguru historical language mapping project, publishing a lexical handbook titled 'An Introduction to the Languages of Moreton Bay, Yagarabul, and its dialect Djandewal, and Moreton Island's Gowar' to celebrate the 2019 United Nations Year of Languages of the World's Indigenous Peoples. The Wulara-Nguru lexical handbook contains comprehensively researched and compiled word lists, surveyed words and cultural insights to assist language revitalisation across Moreton Bay and south-east Queensland. Twelve years of inquiry produced this exceptional resource for language custodians and their partners in reclaiming languages. Gaja Kerry is Indigenous Industry Fellow at the School of Languages and Cultures at the University of Queensland.

Meanjin

Vol 82 No 2
Winter 2023

Meanjin

EDITOR
Esther Anatolitis

DEPUTY EDITOR
FICTION EDITOR
Tess Smurthwaite

meanjin@unimelb.edu.au

CULTURAL AND LITERARY
ADVISORY
Dan Bourchier, Sophie
Cunningham AM, Winnie
Dunn, Samantha Faulkner,
Grace Lucas-Pennington,
Jinghua Qian, Christos Tsiolkas

POETRY EDITOR
Bronwyn Lea

CULTURE EDITOR
Cher Tan

COPYEDITOR
Richard McGregor

PROOFREADER
Jack Callil

ARCHIVES ASSISTANT
Emma Sutherland

INTERNS
Eliza Callil
Tah Ai Jia

DESIGNER
Stephen Banham

LAYOUT
Patrick Cannon
Set in Berlingske

COVER DESIGN
Stephen Banham

Printed and bound by
Printgraphics
rod@printgraphics.com.au
Distributed by Penguin
Random House
AU ISSN 0025-6293

FOUNDING EDITOR
Clem Christesen
(1911–2003; Editor
1940–1974)

Meanjin was founded in
Magandjin (Brisbane) in 1940.
In considering the journal's
name, Christesen felt (after
Lawrence Durrell) that 'the
important determinant of
any culture is, after all—the
spirit of place'. For this reason,
Christesen chose the name
'meanjin' (pronounced
MEE-an-jin), a Yagara word
for the site where central
Brisbane sits.

SUBSCRIPTIONS
BACK ISSUES
CONTRIBUTIONS
meanjin.com.au

WRITING FOR *MEANJIN*
Submissions are welcome
and guidelines are on our
website. Please join the
mailing list to be notified
when submissions open.

Meanjin is an editorially
independent imprint of
Melbourne University
Publishing (MUP). The
copyright of each piece
belongs to the author;
copyright of the collection
belongs to *Meanjin* at MUP.

WHERE TO FIND US
Meanjin
Melbourne University
Publishing
Level 1, 715 Swanston St
Carlton VIC 3053 AUSTRALIA
+61 3 9035 3333

What is language doing?

How does it enlist us into its project? What does it presume to fix for all time? What is it constantly unsettling?

What is literary about oral culture? Does oral culture only become literature once it's written down? Is literature reading, or writing, or learning?

Is the arbiter of spelling the printing press, the dictionary, the style guide, the spelling bee, or the legislature? Do typefaces have intention?

How does transliteration undermine the authority of the word? How does it make visible what language strives to hide?

What is private about language? What is public?

What makes a place public? Does that make it ours? Or everybody's? Or nobody's?

Has *Meanjin* helped normalise a place name spelling that was never intended to become authoritative?

What is this place called? Why did this place need a name? What gives someone the right to name something? Where in Magandjin does Meanjin exist? Who held the digging stick, what is the spike, and where are the tulipwood trees?

What is cast up into the air the moment a sentence has formed itself into a question? How does your breath change? What does anticipation feel like?

How does your accent belie your politics? Or someone else's politics? «Τα ελληνικά σας είναι τέλεια», they say to me. «Πού τα μάθατε;»

What escapes—and what is exhausted by—the constraints of this language I never chose? Can't I play with it ... just a little?

Are the tools of the writer too hidden (in plain sight) for their work to be recognised as a profession? How do we champion the writers of the future?

Who writes the future? Who wrote the past? What happens when we try to write the present?

Ἐν ἀρχῇ ἦν ὁ Λόγος, so how have we come instead to privilege the Word? How does the Dreaming dissolve any question of beginnings? How does Country speak today? Who should we ask to tell it to us? 'Wirrepi': In returning, in giving back, how might we create something new?

What does writing perform? What does it co-opt? What does it colonise?

Is it possible to be heard without a voice?

• • •

Esther Anatolitis

Σταθία Ανατολίτη

Journalism and the Referendum

'A Proposed Law: to alter the Constitution to recognise the First Peoples of Australia by establishing an Aboriginal and Torres Strait Islander Voice. Do you approve this proposed alteration?'

This is the question all enrolled Australians will be asked later this year. Yes or No. They are the options you will have in the privacy of the ballot box—to make your determination. When you look at it like that, it appears a simple prospect. And a very simple question. But it's not.

Sitting behind that question is the much more complicated pathway that led to this vote: the complexity of colonisation and its lasting impacts; the pain and intergenerational trauma of the White Australia policy; the forced removal of children that led to the Stolen Generations. Then there is the crippling disparity in life expectancy, health and education outcomes, overincarceration in prison—just some of the measures of Closing the Gap, the majority of which are going backwards. The annual reporting of which Professor Marcia Langton described as a 'misery fest'.

That 'a young Aboriginal man of 18 in Australia is more likely to end up in jail than university', as then-opposition leader Bill Shorten noted in 2015, should ring alarm bells and prompt a jarring halt in the status quo—regardless of what the next steps are to address that. Arguably the dial has hardly moved in the eight years since Shorten said that.

'Yes' campaigners say a Voice to Parliament is the circuit-breaker to address the disparity, while 'No' campaigners say it will be another layer of bureaucracy that will lead to talk-fests without outcomes.

The impact of all of these realities isn't academic to me, they cut close. I was born and raised on Warramungu country in Tennant Creek, while my Indigenous heritage comes from my Mum's side of the family in Victoria. The story of where we are as a nation right now is as much mine as it is all of ours—the good and bad, success and failure intertwined like the threads of a rope.

I began reporting at the *Tennant and District Times* when I was thirteen, almost 25 years ago. I made mistakes and grew as a reporter and a person with strong and generous members of the community investing their time, energy and wisdom in me. It was the making of me.

I'm charged with making sense of all sides and bringing voices and perspectives to the fore, in my role leading the ABC's

Dan Bourchier

Dan Bourchier is an award-winning journalist and broadcaster with the ABC. He is a host of current affairs show *The Drum* and special correspondent for the Voice referendum.

Illustration by Lee Lai

coverage of the Voice to Parliament as Referendum Correspondent. I see my job as navigating all of that complexity—and to distil and help explain each step of the process. To bring all Australians into the conversation about the constitution, the proposed amendment and the broader discussion about the proposed Voice to Parliament. And to bring humanity to the reporting of both sides.

Obviously, I have a view and a range of perspectives, but it's crucial that I don't take a side—which I haven't. As journalists, we are naturally curious—you could even say sceptical, and in spite of whatever my own views are, my job is underpinned by the deliberate action of putting what I think aside to ensure I hear all perspectives and in turn share them with all Australians. No-one should assume my views are either for or against.

But I also see my role as doing something bigger than just covering this referendum and this debate—I see it as helping to navigate a bigger discussion about who we are as a nation, and the place of Indigenous Australians and where we all fit in.

I wanted to write about what I'm observing. I'm concerned that we have lost the ability to respectfully disagree. To be abundantly clear, this doesn't mean we need to agree. It's important that we can disagree, that we can have a robust contest of ideas. It's all a question of how. I'm increasingly concerned that there is such polarisation around the debate that it has become a binary of 'with or against', which mutes nuance and discussion.

A friend—a senior leader in the public service who is familiar with navigating difficult matters of politics and policy, and often with politicians of all persuasions, told me of a dinner party she was at when the learned people she was dining with became so heated on both sides of the debate that the night came to a crashing and jarring holt.

Another, a governance expert, lamented to me how she had recently called time on discussions about the Voice amid a group lunch, such was the deterioration in the tone and the aggression that was emerging. These are just two examples of a litany of experiences shared with me, or that I've observed and experienced myself.

I've been fortunate to have a powerful vehicle I can use to discuss and debate the Voice to Parliament and the referendum, and have found *The Drum* more broadly to be central to having respectful conversations about contentious or layered topics that don't shy away from conflict, but facilitate discussion in a way that's about the idea and policy, not the person.

'My heart is filled with joy on one part and trepidation on the other,' Deputy Vice-Chancellor of Indigenous Strategy and Services at the University of Sydney Professor Lisa Jackson Pulver, told *The Drum*, when I asked about the tabling in federal parliament of the legislation including the words all Australians will vote on in the referendum:

> This has been such a long time coming, and we have been pushing on to future generations for such a long time the huge matters of our times. The trepidation is very much around the behaviour that I'm seeing in some quarters where people are promoting

a lot of misinformation, people are waging a fear campaign against the Voice and what it means. People are using it as a lever to create hostility when in fact a decent conversation needs to happen, and when people ask a decent, innocent question about, 'What does this mean?' 'How can I understand better?' I've seen some very, very unpleasant responses to that.

I put to Professor Jackson Pulver my concern, that generally speaking, we are losing the ability to disagree respectfully.

'Arguing well is one of the real characteristics of intelligence and a real characteristic of an intelligent nation, and we are seeing a lot of democracies at the moment not being able to do that,' she said.

I'm really grateful to have the time and space on *The Drum* to be able to dig deeper into all perspectives of the debate. I knew that this year would be heated. How can it not be when as well as the Voice to Parliament, the matters being debated are about identity, acceptance, place and belonging. What I didn't expect was the ferocity of the debate, and in some instances character attacks, or how early they've come.

If I was ever unsure or wavering that I was doing my job of providing balanced and fair coverage, it was made crystal clear across a single week at the end of February into March. I faced threats of formal complaint from a 'progressive No' campaigner, which was aimed at intimidating me into changing an accurate analysis piece. This person later privately apologised.

I was accused live on air of campaigning for a 'Yes' vote, by a prominent 'No' campaigner, because of my 'body language'. The person publicly apologised, and privately told me that they thought I was navigating the complexity of the different views of the Voice with fairness. Then a prominent 'Yes' campaigner publicly wrote, 'the ABC's platforming of regressive "No" advocates is wrong'. It was an independent Indigenous senator not without power or platform whom the 'Yes' campaigner was describing as 'regressive'. I sought to interview this campaigner live on air—they never responded.

It's not lost on me that some who are advocating for or against appear to seek to advance their case by shutting down the voices of others. I'm not sharing these experiences for pity, far from it. I'm sharing them to show how fraught it is being a journalist, navigating this debate and seeking to elevate all voices. Critique of reporting—mine or others—isn't new, and is actually crucial as a check and balance. Some of what I'm seeing and hearing, though, has hammered home how entrenched some people are—so determined to get their point across that they are almost insisting their point of view is the only one.

Lucky I grew up in Tennant Creek, which taught me great strength and to trust my instincts. I'm grateful I bring to my job and life a long and unflinching heritage of resilience.

•••

Stayin' Alive

You rock up to the emergency department of your local hospital with a jagged piece of bone protruding from your leg. Despite seeing the inside of your body on the outside, the medics who made an oath to do no harm tell you to practise mindfulness, exercise for endorphins and see a therapist.

Jasper
Peach

Jasper Peach is a trans, non-binary and disabled writer, speaker and parent. Their first book, *You'll be a Wonderful Parent* (Hardie Grant), was published in March 2023.

You point to the bone and politely describe the impact the situation is having on your life, somehow finding your manners while in blinding agony in the hope that you'll be treated better, but they speak over you and repeat the same nonsense over and over. You see a specialist after receiving a referral who repeats the fable you've heard already, then charges you many hundreds of dollars for the privilege of hearing it. You now live with the most intense pain you've ever experienced, as though there are flames inside your marrow and your limbs now weigh more than a piano, and you begin to hope nothing is real in order to cope.

It's an extreme metaphor, but replace the visible broken parts of you with invisible chronic illness and you'll pick up what I'm putting down. This is a story of gaslighting and neglect that doesn't have to be your life—but as COVID-19 continues to disable people at a rapid rate, it soon will be if it isn't already.

At the time of writing, multiple articles are being published in response to the parliamentary inquiry into long COVID. I bookmark them all then decide not to read them. The most recent article in *Good Weekend* asks how much we can expect from science when a new medical condition is identified. It would be a valid question, except long COVID isn't new by any stretch of the imagination. I need to keep my path clear—it's me talking to you, not a bunch of research and reporting I want to set on fire that's easily found online. I also decide not to read articles on long COVID because when I attempt to they look like soup and I feel I'm dying. I rest for a few days and try again.

In 2005 my health became noticeably complex and although diagnosis took a long time I exist under the umbrellas of fibromyalgia and myalgic encephalomyelitis (ME). I won't use the phrase chronic fatigue because this minimises the reality of being in a body with this illness—it doesn't even touch the sides. I'm not sleepy; I'm in a living hell. I'm the guy in the broken leg metaphor, and so are a bunch of my friends.

We all grew so tired, didn't we? Of being at home and afraid or bored, or both. We experienced disconnection from our families and communities, workplaces and things that gave us joy. We washed our hands and sang 'Happy Birthday' or 'Closer' by Nine Inch Nails while scrubbing germs away. For some people in so-called Australia, there was blessed relief that spread like warmth in your belly after a good meal once the restrictions were reduced, then lifted and melted away. It feels annoying to have to go back to that time, doesn't it? Before you decide you've had enough of this subject, I just want you to stick with me here.

I can't tell you what it cost me to write even this short essay because if you don't have the lived experience, you'll never understand. I don't want you to. I want you to be safe, and not to live with the delusion that 'optimal health' is your birthright.

I'm a disability advocate and activist, and wonder if I'm skirting too close to ableism here—telling people to avoid a life like mine. But to assume the issue is black and white would mean a complete disregard for the gold in the grey, the joy and love and euphoria in my life that has exquisite value. I have found these places within that coexist with a disease nobody can help me recover from. Every day feels like walking a tightrope above flames, as I try balancing my family, my career and my sanity, without getting burned. If the world were accessible and the social model of disability applied, that would be great. But that's not how it works, and I can't see that changing overnight. Maddy Ruskin, a writer and screen developer also living with ME, has said:

With COVID running rampant while the government does nothing, more and more people are going to experience the hell of long COVID

and our disbelieving healthcare system. And they won't all have the resources and privilege—family help, supportive workplaces, limited responsibilities—needed to reach a level of health that isn't completely debilitating to their life.

You can live well with post-viral illness, but you'll need to make peace with a constrained lifestyle. Tiny amounts of energy that waft by before you can raise your hand to grab them; brief windows of the day when you can function; minimal income coupled with massive expenses to establish a level of care that keeps you alive. Are you getting the picture? What is secure can become out of reach once you're sick—housing, access to treatments, people who believe you. If you have the means, it's possible to configure a life where you cope with the hand you've been dealt. The alternative means disappearing, one way or another. We don't want this to happen to you.

Writer and disability activist Natalia Hodgins submitted a clear and specific submission to the parliamentary inquiry. Hodgins contracted ME six years ago and has lost almost half a million dollars in earnings due to her disability and faces a lifetime of scraping by on the Disability Support Pension. Her recommendations are evidence-based and make water-tight sense. They include but are not limited to:
- Ensuring all actions are patient-led and informed by health consumers with lived experience of post-infectious chronic illness
- Reinstating mask mandates indoors and implementing minimum

standards for air-flow and filtration in all public buildings
- A public health campaign to educate Australians about long COVID and the health risks associated with repeat COVID infections
- Education for all Australian GPs, nurses and allied health practitioners
- Up-to-date national clinical guidelines for long COVID and ME that clearly state how exercise harms patients.

Hodgins said in her statement, 'It is incomprehensible that the group of people who have been most severely affected by post-viral illness are being erased from this conversation.'

Hundreds of thousands of Australians have experienced life dropping out from under us when we got sick and didn't recover. We saw the pandemic roll in and witnessed those same mistakes of gaslighting and denying care to people with long COVID. We're offering you a parachute in the form of information, but you're jumping on a plane scheduled to crash without bothering to look our way. It's infuriating and devastating.

Kaitlyn Blythe is a writer, performer and producer who has had ME for 20 years and had this to say: 'Immediate death is not the only risk with a viral infection. ME cuts 25 years off your life expectancy. So, what's the number? How many years of your life are you willing to risk so you can pretend the pandemic is over?'

Flic Manning, author of *Living Human*, a memoir about sustainable strategies for invisible illness, wrote:

It feels like a purposeful leadership decision to let us die. I moved to the beach after two years of living in lockdowns because my mental health could not bear it anymore. Not the lockdowns or isolation, but the willingness by everyday people to buy into the story being sold, and as such their willingness for people like me to die. How did we become a species so willing to support our own demise?

There have been times when my illness has been very difficult to live with, and others when it felt like living couldn't be possible—that my system (in a bizarre mirroring of the health system under COVID-19) would buckle under all the pressure and cease to be. But I am still here. I matter and I want to live. All the finite, energised time I have I spend loving the people dear to me and doing the work to make a kinder world.

It's hard to know how to get the message through. Person to person—will you stay safe for as long as you can? Guard the baseline of your health and do not let poor management choices shorten your lifespan or create unnecessary illness that throws you in the deep end of our healthcare system. It is a powerful industry that promises treatment and cures for some, while perpetrating profound medical trauma on people like me with health issues seen by those in control as unworthy of investing time and research on, such as long COVID and ME. We didn't think this would happen to us until it did. Your story can be different.

•••

My deep thanks to Natalia Hodgins for her outstanding editing assistance when I hit a wall, and to all the contributors.

Prised Wide Shut

It's not the end of the world at all. It's only the end of us. The world will go on just the same, only we shan't be in it.

—Nevil Shute, *On the Beach*

Political winds swirl wildly these days. Key allies elect gauche grifters and slip into disarray. Activists fight back. A virus swept the world and showed who and what was essential and who and what was not. Climate havoc is wreaked as fire roars across Australia, Pakistan slips under water, cyclones rip through Auckland and snow blankets Los Angeles.

The icesheets of Antarctica groan impending collapse. And as we the people squint fearfully through newly descaled eyes, political landscapes rupture. The Overton Window—the range of political ideas that the public is willing to consider and accept—shifts. As the calamitous state of our polities and planet becomes starkly clear, the parameters of political possibility widen. We're demanding change, we're demanding better, we're demanding it quickly.

When the Labor Party implemented its election policy of abolishing Temporary Protection Visas on 12 February, we took an unwelcome trip down memory lane as the Opposition waspishly warned of opportunistic people smugglers dusting off dormant business models should the government tamper with Operation Sovereign Borders.

The Minister for Home Affairs was having none of it. Regional processing, said Clare O'Neil, is 'settled policy on both sides of politics'. So if one were hoping for a Brave New World under Labor, that was one hope that sank like a stone.

There is lots to like about our new government and its comforting veneer of change. There's a definite improvement in presentation. National integrity has been restored by men and women of intellect and goodwill. But while the nation will forever be grateful to Anthony Albanese for wresting the prime ministerial reins from the abject Scott Morrison, and relieved he leads a government both competent and conscionable, if one digs too deep, with hopes too high, soon enough one hits the bedrock of settled policies on both sides.

Labor trumpets its climate credentials as it opens up 47,000 square kilometres for offshore oil and gas exploration, approves donor Santos's request to launch 116 new gas wells, and allows vast seismic testing for oil and gas off the

Jo
Dyer

Jo Dyer is a writer, producer of theatre and film and former director of Adelaide Writers' Week.

east and southern coasts in fish-dense waters as the Twelve Apostles look on. The states join in the exploration frenzy. A hundred and seventeen further projects lurk malevolently in the wings, apparently needed to protect our energy supply, as 80% of our gas is exported annually for rocketing profits while at home we fork out for leftovers at prices set from afar. As we're carpet bombed with carbon bombs, it doesn't matter if we like this bomber more.

The signature policy the government sought to ram through parliament by warning of the futility of perfect versus good has at its heart a 'safeguard mechanism' invented by former energy minister Angus Taylor: a cap-and-trade system without a cap, promoting imaginary offsets with imaginary impacts on emissions reductions; trees to be saved from logging that go on to be logged secretly; money given for forest regrowth as forest cover declines; farmers remunerated for not clearing land they never intended to clear.

Conflicted fossil-fuel players rebadge as carbon-credit providers and enrich themselves in the new brisk markets for phantom offsets. It's a paper-based carbon capture and storage without even failed technology to show for it, direct action all over again, ten years closer to the apocalypse. That decarbonisation might require us to cease burning carbon is kryptonite to a government that fends off a desperate, desperately disappointed nation with implausible deniability that the actions that it takes, and those that it does not, don't pour fuel on the gathering inferno.

If it's the planet's slide into uninhabitability that will kill us these days, growing up as a Gen X-er in the shadow of nuclear annihilation, it was the spectre of *On the Beach* that haunted my dreams— ripped banners claiming 'There's Still Time' wafting forlornly in the nuclear breeze as the last humans embraced and laid down to rest overlooking the ocean, poison pills beneath their tongues.

Under-the-desk drills to combat nuclear Armageddon are no longer taught in schools but the drums of war as a necessary soundtrack to the preservation of peace remain popular. Admonitions to be alert not alarmed at the Islamic Menace have been replaced by a sky-high Red Alert. Encircled as they are by expanding US bases, nonetheless China is condemned as belligerent and the country from which we need protection. More settled policy on both sides.

It is also settled policy on both sides that we repay the United States for their expected but not guaranteed defence of us in the event of a neighbourhood skirmish they're slaveringly predicting by privileging their interests above our own and our region's. It is settled policy that a unilateral invasion of Taiwan should be robustly rebuffed by all in a way that other illegal invasions did not require (see Iraq, 2003). Into this febrile debate came the quickly settled policy of the AUKUS agreement, a thought bubble from the most inconsequential prime minister of our time announced mere months before the election that turfed him out. The British seized upon it, desperate for a global role beyond a post-Brexit punchline. The cavalcade of retired US admirals paid handsomely as Australian government 'defence procurement consultants' performed well for their country, their whispers finding receptive ears that it is American know-how we need, and American companies that should build our submarines, and, once built, American officers who should ride in them on stand-by. That these ex-admirals were often also on the payroll of the defence contractors that stood to gain by our abrupt and unheralded change in strategic direction escaped comment.

AUKUS became sacrosanct in seconds, Labor criticism restricted to the then-PM's diplomacy-by-SMS. Sympathy was expressed that the French learned by text message that their $55 billion submarines contract endorsed only weeks before would be trashed—but not for the fact that we were trashing it, nor that this trashing undermined French strategy in the Indo-Pacific for which we'd promised energetic support. Enthusiastic subscription to the American 'with us or agin us' world order is once more the order of our day, considered objections from our generation's most important foreign policy prime minister dismissed with condescension, as Paul Keating is shepherded hurriedly offstage by a Labor Party desperate its national security credentials be unassailable from the feisty featherweights opposite.

Visiting Australia for Adelaide Writers' Week in March, playwright and contemporary chronicler David Hare spoke of his student days at Cambridge, when his intellectual idol, leading literary critic and Orwell-with-jokes Raymond Williams, warned him against putting faith in Labour governments. On the evening of Harold Wilson's first election as prime minister, Williams remarked that now, on this night of victory, the students should 'prepare themselves for the coming years of disillusionment and steady themselves for a longer and longer fight'. To the young firebrands, his caution was as salutatory as it was prophetic, a passion for the moment qualified by an exquisite sense of history. Albanese's victory night was an evening that will linger longer than Kevin Rudd's tea and Iced Vovo buzzkill, but whether his government will rise to the wretched challenges confronting our planet remains in question as the seismic shift we felt beneath our feet on 21 May 2022 steadies swiftly.

However hot it gets inside, Labor wants the Overton Window prised wide shut.

•••

Greedy

Kirli
Saunders

Kirli Saunders OAM
is a proud Gunai
woman and award-
winning author,
multidisciplinary artist
and consultant. She
has four books out,
including *Bindi*, and is
working on her novel,
'Yaraman'.

I come from a long line of salt water women—
Gunai and Yuin on Nan's side,
Biripi and Dharawal on Pop's.

Up and down this coast—we are sea people,
at one with the rhythms of guriwal or muriyira, the whale, and her
calendar flowers

At one with grandmother moon
and her tides

fullest in every sense
when nourished
by Gadhu
with a swim
and a feed.

I learned to separate fishbones from flesh with my
tongue as toddler.

Watched my expert mother elegantly rock
hop, shuck and gulp oysters.

The aunties taught us to pippy dance
in golden sand—
twist and sway

to harvest and clean abalone
wulkan—
a delicacy for our mob,

to cut away,
gut, and scrub the black on rocks
to beat sweet flesh
to cook over crackling coals
as the sun sets.

They tell me this is Women's Way

and that when Cook came, our fishing changed
in the name of greed,
that what was once abundant and free
was now a commodity and our people were kept out of the economy despite
being industry leads
in the sea that raised us.

Where abalone are overfished
there are urchins—
thorny black infestations
who feed on the same seaweed and modify reefs
with colonisation
causing baron ground,

so proud aunties can't hand down
this saltwater women wisdom

and our daughters
at one with the sea

are consumed
in the place we used to feed
by a greed
that longs for sweet blak lipped flesh.

I named her naturally because I love castles

Dan
Hogan

Dan Hogan (they/
them) is a writer
from San Remo,
NSW (Awabakal and
Worimi Country), living
on Gadigal Country.
Dan is the author of
Secret Third Thing. See
<www.2dan2hogan.
com>.

'Dig a hole for the windchimes? Thought you'd never ask.'

'When you dig don't lean down like that. Bend your knees or you'll stuff your back,' said dad, snatching the shovel from my hands, plunging it into the lawn. 'Watch.'

Haunted as I was by the clang of windchimes in the kitchen of my childhood, dad'd be knocking around at five in the morning because the bloke can't sleep for all the alcohol he needs so he's always drinking; noisy ghosts barnacled to my memory hull less as menace and more as commensalism. Dad's head striking the chance-based percussion instruments suspended from the kitchen ceiling at a time rendered impossible to the sun and held in disdain by the moon. *Fuck ya*, he'd curse the tintinnabula. This dadsound—hiss of a beer twisted open. This ... rude epoch. *Mongrel things.* The ting ting ting of a bottle cap dancing across the sink. *Flap jacket farter. What wind is there?* New South Ales, his piss of choice. *Good as a dead dog in spring.* Beer frothing until the pressure inside the bottle matches the pressure outside the bottle. *Fucking shit bucket shadow of death.* Dad throwing open the screen door. *No wind? No worries.* Dad casting the chimes into the darkness wet on the lips of dawn. *Fuck ya.* The predawn sky splitting up like parents. The sound of windchimes forged from cutlery and utensils discarded by San Remo Neighbourhood Centre crashing into the damp lawn, clammy fingers of grass haloed by vapour. More curses. More

THE NARRATOR: shit bucket shadow of death?

shit bucket shadow of death.

THE NARRATOR: What's up? Accusative plural?

Mum'd tinkered all manner of chime. Gnarled spoons, sporks, forks, never a knife, spatulas, egg rings, metal teapots smaller than could be occupied by a teabag. *Little teapots make good central clappers.* Nondescript metals, tubular and plate-like, a domestic collision of untunable and undetectable acoustic waves propagated through a transmission medium like a homing missile of small, daggering sounds shot into the ear canals of Cloudcuckoolanders being beautiful and bourgeois on the other side of the Entrance Bridge. *I should set up a stall at Toukley Markets.* Hinges past their best. A Coca-Cola tin from the 1980s. Fishing line. *Tell you what.* Deranged whisk. *They don't make Coke cans like they used to. When I was your age you could brain damage a considerable fish with one whoompa from a Coke can. Whoomp. You want that fish breathing when you put it in the hands of the monger. It pays better. What happened to the good ol' days of steel?* Ladle handle. Seashells. Keys. Washers. *Aluminium? Take it or leave it. No wonder bells don't ring like they used to. I'll leave it.*

THE NARRATOR: This parentsound? This brusque epoch? Dare I characterise this second moment of area? Consider for one second the kitchenchimes as unsupported free-free beams, which is to say in no uncertain terms,

$$v_1 = \frac{\beta_1^2}{2\pi}\sqrt{\frac{EI}{\mu}} = \frac{22.3733}{2\pi L^2}\sqrt{\frac{EI}{\mu}},$$

where L is the teapot's size, and I is the second moment of area for the modified forks, and μ is the Coke cans' mass per mornings spent parsed by dad's head, and E is the Dadsound Modulus for the chime material, collapsing the perceived and objectively tangible, forming the third moment of area for matter to command resonance.

Jar lids. *Do any bells ring?* Inverted soup tin, painted, adorned with diamantes. Phone cases. Dead batteries. AAA. A deconstructed iPhone 3, dangling. *That's not an iPhone.* Nowhere devices, really. *It's a Samsung Galaxy.* She loved that stuff when she was alive and I reckon she probably loves it wherever she's gone.

THE NARRATOR: What's that smell?

Dad's talk was ball lightning talk: spontaneous discharges of poetical information emitted sideways along the present situation, sometimes presenting as a spherical object hung in the air like a driverless Tesla suspended in the sky at the will of violent rotating winds, other times pea-sized and unmoving and green, nonetheless aglow, acting like a moat around him, present for however long and always ending in a jump-cut disappearance, an exit rarely witnessed and, if knowable, detected by the characteristic lick of sulphuric odour it leaves behind. Charged with an unproven existence by those who think they know how to read and yet here's dad, talking about mum.

'You know you've made it when there's a frozen pizza in the tree behind you.' Dad pointed to the frozen pizza stuck in the brigalow at the end of the back yard.

'What's it doing up there? Bird food?'

A pair of cockatoos pecked at the frozen pizza, crests low, chatty. More curious than hungry.

'Crouch close enough to the lawn and you'll hear the wind whisper between the leaves of grass: *there is a frozen pizza in the tree behind you*. That's when you know you've made it.'

'Made what? Look, I'm not going to ask the lawn questions again, if that's what you're suggesting. Not after what happened last time.'

'Fair enough. That's fair. I just thought you might want to have a little back-and-forth while you're down there tying your shoelaces.'

Dad was right. My shoelaces were undone. But to what end? Who could say? The moment I knelt, dad rushed to my side, aggressively whispering into my ear. 'If dolphins could fly as good as they swim, we'd experience things like dolphin shadows while we went to the ground to tie our shoelaces,' he said.

'You're not wrong,' I said. 'Dolphin shadows would be preferable to the crap you get these days.'

'Come. Let's cut jib and leave the lawn to undo itself,' he said. 'I'll show you what I'm working on.'

THE NARRATOR: Gaston Bachelard points out in his essay on the imagination of matter, *Water and Dreams*, that 'in a little while, the vegetable world itself grows quiet, and then, when sadness falls on the stones, the whole universe becomes mute through an inexpressible terror'.

Dad's back shed was a hut fastened together from sheets of corrugated iron, timber and a few bags of concrete he'd nicked from a building site decades ago. I always bring it up. Keeps the oil on his corroded synapses.

'Can't believe it's still standing after all this time. Feels like at least two lifetimes ago when you swiped this stuff. Who'd have thought it?'

'Surplus materials. It's not stealing if it's possessed by a boss who doesn't know if he's coming or going.'

'Was the giant ceramic fish surplus material as well?' I pestered, pointing to the waist-high fish sculpture propped against the door of the shed.

'That fish,' started dad. 'For 20 years that fish has followed me.'

The globose stare of the fish hunted us both as dad spoke.

'A lawn I've been mowing for 20 years. Like the metric fucktonne of weeds I've pulled from their gardens, they won't even notice it's gone.'

'I'm not having a go or anything. I think it's good.'

'The fish isn't stolen goods if the fish is following you.'

'You've put up with enough exploitative bullshit from those people over the years.'

'You know what it's like. Those people have more dollars than sense. Better a giant blue fish guarding my shed door than gathering dust in Cloudcuckooland,' said dad. 'Just watch the door as you come in. I don't want Castle to get out.'

Truth was Castle was already out. Dad fell out of bed last week and some fingers broke on both his hands. He'd fallen on Castle, too. Castle had been gone almost a full week but she'll be back. She always comes back. Plus, she's seen dad fall out of bed a million times. I reckon once the spook recedes she'll know it was an accident.

'Worst part is ...' dad giggled, spurred by the sudden recollection of Castle's absence, readying the delivery of his new catch phrase, 'I lost my job at the Twinkle Twinkle Little Star factory.' He chortled on, hands raised, splintered fingers trembling.

Resting by the big blue fish was an open can of corn, bright yellow kernels forwarding light like push notifications, messages from the glistening brine, cc: Castle. Castle loved corn. But only the stuff that came from a tin. Probably because when we were kids dad used to chuck her a dollop at dinner. Expired army rations were always falling off the back of trucks in San Remo. A free meal is a free meal even if it is leftovers from the Gulf War. PK chewing gum branded to include the words *Kuwait* and *Operation Desert Storm*. Dad telling us Operation Desert Storm was some yankee doodle nonsense and Operation Hurry up and Eat. I still think Castle is a pretty good name. I named her naturally because I love castles. Or at least when I was a kid I loved the counterfeit castle over in Buff Point. In technical terms it wasn't a 'real' castle but a house made of bricks, a bootleg fortress, a knock-off miniaturisation planted in a suburb of asbestos-laden fibro and drywall.

It wasn't home to royalty or nobility, of course, but it was built as a holiday home by a Cloudcuckoolander from Sydney. Or so the story goes. It was abandoned before construction was complete for reasons only remembered by creepypastas and urban legends: the murder-suicide, bikies, the San Remo Slow Walker, the Barefoot Investor II: Bride of the Barefoot Investor. Left to ruin, the Buff Point Castle was ruled for decades by bonglords and working-class kids who would mine the site for rocks for rock wars, tales of ghouls and insurrection, tormenting the Cloudcuckoo neighbours when they came from Sydney to sit in their holiday houses while wearing white linen pants to make pasta from scratch, draping snakes of spaghetti on a contraption that looked like a clothes horse but wasn't a clothes horse. *Do they know a packet of spaghetti costs like eighty cents?* Today the Buff Point Castle is long gone, the site underwater, a multistorey houseboat duplex floating in its place.

Dad didn't much care for Castle when we were kids but since mum's death, Castle has been a lifeline of sorts, a conduit for dad's projections and the particular nonsense he needs to keep going. If the rust and mould were the only thing holding together his back shed, Castle was the only things holding him together. *Castle knows how to read*, he'd tell me whenever I visited after mum died. *I caught her reading the letters to the editor again,* he'd announce before retelling the same letter to the editor he'd read a year ago. Someone'd written in describing how their family friend was swathed in leeches. They said it was the council's fault their family friend was swathed in leeches and no family friend should ever be swathed in leeches. The family friend had fallen into a ditch drain and broken their ankle when the embankment, without warning, rearranged itself underfoot.

Get this, said dad. *The family friend was stomping around the nature strip in rollerblades.* The letter writer complained how a full canister of table salt was wasted on exploding the leeches. After detonating the leeches the family friend was swathed in leech blood and *it was the council's fault the family friend was swathed in leech blood and no family friend should ever be swathed in the blood of leeches.* Dad was of the opinion the council should at least replace the rollerblades. *If they're never going to give us concrete kerbs and drains they would want to be forever prepared to fork out for family friends whose ankles snap inside rollerblades when the nature strip collapses and drops them in a slap of gutter leeches.*

I got where he was coming from. When I was a kid I'd get down in the gutters with Aaron Warren, the kid with two first names, who lived a few houses down. We'd catch thumb-sized tadpoles in disused jam jars. One scoop of drain water and you'd have a hand-held aquarium brimming with life. Aaron Warren always pointed out how when a tadpole writhed in his open palm it resembled his step-dad's signature. I didn't know what a signature was then and I didn't want to ask Aaron Warren because I sensed his regular announcement of this observation was his way of baiting me into participation in some low-level nefarious activity, like the time he convinced me to help him break into our school to steal a hose and a tote tray he'd hidden in a wattle bush before the summer holidays. One time I went tadpoling solo and showed Aaron Warren my catch at school the following day. I handed him the jar, expecting him to be impressed by the number of tadpoles sporting fresh legs.

Aaron Warren looked me dead in the eye and shook the jar, grinning like a possessed folk instrumentalist shaking a tambourine as the audience heaped roses on the stage. He jerked the jar between our faces, between our eyes, as the tadpoles were shredded by the vortex. When the thinning tentacle of spun water dissipated, scattering the dismembered remains of the tadpoles from its violent torrent, my stomach hurt. *Those tadpoles were going to be frogs one day*, I said. *We needed those frogs in case we had to scare my grandad into continuing to live.* Aaron Warren shook the jar again except this time he shook it like a tambourine at the dawn of the golden age of competitive edges. As the maelstrom slowed down, Aaron Warren's grin spread to the brink of his face and kept going, continuing outwards, burrowing into the plasterboard walls of the classroom, filing straight through to the outside and across the playground, stopping only when time stopped, when the bell rang for recess.

I didn't like Aaron Warren much after that. He would be knocking on my door every other arvo but because I was scared shitless of him I couldn't turn him away. One arvo I showed him the chickens we had and he said my family was weird because we had chickens but didn't live on a farm. I showed him the chicken feed in the tall white bucket in dad's back shed. I always remember that bucket because dad had to kill mice in it. The mice'd been rooting around the house and eating the curtains and shitting in the pantry and eating Castle's corn and had arrived in the tall white bucket to begin the grisly but nonetheless necessary procedure for forming a rat king capable of ruling over San Remo for centuries to come. Aaron Warren picked a kernel of dehydrated corn from the chicken feed and asked me to dare him to do something with it. *You dare me ... to dare you?* He inverted the skin of one of his eyelids and nestled the corn kernel under there. I could see a little square-ish bump on his eyelid where the corn was stored.

THE NARRATOR: Corn is a fruit-producing grass of the Poaceae family. Not unlike most species of grass (the exception being QuarkGrass and other artificially intelligent ghost grasses), the corn plant is an angiosperm, growing ovuliferous inflorescences or 'ears' pregnant with cereal yields. Corn kernels are the fruit of these ears.

I can't even remember if he took the corn out before he went home. I had a joke with mum where we'd say Aaron Warren is out there somewhere, successful and handsome, tall and fertile, eyelid pregnant with the kernel from the tall white bucket, pregnant in perpetuum—eye of corn, fruit of retina—delicate and irretrievable like the inner contents of an ancient fossil. And the only reason he was successful and handsome was because of the corn. The corn was his *point of difference*. His *competitive edge*. We'd call it the *Enchanted Corn* and *Aaron Warren's Corn Feast*. If the corn ever left Aaron Warren's eye, everything he held dear to his heart would be sucked into a watery vortex, or so mum said. Sometimes we would deploy a variation of this joke in which we'd say something like: *I could really use an Enchanted Corn right about now.* Mum'd say this whenever her health was playing up and I'd say it every time work stuffed up my pay. Sometimes mum would text me a picture of corn she'd ripped from Google Images and I'd know what that meant and what I had to do.

I still eat corn. I don't like it but I eat it. Despite seeing a pile of Aaron Warren's bumpy eyelids blinking back at me from a dinner plate decorated with the words *Operation Desert Storm*, I still eat corn. And I hope Castle returns, for dad's sake. That open tin next to the big blue fish isn't going anywhere soon.

THE NARRATOR: Evening Meggett died due to a supply shortage. Despite claiming to be the greatest economic managers ever to grace government over the federation of colonies, the colonial-vectoralist class did a bad capitalism. A terrible, horrible, no good, very bad capitalism. Some have dared to call Evening's death—as with so many others—a form of social murder. The colonial-vectoralist state rerouted positive health outcomes from the poor to increase the life expectancy of the rich. An old hat worn by a new ruling class. What's that smell?

'Those seeds I gave you,' started dad as we stepped inside the shed.

'The chondrilla ones? Yeah. I've been doing what you said.'

'Good stuff. Good stuff. You know how I said the seeds could infest a QuantumLawn with weeds?'

'Yeah. To slowly break them down. Make unmowable lawns mowable again. Neutralise their patents and to—'

'To rewild QuantumFantastic's intellectual property. To weaponise nature as a means of abolishing private property. To expedite the product's discontinuance. And to—'

'Rewilding. That's the word I was trying to remember. I was explaining it to Wes but I kept calling it rewinding.'

'That's not far off, really. It might even be more accurate when I show you how it will go down.'

THE NARRATOR *extremely Wikipedia voice*: QuantumFantastic, Inc. is a multinational conglomerate, to which is largely attributed the definition of the colonial vectoralopocene. QuantumFantastic resulted from the merger of agri-businesses QuantumBarn and Fantastic Solutions. The conglomerate specialises in domestic and commercial gardening and maintenance products, agricultural commodities and agri-asset monitoring and surveillance technology. The merger saw CEO Karen Chadtop become the third earthling in history to gain quadrillionaire status and the first 'Earth-only' quadrillionaire whose wealth is entirely contained in 'on world' accounts and economies.

'Did you drop your guts or what?' I declared, walking deeper inside the shed. 'The hell is that stench? My god.'

Dad clicked on the light and the usual cockroaches scattered: Gary, Louise and Brigadier Francis, big as plates, Brigadier Francis losing his bejewelled toe ring in the frenzy. Expired New South Ales had very obviously organised with the clandestine workings of vermin, a solemnity and freemasonry in its own right, lending dad's back shed its characteristic atmosphere. Aromatics aside, the tall white bucket. Dethroned of its handle but no longer haunted by chicken feed or nascent rat kings, the plastic repose didn't look a day over a hundred, stationed in the middle of the room, collecting empty beer bottles for dad to cash in later.

'Here,' said dad, mashing the keypad on the repurposed vending machine he'd installed in the furthest corner, 'have a beer.' A metal spiral clanked and a stubby emerged, dropping into the machine's collection tray, shattering.

'Shit. I didn't think of that,' laughed dad. He opened the front of the vending machine like a door, retrieving a beer with his good hand and lobbing it over to me.

'Cheers.'

'Anyway. The seeds. Have you ever seen one of these QuantumLawns being installed?'

THE NARRATOR [From Wikipedia, the free encyclopedia]: The quadrillionaire status of the 'first' quadrillionaires, Elon Musk and Jeff Bezos, is contested and rejected by some capitalist sovereignties. Although recognised as 'legitimate Earth-only trillionaires', the off-shore tax haven that made them quadrillionaires has received heavy criticism for being 'a crime against humanity'. During the climate-induced recession, Musk and Bezos established a scheme in which residential landlords were paid large sums to coerce their tenants into participating in their Mars colonisation program. In so-called Australia, federal and state governments partnered with the scheme, allowing it to function at the edges of the law. Dubbed FreedomSeeker, the program saw tenants on JobSeeker charged with automated debt notices known as 'robodebts' and landlords encouraged by cash incentives or 'luxury finder fees' to issue eviction notices. Landlords were paid three years' worth of rent for every evictee they inducted into FreedomSeeker.

Although official numbers are presently unverifiable, it is estimated that at least two-thirds of these bounty immigrants died while in transit to Mars. Documentation obtained during activist raids of government informational infrastructure stored on servers rented from Amazon Web Services confirmed that so-called FreedomSeekers were promised a 'work-free paradise' but in reality were tricked into manning the off-planet tax haven under sustained duress. When questioned by press gallery journalists about his government's ongoing support of a scheme described as 'tantamount to industrial-scale interplanetary human trafficking', Prime Minister Paul Paulson replied: 'I reject the characterisation of a scheme that has lifted so many out of precarity, out of uncertainty, out of debt and out of poverty.'

Documents obtained in the so-called 'seize the means of information' raids on AWS and Google revealed the government's implementation of sloganeering was recommended by PR firm F*ckface! International at a cost of $7 billion to taxpayers. The recommendation from F*ckface! International rested on a legal technicality that allowed the government to justify the use of phrases such as 'the program has literally lifted thousands out of uncertainty' since they were physically lifting many thousands of workers into outer space, indefinitely. The scheme has significantly reshaped unemployment and productivity statistics that, owing to legislative changes introduced by the Paulson government and supported by the Opposition, only include 'on-world numbers'. They told us outer space was the final frontier; a beautiful temple to be repossessed. But they lied. Outer space is no beauty and no temple. It is feral. Outer space is feral, and it is fair.

'No ...'
'Exactly. Nobody has ever seen one of these QuantumLawns being installed. Where are all the ghost grass turf farms? They're nowhere. And I'll tell you they're nowhere because a quantum is only virtually real.'
'A simulation? More Matrix than ghost?'

'No, no. More like ... an app. A bit like Hardlyany except ten steps further. How do I explain?'

'Oh I get it. The lawn is like a kind of software.'

'Like? Come on now. You know as well as I do that all lawns are software, be it ghost grass or regular old grass. We're the hardware. Difference with these ghost grasses is they do not speak to nature, on any level. They're not your traditional AI, like Hardlyany. I don't know. It's just another annoying thing in the world.'

'Oh.'

THE NARRATOR: Aduantas did know. He knew very well every single QuantumFantastic QuantumLawn with its QuarkGrass was an enclosed space of computational reducibility. The infrastructure of another reality grafted onto the generally accepted one. Or something. I don't know. I'm not an expert but I am a nondescript prism, hurtling.

'What I've worked out is these seeds.'

'The chondrilla rush skeletonweed?'

'I'll tell you now they're not chondrilla. Well, sort of. For appearance sake, they are chondrilla. But if you pop the hood you'll see the skeletonweed is only part of the story. Chondrilla is the template but they're really something else entirely.'

'What are they?'

'An even more annoying thing in the world.'

THE NARRATOR: Malware. The old son of a 3D-printed gun has done it. He doesn't know how he's done it.

'I don't know how I did it but the deed is done and done again as the deeds are always done in corn sugar. I will tell you about it because I am here and you are distant.'

'Dad. I'm right here.'

'I wasn't talking to you. I was talking to my Evening.'

THE NARRATOR: What's that smell?

Dad's demeanour had turned a horrible corner. I could tell by the way he misquoted lines from his favourite book. He always does this when struck by certain recollections; the ocean between his ears raising old wrecks, turning them over and over in the surf between beers and beached before blacking out.

'Sorry. I'm having a mild memory attack. I'll tell you something—never get old. It's not worth it.'

'Please. No need to apologise. I get it.'

'You know how QuantumFantastic goes on about their ghost grass. FantasticTurf and QuarkGrass and all that being manufactured from materials extracted from an extinct grassland that was transformed into a field of glass by lightning and fire and a barrage of asteroids. Those sponsored ads where they crap on about their QuantumLawns being 15,000 years in the making. You know the ones. With the quadrillionaire girlboss wearing a hoodie, whose parents owned—'

'Yep, yep. I know those ads. Awful. Really awful stuff.'

'Those ads are the reason I must cringe for a million years. Thing is this. I thought it was all a bunch of marketing fart but turns out even a cob of lies can grow a kernel of truth.'

'Edeowie glass? I read something about secret edeowie glass farms recently.'

'I'm not sure if they're mining edeowie glass from a stolen place passed down to them or if they're simply replicating ancient conditions to a desired effect. Whatever. There's something in what they're saying because their ghost grass is silicate-based.'

'How do you know that for sure?'

'Because those seeds I gave you, the ones you've been casting about, those seeds can transform a QuantumLawn into this.'

Dad walked over to a towel draped over a stool concealing something box-like. The towel was older than me, stained by the unceremony of age, emblazoned with the cartoon family from *The Simpsons*. We used to sit on it at the beach. Now it sat at the end of a long life, consigned to anything but a beach, a swatch of atrophied nostalgias at various stages of decay. Dad lifted the towel, revealing a tote tray filled with a globby, fluro-beige substance.

'Porridge?'

'No. Quicksand.'

'Holy shit. That muck used to be ghost grass?'

'Yep. How good's that?'

'So good. But can't quicksand, like, kill a person?'

'I wouldn't worry your conscience too much. Quicksand has only ever been the enemy of cartoon characters and those who go looking for gold on stolen land.'

'I mean it's great and we should definitely keep distributing the seeds. I'm just worried about how traceable it might be?'

'Be patient. Wait for the image to take hold. It shouldn't be long.'

'Image of what?'

'The image of malfunction. The appearance of a dangerous defect.'

'A product recall.'

'You got it. But once the image takes hold it will be a bigger disaster than your run-of-the-mill product recall. Want another beer?'

'I'm good. I actually wanted to ask if you had time to mow the rooftop lawn over at our place. The landlord will pay you but I reckon you should invoice her for more than you did last time. She's loaded, you know.'

'Sounds good. You have to help me get the mower up all those stairs though. Shocking things. Never seen a houseboat with so many bloody stairs.'

'I'll mow if you whipper snip. But you have to charge my landlord a proper Cloudcuckoo price, yeah?'

'Cluain, I don't want to get into this again. I know what you're saying but you have to remember I'm competing with the likes of QuantumFantastic and Jughead's DK Mode Mowing. Best thing I got going is my price.'

'Your exploitation is not the best thing you've got going, honestly. I doubt you'll lose the gig if you raise the price. Trust me. My landlord doesn't know if she's coming or going.'

'They rarely do. We'll see. You finished with that?'

With the composure of a surgeon lowering a pacemaker into the open hole of a patient's chest, dad placed the empty New South Ales bottles in the tall white bucket.

'I don't want the bottles to break, you see. I got 50 bucks last time I cashed them in. Those bottles are my superannuation.'

'That's 500 beers. So every 500 beers you get a free case.'

Dad laughed. 'That's one way of putting it.'

'You wouldn't believe how long our lawn's got. We lost Hardlyany in it for a few hours the other week.'

'How is Hardlyany?' asked dad, twisting the top off another beer.

'Good except that Wes' aunty changed her operating system again.'

'You're joking.'

'I kid you not.'

'I'd be having a word with Wes if I was you.'

'He's a difficult one to catch. I swear his aunty is at our house more than him.'

'His aunty is that Gloria Throckmorton, yeah? I like her. Come good then went back to bad. She's good fun. Went to school with my Evening. Had an interesting chat with her last time I was around to do the lawn. She's not the villain you think she is, Cluain. Look. I know your mother had it in for Gloria but Gloria was different back then. She was married to that dickhead and that dickhead was a pretty big dickhead.'

'Yeah. I know. Elvis impersonator, too.'

The tin roof lit up with the pitter-patter of a downpour.

'There's a low off the coast. Could use some rain,' I said.

'That's not rain you hear falling. It is frozen pineapple pieces. The cockatoos hate pineapple on pizza.'

• • •

Reading Blanchot at Neutral Bay

In memory of Robert Adamson

Kevin
Hart

Kevin Hart's most recent book is *Lands of Likeness* (Chicago UP); his memoir, *Dark-Land*, is forthcoming from Paul Dry Books. Among his new collections of poetry is *Carnet Beaune*.

No shit we're off low slung a car that sings
Of money mangroves leather and slow blurs
Of suburbs Hornsby Pymble Artarmon

Until we've reached the wharf so out at Hayes
For wine John Dory and some creamy light
You wanted us to talk of angels ah

I spoke about their death as Bernard did
We have escaped just as a bird that flees
A fowler's snare you smiled golden bird

And recalled Mallarmé who saw himself
And saw an angel felt that death was close
And it was then I showed a little book

La folie du jour and perched it on my hand
And what of death I'll feel the greatest joy
I think of women lovely creatures who

Would never say piss off to life or death
Yet when we die the margins of our books
Will stretch towards the centre and those lines

Of heat and rivers oysters herons God
Will shrink a little no take back the day
And let us have our grief no angel near

Except for you bird spirit with your smile
Your fingers filleted by steely hooks
All that was real take note the creamy light

Already going grainy wild dark wind
Shaking the Bay and almost saying then
No poems no no poems ever again—

We are hoping Australians will vote 'Yes'

The fate of future generations is in the balance

Marcia
Langton

Marcia Langton AO
is a descendant of
the Yiman people
of Queensland. She
is the Foundation
Chair of Australian
Indigenous Studies
at the University of
Melbourne.

'A Proposed Law: to alter the Constitution to recognise the First Peoples of Australia by establishing an Aboriginal and Torres Strait Islander Voice.

Do you approve this proposed alteration?'

Australians will vote 'Yes' or 'No' on this question in late 2023, and it will be their first referendum since 1999 when they were asked if they supported Australia becoming a republic. That was 23 years ago, almost a quarter of a century.

The Australian Republican Movement lost that referendum in 1999 because then prime minister John Howard confused the 'Yes' voters into believing that there was a better model; they should vote 'No' for the question being put to them and wait for the next referendum to vote for a better model. They are now boomers and it is highly unlikely they will see Australia become a republic.

Young Australians who have come of age and obtained the right to vote a few years ago will have no memory of that tortured, tricky debate. Yet they are witnessing the same tactics now, with Opposition Leader Peter Dutton proposing that his party room supports a different model for the Voice and has committed to advocating a hard 'No' for the question that will be put to Australians later this year.

The proposed law that Australians are being asked to approve at the referendum would insert a new section into the Constitution:

'Chapter IX Recognition of Aboriginal and Torres Strait Islander Peoples
129 Aboriginal and Torres Strait Islander Voice

> In recognition of Aboriginal and Torres Strait Islander peoples as the First
> Peoples of Australia:
> 1. There shall be a body, to be called the Aboriginal and Torres Strait Islander
>   Voice;
> 2. The Aboriginal and Torres Strait Islander Voice may make representations
>   to the Parliament and the Executive Government of the Commonwealth
>   on matters relating to Aboriginal and Torres Strait Islander peoples;
> 3. The Parliament shall, subject to this Constitution, have power to make laws
>   with respect to matters relating to the Aboriginal and Torres Strait Islander
>   Voice, including its composition, functions, powers and procedures.

This is a modest proposal, designed over many years of consultation, research and debate to empower Aboriginal and Torres Strait Islander people to have a say in the laws and policies that affect them. History shows, the Close the Gap reports show, successive royal commission reports show, and the statistics show, that for most Indigenous people those laws and policies have failed to improve their lives—and in many cases, further marginalised them from the opportunities enjoyed by other Australians.

Dutton's special trick in his drive to persuade Australians to vote 'No' relies on several old hacks that former prime minister John Howard turned into weapons of war against decency and humanity. He learnt the dark arts of misleading the voters to retain power, not only from his Australian-born backroom boys, but also from an emerging class of influencers who respectively succeeded in winning power for their masters by getting Donald Trump elected to the presidency in the United States and Boris Johnson to the prime ministership in the United Kingdom. They also persuaded the British to vote against their own economic interests in the Brexit plebiscite with the result that the UK has fallen to the bottom of the OECD economic rankings and ordinary Britons are sacrificing meals for heating. The *Financial Times* reported in November 2022 that the economy 'is set to be the worst performer in the G20 bar Russia over the next two years'.

Just as Nigel Farage and Boris Johnson conned the voters into voting for a fantasy about the Britannia of their private school days, so Dutton is appealing to the old frontier days beloved of Queenslanders who remember when Aboriginal and Torres Strait Islander people were kept in their place by Joh Bjelke-Petersen. I remember too. I grew up in that racist system that classed me and every other Indigenous person as a 'ward of the state'. That authoritarian control of our lives may have lessened, and the formal racist laws ended two or three decades ago, but the logic of paternalist control lives on in Dutton's Liberal Party, and alarmingly in what he says is the policy position of his party room on the Voice proposal.

The Opposition Leader has announced that his frontbench is bound to the 'No' case as he has outlined it, and indicated that backbenchers would be free to have a conscience vote. It is clear that some members of his party room dispute the outcome, and several are refusing to advocate the 'No' case. Premier of Tasmania Jeremy Rockliff has also refused to advocate for the 'No' case. Dutton represents the hard right of Queensland Liberal and National Party members, and this is his strategic error.

Rather than John Howard's much cruder lies about 'children overboard' in demonising the 433 refugees on Norwegian freighter MV *Tampa* and refusing to accept them, Dutton is purporting not concern for the children of the despised Muslims on boats but instead concern for the remote Aboriginal people who are being manipulated by a 'Canberra elite', '24 academics'. He purports to support closing the gap on our disadvantages but insults all 25 of us serving on the Referendum Working Group as the 'Canberra elite'. This was especially shocking since one of our members was the great Dr Yunupingu, elder and statesman from northeast Arnhem Land who died just days before Dutton made these disgusting statements. Moreover, only three of our members live in Canberra, and all are Elders born and raised in the Northern Territory: Professor Tom Calma AO, and Senior Australian of the Year; Pat Anderson AO, former ACT Senior Australian of the Year; and Pat Turner AM, CEO of NACCHO and the Chair of the Coalition of Peaks. The majority of the members live in and represent Indigenous constituencies in the Torres Strait Islands (Pedro Stephen), the Kimberley (Peter Yu) and Quandamooka, south-east Queensland (Dean Parkin), as well as the Kaurareg Aboriginal and Kalkalgal, Erubamle Torres Strait Islander, living in Darwin (Thomas Mayo) and the list goes on, with the contributions of each outclassing Dutton's in compassion and good works manifold times.

Let's think also for a moment about his insult to his parliamentary colleagues who serve on the Referendum Working Group. The Referendum Working Group is co-chaired by Indigenous Australians Minister Linda Burney and Special Envoy Senator Patrick Dodson, and especially his former cabinet colleague Ken Wyatt, who resigned his membership of the Liberal Party after Dutton and Ley announced their opposition. The full list of non-parliamentary members insulted by Peter Dutton can be read here:

Mr Dale Agius, SA Commissioner for First Nations Voice

Ms Pat Anderson AO, Co-chair of Uluṟu Dialogue; Chairperson, Batchelor Institute

Ms Geraldine Atkinson, Co-chair (outgoing), First People's Assembly of Victoria; Member of Indigenous Voice Co-design groups

Professor Tom Calma AO, Co-chair, Indigenous Voice Co-design groups; Chancellor, University of Canberra; and Co-chair, Reconciliation Australia

Professor Megan Davis, Co-chair of Uluṟu Dialogue; Balnaves Chair in Constitutional Law UNSW

Mr Rodney Dillon, Chair, Tasmanian Aboriginal Heritage Council; Co-chair, Tasmanian Regional Aboriginal Community Alliance

Mr Sean Gordon, Managing Director, Gidgee Group; Councillor, University of Newcastle

Dr Jackie Huggins AM FAHA, Co-chair, QLD Treaty Advancement Committee; Co-chair, National Apology Foundation

Professor Dr Marcia Langton AO, Co-chair, Indigenous Voice Co-design groups; Associate Provost, University of Melbourne

Mr Thomas Mayo, National Indigenous Officer, Maritime Union of Australia; From the Heart

Mr Tony McAvoy SC, NT Treaty Commissioner; Barrister

Ms June Oscar AO (ex officio), Aboriginal and Torres Strait Islander Social Justice Commissioner

Mr Dean Parkin, From the Heart

Mr Noel Pearson, Founder of Cape York Institute; From the Heart; and Member of Indigenous Voice Co-design groups

Ms Sally Scales, Uluṟu Dialogue member; APY Artist

Mr Napau Pedro Stephen AM, Chairperson, Torres Strait Regional Authority

Mr Marcus Stewart, Co-chair, First People's Assembly of Victoria; Member of Indigenous Voice Co-design groups

Ms Pat Turner AM, Convenor of Coalition of Peaks; CEO, National Aboriginal Community Controlled Health Organisation; and Member of Indigenous Voice Co-design groups

The Hon Ken Wyatt AM, former minister for Indigenous Australians

Professor Peter Yu AM, Vice President, First Nations at ANU; Member of Indigenous Voice Co-design groups

Yunupingu (1948–2023), Chairman, Yothu Yindi Foundation; Member of Indigenous Voice Co-design groups.

Leaving aside Dutton's utter ignorance of the biographies of the members of the Referendum Working Group and the parliamentary process, there is the chilling innuendo in his statements that send a very nasty message: those of us who have managed to close the gap in our own lifetimes by standing up to racism and working hard against the odds are now 'manipulating' the vulnerable Aboriginal and Torres Strait Islander people who have not closed the gap, even though each one of our life stories demonstrates decades of hard work to improve their lives. It is worth reminding readers that Professor Tom Calma AO was the main protagonist who convinced Australian governments to formalise the Close the Gap strategy. Pat Turner AM convinced Australian governments to sign the national partnership to Close the Gap and collaborate to achieve the new targets.

This hack of the 'real Aborigines' versus the alleged frauds has been borrowed from a long line of politicians, haters, shock jocks, grifters and Murdoch opinion writers, including Pauline Hanson, Mark Latham, John Howard, Alan Jones, Gary Johns and Andrew Bolt. The stock in trade of the racist who purports to love the 'real Aborigines' is to cast all the Indigenous people they hate as frauds, as Andrew Bolt did in his famous 'It's Hip to be Black' articles that were found by Federal Court Justice Bromberg to be racist and based on lies, and ordered to be removed permanently from the internet. Dutton's sneaky version of this is 'We shouldn't be voting for a divisive Canberra voice, that's the issue. We should be listening to what people are saying on the ground', as reported in most of the media, including on the ABC's 7.30 in an interview by Sarah Ferguson with me on Thursday 6 April 2023.

The announcement of the Liberals' party room opposition to the Voice question by Peter Dutton and Sussan Ley was a jumble of deceitful propositions, glued together with the usual contempt for Indigenous people who won't bend over and smile while being punched down on with their paternalism. Lucky for them there are a few who will.

There are several obvious points to make about their announcement and its messaging. The first is that it came just days after the Liberal Party lost the seat of Aston, creating a historic record—it was the first time in 103 years that a federal government had won a seat from the Opposition in a by-election. The swing against the Liberals shocked even Labor; at more than 6%, it demonstrated that the Liberal Party had lost touch with its traditional constituency and also everyone else, including most women, young Australians, the children of migrants, Chinese Australians, and other ethnic groups that had been demonised in the brutal years of rule by Howard, Abbott, Turnbull and Morrison. As Minister for Indigenous Australians Linda Burney MP said on the ABC, 'Today's decision is about Liberal Party internals. It has nothing to do with Aboriginal and Torres Strait Islander people or taking Australia forward together.'

At the core of the Liberal Party opposition to the Voice is the very idea of the recognition of Indigenous Australians, even if Dutton denies this. His slippery, two-faced approach is to pretend to support a 'symbolic recognition' and the 'practical implementation' of local and regional bodies to give advice. Dutton has tried to deceive Australians into believing that the Liberal Party supported the Voice. He has lied about this in several ways. He is banking on most Australians being ignorant of the fact that every Coalition government for the past ten years—and he served as a cabinet minister in every one of them—deliberately and viciously opposed both. Former minister for Indigenous Australians Ken Wyatt took the Interim Report and the Final Report of the Indigenous Voice Co-Design process (led by Professor Tom Calma AO and me) to Cabinet in 2020 and 2021, and both times, Cabinet declined to approve the implementation of the regional and local voices. Further, Dutton now claims incorrectly that the proposed Voice to Parliament will be a 'new arm of the government' and will require 'thousands of new public servants' and 'cost billions to run, without improving outcomes for Indigenous Australians'. These matters will be settled by the Parliament should the referendum be successful, and he knows that. The question itself does not concern these matters.

Dutton plainly set out to deceive Australians on his claim to support what is now referred to as the Calma–Langton Report, suggesting that I support his contention about regional bodies being preferable over the national Voice. That is not supported by the evidence. The Calma–Langton Report recommends an integrated system of regional bodies that would appoint a National Voice. Our terms of reference explicitly ruled out any consideration of constitutional matters. Our report was devised by a group of 52 people, mostly Indigenous, relying on consultations with thousands of people, and is largely technical in its recommendations. Dutton has misrepresented our recommendations. They are there for all to see in our Final Report on the Aboriginal and Torres Strait Islander Voice website.

This will be the basis for parliamentary debates following the referendum, should it be successful. We include: a summary of our recommendations; and a graphic overview of the local/regional Voice arrangements which would nominate members to the National Voice; that the Voice would have no responsibilities for funding or programs; it would be advisory only; it would provide advice to the Parliament and to government. We accommodated remote regions, youth, people who live with disabilities and Torres Strait Islanders who live on the mainland; ethics and a system for determining who is a fit and proper person; and how the Voice would give advice.

Sarah Ferguson noted that Dutton says his decision to oppose the Voice to Parliament is based on his view that it is an elitist 'and I quote, "Canberra" model, that it won't improve the lives of Indigenous Australians'. She asked me to respond to that, and I replied: 'He couldn't be further from the truth, and I deeply resent that deceitful opinion that he's expressed.'

Tom Calma and I were co-chairs of the senior advisory group in the Voice co-design process appointed by Ken Wyatt, and we chaired meetings of 52 people including a National Voice Co-design group and a Local and Regional Voice Co-design group from all over the country, from rural and remote Australia and from the cities, from every state and territory. It was a collaborative effort—and yet a lot of people say it was a government report. No, it was not. It is the report of the 52 people on that Voice Co-design Committee, and we presented two reports to Ken Wyatt.

He has explained this in public a number of times. He took the Interim Report to Cabinet: no comment. He took the Final Report to Cabinet: no comment. It was my view, shared by several informed observers of federal politics, that Peter Dutton would never support the proposition for constitutional recognition through the enshrinement of the Voice. His early days in the Queensland Police Force shaped his world view and his approach to Indigenous Australians, as he himself admits. I made my views clear to Sarah Ferguson:

> At no time in our history has Peter Dutton ever acted in a way that has, you know, resulted in a measure that would close the gap on our disadvantages, that would benefit us, that would enable Aboriginal and Torres Strait Islander people to fully participate in Australian society. That's just not his track record.

In fact, to the contrary—many of his decisions, including walking out rudely on the apology to the Stolen Generations, rather typifies his history, and even though he much, much later apologised for that, one, of course, has the feeling that he did so under pressure to rehabilitate his reputation.

In contrast, Prime Minister Anthony Albanese has been positive and transparent in his commitment to the principle of constitutional recognition through the enshrinement of a Voice for Indigenous Australians: 'We've waited 122 years to recognise in our Constitution the privilege that we have of sharing this continent with the oldest continuous culture on Earth. I say to Australians, do not miss this opportunity.'

I have been particularly surprised at the way that Julian Leeser, as the former shadow minister for Indigenous Australians, twisted history and participated in a lie-fest to oppose the Voice, given he co-chaired with Senator Patrick Dodson the Joint Select Committee on Constitutional Recognition relating to Aboriginal and Torres Strait Islander Peoples. It shows some integrity on Mr Leeser's part to have resigned the shadow ministry to move to the backbench, knowing that it took more than a decade of work to propose constitutional recognition of First Peoples by ensuring the Voice. He shows some familiarity with the Calma–Langton report, which results from the recommendations he made when co-chairing the Joint Select Committee with Senator Patrick Dodson. However, he insists that he will push for changing the referendum question. He has not made the task of advocating for a 'Yes' vote easier. I will be interested to see his submission to the present Joint Select Committee considering the Bill. He remains confused and unable to arrive at the logical position of supporting the Bill as it is, despite his protestations about his positive commitment arrived at ten years ago.

Dutton also claims that the Solicitor-General argued against the Voice being able to make representations to executive government. It is central to the case that Dutton is making. He is not correct, and is devising a false case to frighten the voters. He is relying on voters to believe his web of deceit and ignore the Aboriginal and Torres Strait Islander leaders who are advocating for constitutional recognition through the enshrinement of the Voice.

The Solicitor-General gave us a briefing on a particular set of words. Some of the members of the Referendum Working Group were concerned about the wording and how those words might confuse voters, and especially the majority of Aboriginal and Torres Strait Islander people who were relying on us to settle the referendum question to their satisfaction, after years of consultations. We debated a second set of words proposed by Attorney-General Mark Dreyfus. After debating this proposal, I believe that we settled on a constitutionally sound referendum question that clarified the scope of the Voice and the powers of Parliament that does not derogate from the power of the Voice to make representations to Parliament and the executive government, while also clarifying and confirming the powers of Parliament. The question is clear and comprehensible to anybody in the community and we are able to defend it. The constitutional alteration defines the powers of the Parliament to design the Voice in legislation and, should we be successful in the referendum, it will become the subject of a parliamentary committee and a design process. The Second Reading Speech, which will be relied on by courts, makes this clear, but it has been misrepresented by Dutton.

Australians will be consulted, and parliamentarians will have their say in the House of Representatives and the Senate on the design of the Voice. The referendum can still succeed without bipartisan support. The electorate has changed over the past two decades, and I believe that Dutton has made a strategic error in banking on the confusion and contempt that Barnaby Joyce, Andrew Bolt, Pauline Hanson and others are causing with conspiracy theories that are not justified by the Constitution Alteration Bill and the Second Reading Speech. These are now the subject of a Joint Select Committee, and any member of the public can make a submission.

Most Australians rejected the hard-right policies at the last federal election, in the NSW election and in the Aston by-election. The constituency of the Liberal Party has changed dramatically. Dutton seems unaware or cavalier in his misreading of the electorate, hoping for a swing to the 'No' case based on fear-mongering and contempt for Aboriginal and Torres Strait Islander people. We who advocate for the 'Yes' case are hoping that Australians are better than this, and more aware than ever before of the case for empowering us to make representations to Parliament and government that have historically imposed laws and policies that continually fail us, and fail all Australians. Aboriginal and Torres Strait Islander people deserve better than Dutton's gaming of a very straightforward and modest proposal.

• • •

Picture of a Peanut Gallery

Mohammed
Massoud
Morsi

Mohammed Massoud
Morsi is an Egyptian-
Danish-Australian
photographer,
journalist and
writer. His work has
been published
in all three of his
traditional languages.
Morsi looks to
important questions,
finding what is
quintessentially
human in broader
struggles.

Small rice lamps in splendid colours showed the way. The woman and the foreigner walked past two cars, a boat and a spot-lit carport. An open gate welcomed them to the back of the house. Soft music was playing. Up against a rustic brick wall, a grand barbecue was surrounded by a large group of people. Most of them had a drink in hand. The woman and the foreigner made their way to the crowd where couples and smaller groups were scattered under deliberately flaccid lights. The foreigner took the bottle of wine he was holding and put it in a tub with the other drinks. Melting ice overflowed the edge and fell onto his feet. He curled his toes against his thongs and smiled to himself.

'What would you like to drink?' the foreigner asked the woman.

'An apple cider, ta,' she said.

The foreigner pulled up bottlenecks from the ice until he found the right one. He twisted it open and handed it to the woman. She blew him a kiss in return.

The noise of the party was humming, like a sort of mooing only broken by the odd squeal of 'Jesus!', 'You're kidding me!', or 'Oh my God!' The foreigner stood for a while, smelling the bacon-wrapped sausages. He watched as the fat dripped and burst into flames. He saw the woman walking over to a couple and hugging them. She wrapped her arms across toward them, but kept her body away—a sort of an A-frame hug. She turned around and signaled for the foreigner to join them. As soon as he had greeted the couple, the women turned to each other and started talking. The foreigner and the man glanced at each other.

'What are you drink—oh—shit—sorry mate! I didn't think about it. You guys don't drink, do you?'

'I am driving,' said the foreigner. He smiled briefly and looked across the garden.

The crowd was shoulder to shoulder, grouped in small flocks, moving in a leg-cuffed pace around each other. A hiss from the barbecue slithered across the garden.

The foreigner, an avid photographer, had a small film camera with him. He took it out of his pocket and placed it in front of his right eye.

'Good shot?' asked the man.

'Last shot,' the foreigner replied, listening to the film rewinding. 'It kind of looks like a peanut gallery—what do you think?'

'What's a peanut gallery?' asked the man. 'I don't think I've ever heard of that.' The foreigner removed the camera from his eye and kept looking across at the people.

'It's where ...' the foreigner paused. 'Never mind, don't worry about it,' he said.

'Too easy! What are you drinking, mate?' asked the man.

'I'm driving,' said the foreigner.

'Faark! Sorry mate! I've already had a few,' the man said and slapped his own face. The foreigner turned briefly and smiled at the man, to let him know it was fine.

'So... I've heard things aren't that great back home,' said the man.

The foreigner was still watching the large group of people. What were they all doing, he wondered. Standing and talking, sitting and talking, talking and talking. There was no dancing, no playing, no cards being shuffled, nothing. Just the draping, dawdling and drinking.

Something needed to happen.

'Yes, something needs to happen,' said the foreigner.

'Do you think there will be another revolution?' asked the man.

'Maybe, I don't know.'

'I reckon it'd all blow up if that happens.'

'Why is that?'

'Well, they're all crazy!'

'Who is crazy?' asked the foreigner.

'The fucking terrorists, all them Bin Ladens—no offence, mate!'

The foreigner paused, thinking. 'None taken,' he said.

Something definitely needed to happen. A demonstration, a revolution—the man was right. Yes, a revolution! The foreigner was sure of it. We should break out of the rythmns of life, of this party. We would all get naked. We'd look into each other's eyes. We'd be dancing and playing. We would come to life! It would make sense, it would justify everything!

People crowded closer around the barbeque. There was a clinking of cutlery.

'Time for some snaggers!' said the man. 'Follow me!'

The foreigner followed the man, and the two women strolled behind them. The man grabbed a beer from the icy tub. He cracked open the can and quickly put it to his mouth. He gulped down the froth and some more. His cheeks bulged for a moment before he let out a loud burp. The man laughed at himself.

'What can I get you?' the foreigner asked the woman.

'I'll have one of those wrapped ones, babe, ta!' answered the woman before returning to her conversation with the other woman. The foreigner took a paper plate and dressed it up with the sausage, a colourful salad and a handful of fat, gleaming prawns.

'Pretty good setup you got there!' said the man.

'Yes, not bad,' said the foreigner, wielding a brief pulling of his lips.

'Mate, I knew you were all right,' said the man before he gave the foreigner a wink.

The foreigner didn't answer. He stared at the man busy picking his food. He turned around and handed the woman her plate, who returned him a kiss, a peck on his lips.

'Are you alright?' she asked.

'I'm—,' he began to speak and stopped, staring into the woman's eyes. The foreigner put his head forward and kissed her. The woman and the foreigner both closed their eyes until the foreigner pulled back. He didn't take his eyes off the woman and said, 'I'm ... not hungry—not yet—but I'm getting there.'

The woman smiled and turned to her friend. The foreigner looked at her back, her bare shoulder blades. Her dress was red, the fabric light. His eyes followed her spine, traced the outline of her underwear. For a moment the foreigner was lost in thought. Then it snapped to him. How dare he just stand there without starting that revolution, without getting naked? He would not waste this opportunity.

He took his clothes of. Right there. Right then. And everyone clapped. Everyone cheered. The woman blew him yet another kiss. Her lips glistened. He smiled.

When the foreigner woke up, he was all alone. There was no woman. He got out of bed. In the kitchen he flicked the kettle on and looked out the window. There were no cars on the verge, no gleaming prawns or snaggers dripping fat. No fancy barbeque, no soft music or tub with daftly named beers sticking out of ice.

A car drove past, then a van appeared. It stopped, outside the foreigner's house, idling. After a while, the driver jumped out. He slid the side door open and began offloading bundles of junkmail onto the curb. Once he had finished, the driver walked towards the house with a slip in his hand. The foreigner opened the front door.

'Mornin' mate,' the driver said. 'Sign here, mate.'

The foreigner rolled the pen on the paper. The driver wasn't the usual guy, but he was Asian nonetheless. The foreigner wondered whether he could also be a delivery driver or whether he had to be Asian, too.

'We need the rain,' the foreigner said.

The driver stopped, clearly confused.

'What mate?—What did you say mate?' asked the driver.

'That we need the rain,' said the foreigner, gesturing towards the bundles of junkmail. The driver scratched his head for a moment, then pulled a smile:

'I'm all good in there—mate,' and pointed to the van as he turned around and walked away. He took off, staring at the foreigner as he sped off.

The foreigner walked out to the curb. He curled his toes against the wet grass and stared at all the papers piled up before his feet. He gazed up and across the sky. The sky was intensely blue. He walked back inside.

The foreigner sat down with a cup of tea and listened to the ticking of the kitchen clock. It was Sunday morning. It was quiet. Something needed to happen. A month had passed since he'd come back from back home. He recalled going through the passport control at Perth airport. He remembered the immigration officer who had glanced at his name and with a smirk, quickly added: 'You just need Bin Laden in there, and it'd be perfect—mate!'

The foreigner was about to take another sip of his tea when he noticed a red piece of fabric draped over the back of the chair in front of him. He put down his cup and walked across to it. He picked it up—the woman's red dress. He put it to his nose. It smelt nice, a mixture of perfume, meat, and mostly sweat.

The foreigner put the red dress on. He had broad shoulders, a firm chest, dappled with hair. He stepped out to the hallway mirror and looked at himself. The red dress stretched out like a tank top. It matched his blue underpants. He liked his frumpy look.

The foreigner walked out to his car in the driveway. There on the dash was his camera. He bent over to grab it. His arm was still inside the car when he heard his neighbour across the road. The neighbour was laughing hysterically. The foreigner froze until he heard the sound of a car door slamming. The neighbour honked the horn as he drove past. He was still laughing, now a muted laughter behind closed windows. The foreigner straightened up. He took off the red dress and his blue underpants. He stretched out his arms and did a full circle. Nothing happened. He went back inside.

The foreigner developed the film in the kitchen sink. He swiped the water off the negatives when they were ready and held them up against the window. There. He placed the magnifier on a frame and squinted through the eyepiece. Something *had* happened.

In the photo was a large group of people. They were all over each other, hurtled helter-skelter into the small rectangle of the picture. They were all naked. The foreigner was, too. His smile was wide. The woman was there. But she was throwing something at him. She was angry. They all were. They were drunk, and they were angry. In the negative, the foreigner was the only white man. In that frame, it was them who had no voice. They were the black ones now—in that picture of a peanut gallery.

● ● ●

Smoke and Mirrors

Stephen
Edgar

Stephen Edgar's most recent book, *The Strangest Place: New and Selected Poems*, received the Prime Minister's Literary Award for Poetry in 2021. He lives in Sydney.

That worst of summers,
When the whole eastern seaboard was ablaze
And the air was blind with smoke,
Thick as a sifted fall of powdered pumice,
Yet our brief holiday's
First evening a clear window. Then we woke
To find the Hawkesbury choked in a pall of haze.

A silent cell,
The renovated boathouse where we stayed
You'd fancy was afloat
On the sluggish water, as it swelled and fell.
We stepped out and surveyed
The morning (now a gag lodged in the throat)
And saw the far side of the river fade.

A lurid sun
Smeared its distorting mirror, like a sprue
Of dimly gleaming metal.
The rail bridge was the ghost of an outline spun
From shadow, showing through
A scrim of hanging ash that would not settle.
We were the last ones left, for all we knew.

But that first day
Flourished its sleight of time or latitude,
The lucid atmosphere
Letting its nets of sunlight down to sway
Around the decking, slewed
And stretched beneath our feet in shallows clear
As air, for fish to slip through and elude.

All day, nightlong,
The river's lap and glug and suck combined
To play unerringly
The intricate variations of their song,
As though they'd been assigned
To lodge it in our sleeping memory,
And not to pause, lest it be lost to mind.

Australia in Three Books

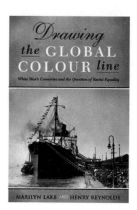

Julianne
Schultz

Julianne Schultz is
Professor Emeritus
Media and Culture,
Griffith University,
founding editor of
Griffith Review and
author of *The Idea of
Australia: A search for
the soul of the nation*.

Reducing my Australia to just three books makes me feel like someone panning for gold in a fast-moving stream filled with the precious metal. If I stand still long enough and shake the pan hard enough, surely just three exceptional nuggets will be left. It's fair to say that I have a privileged perspective.

In my house I have three rooms and half a garage lined with books. Probably about half are by Australian authors, many by friends and colleagues, people I have published and with whom I have had long (and fleeting) conversations. They are about Australia looking in and looking out, filled with research, emotion and analysis. Beautifully curated catalogues of exhibitions, historical tomes, collections of essays, biographies,

books about First Peoples, politics, media, women, migration, environment, policy, economics, war, royal commissions; a room of novels and short stories, shelves of poetry.

It was a collection that came into its own when I was researching and writing *The Idea of Australia*. So many telling details, and stories, waiting to be plucked and applied to my quest to try to make sense of this ancient young nation that is both a continent and an island, but is still a half-formed thing. Because it is in books, and the distilled intelligence and insights of their authors, that the seeds of the imagined nation germinate. Two recent comprehensive surveys of a century of novels and plays, Julian Meyrick's *Australia in 50 Plays* (Currency) and Carl Reinecke's *Books that Made Us* (HarperCollins), are good starting points.

The many books in my library show that the Australia imagined into being is at its best generous and diverse, respectful and inclusive, and at its worst fearful, ignorant and cruel. It is not perfect, but it is not owned by the *oi oi oi* brigade.

In getting to my three nuggets, I need to explain a little of my process, something of my journey and some of the questions left unanswered, which my chosen volumes address.

When I was a child, my parents had invested, by onerous hire-purchase, in the *Australian Encyclopaedia*. Like country children everywhere I had worked my way through the red bound volumes. It is possible they chose this imposing set instead of the more famous *Britannica* out of a burgeoning anti-imperialist sentiment, but truth be known, they were probably cheaper.

When I arrived at the University of Queensland in the mid 1970s, Australian studies were finding a place in the long-established humanities and social sciences curricula. It was not something that came easily; we students heard whispers of departmental debates. But it suited the times. The local version of the decolonising impulse that had reshaped the world after World War II: a growing curiosity about what being Australian meant detached from Britain.

At the time, there was still a long way to go. Much was still invisible. But it was possible to enrol in a contemporary Australian-inflected program in literature, history, government, sociology. In the previous decade a determined cohort of ambitious scholars had begun to open the field, to create a distinctive Australian scholarship. By the 1970s they were still searching for the theoretical framework that would later open many more doors.

In the literature honours class, we read the canon, comparing and contrasting it with the smaller list of 'Australian classics'. We were encouraged to explore the writers who showed there was more going on beneath the surface than the old school realists had allowed— Patrick White, Christina Stead, Thea Astley, Oodgeroo Noonuccal, Kath Walker, Thomas Keneally. A new generation of (then mainly) short-story writers and poets were finding places to be published and a hungry readership, including Frank Moorhouse, Kate Jennings, Peter Carey, Murray Bail, Helen Garner, Michael Wilding, Kate Grenville and David Malouf.

Any sensitive young person who was paying attention knew that there was more to know than was allowed in the public discourse. But finding it and making sense of it was not easy. Silence prevailed. Censorship was still in the air. But awareness of First Peoples was pricking the consciousness and those trapped under the white blanket of assimilation were breaking free. Feminism and civil rights were in the air.

One of my classmates in that stuffy, windowless seminar room at UQ elegantly skewered this years later, and his book is one of my three nuggets. **Ross Gibson's** *Seven Versions of an Australian Badland* was published by University of Queensland Press in 2002. It is, deservedly, still in print and available for sale. Sadly, Ross recently died, but his work lives on. *Seven Versions* elegantly and forensically identifies what was happening beneath the surface of regional Queensland and how the trauma and shame of it lingers, making the history unbearable and even the consolation of myth insufficient.

In the 1970s and 1980s in the slapdash, but punishingly real, autocracy of Joh Bjelke-Petersen and the corrupt National Party and its enabling police force, one of the go-to subjects of newspaper feature writers, television current affairs producers and satirists was 'is Queensland different?' The answer was invariably 'yes', but the explanations were never really satisfactory. The thing the journalists missed was that Queensland was the site of the longest and most single-minded extermination of First Peoples on the mainland. The number killed during the second half of the nineteenth century is now conservatively estimated at 62,000—and that does not count those poisoned by opium or grog or locked in missions.

Even before the historiography settled on the scale of this protracted murderous assault, Ross Gibson took his readers on a journey through central Queensland and showed them the signs. The somewhat desolate landscape is brought to life as a 'gigantic crime scene ... a haunted place'. His publisher describes it as 'part road movie, part memoir, part murder mystery'—and that is all true. It is also a poet's work of scholarship. In this year of the Voice to Parliament, it deserves many new readers and will reward those who read this slender volume again.

Sensing what happened is one thing. Knowing it is another, and another still is trying to make sense of why. For all the noise about the arrival of the First Fleet in 1788 and Cook's journey up the east coast eighteen years before, the formation of the nation by act of the British Parliament in 1900 and a parade up Oxford Street and an official ceremony in a blustery Centennial Park on 1 January 1901, remains little known.

It deserves more attention. Therein lie the origins of many of the issues that still beset the modern nation. It's possible that the Voice debate will provide an opportunity for some more insight into this complex process, but I am not optimistic. *Hamilton* is more captivating.

One of the defining characteristics of the Australian colonies was that people were hungry for news and information. It might have taken a while for the journals to get here, but when they did, they were devoured. People knew what was happening elsewhere, the debates and arguments, intellectual and political fashions and trends. A republic of newspapers, some called it.

By Federation Australia was arguably the most literate and numerate society in the world, with compulsory education and a record number of universities per capita. The colonies were established at a time when much was changing—religion lost its power, science was ascendant, revolutions flared and died, capital was global, slavery ceased, and pseudo-scientific 'race' became the new divide.

Those arguing for a federation of the colonies were keen to create a civic nationalism. Universal suffrage (for men) and the absence of an official religion (for reasons of political expediency) were two markers of this. It was only when the first federal parliament sat that the limits of this civic nationalism became clear. The carefully nurtured fear of racial difference was legislated and shaped the nation for (at least) the next 70 years. The deportation of South Sea Islanders who had been brought to work as (virtual) slaves, the White Australia policy and the disenfranchisement of First Peoples and 'Asiatics' when women were given the vote.

Australians were accustomed to paying attention to debates elsewhere, but in adopting racialist exclusion the new nation was ready to lead the world. My second nugget is therefore the extraordinary book by **Marilyn Lake** and **Henry Reynolds**, *Drawing the Global Colour Line*, published by Melbourne University Press in 2008. It traces the 'leadership' of Australians in this brutal process, and documents how it shaped the nation and influenced others.

Much has been written, quite rightly, about the treatment of First Peoples, but the legacy of these policies touched many other people who did not fit the punitively narrow definition of English-speaking 'whiteness' over decades. It is a foundational flaw, and this important book explores how it happened.

Assimilation was a cruel policy of the past, but it is not completely buried, explored or compensated for.

My final nugget points to the future. It is **Marcia Langton's** *Welcome to Country*, first published by Hardie Grant in 2021 and since republished several times. It is a joyous celebration of the true uniqueness of the country and its complexity.

It is just the antidote we all need. Marcia also survived those curious classes at UQ in the 1970s, when Australian studies was just beginning, and some still persistently believed 'race' defined difference. Her book, rich with collaboration, provides a path to engaging with the truly unique dimensions of this island continent's history, people and possibility.

• • •

The Politics of Home

Transformations on the home front in a post-pandemic world

Rachel
Goldlust

Rachel Goldlust is a researcher, writer, housing academic and occasional natural builder passionate about sustainable design, eco-living and the relationship our homes have with the broader environment.

The world cannot be discovered by a journey of miles, no matter how long, but only by a spiritual journey, a journey of one inch, very arduous and humbling and joyful, by which we arrive at the ground at our feet, and learn to be at home.

—Wendell Berry

I have been spending a lot more time than usual on my front porch. Previously inclined to the protection of our back yard, now I go out front at night (especially if it's raining) and watch the curfew-emptied streets from behind the safety of an overhanging tree. It seems natural, given this 'unprecedented' moment, to want to see what's going on 'out there', even if it is just the comings and goings of joggers, tradesmen, dog walkers, kids on bikes, postmen and delivery drivers.

It has felt important to bear witness to the altered streetscape in this tiny pocket of Melbourne—a vignette of an entirely new scenario being replicated across the city, and across the state, as we continue to 'shelter at home' as the Americans are wont to term it. Whether it has been a conscious transition or not, our lack of commuting and reduced driving to work, sport, social engagements, restaurants, meetings and school have resulted in an inverse increase in foot traffic. Moreover, checking out what the neighbours are up to has taken on a whole new dimension as our visual world has shrunk considerably, especially when any opportunity for sensory stimulation is largely restricted to the digital realm. We may marvel at the endless cornucopia of online content—the talks, seminars, courses and classes, television series and endless YouTube parodies devoted to lifting our spirits and keeping us sated—but it is reassuring to step out onto the porch to absorb something of the real world, limited as it may be.

Reframing this enforced 'staycation' into a positive and meaningful experience has involved a few leaps of imagination. It has meant casting our eyes to the foreground,

This piece was written during the dark winter of 2020 and things are a bit clearer and more hopeful now.

and less to the horizon since it is that faraway place that has wreaked such fear and uncertainty. It has led to us narrowing our hopes, dreams and expectations. It has meant settling and looking for the positives out of the chaos. Our gaze has indelibly shifted—from looking out a plane window or the endlessness of a rural horizon on road trips—to scanning the streets and walkways of our immediate locale: the well-trodden paths of our local parklands, the familiar faces in our neighbourhood, and the businesses in our 5km radius that have become comforting and reassuring. It's the perfect time to consider the benefits, if any, of shortening our vision and limiting our imagination to the walls, fences, streets and blocks. The journey, as Wendell Berry reminds us, may have shortened to that of inches, but it is only by looking to these smaller spaces that we start to deduce some profound, and worldly, realisations.

As we tentatively and guardedly emerge from the most extensive and hard lockdown in the world, it feels both timely and necessary to challenge the vision and parameters of our former prime minister's 'gas-fired future', to shift the impetus and vision of sustainability from a peripheral concern into a central and decisive issue, as it relates to us, the citizenry, and the political debate. If we're not so fond of this plan, which many of us are not, and given the vision for our lives and those who come after us may have been forever constrained, or at least changed, by this pandemic, how do we change what we do with what we have?

It's time to ask which of the habits or ideas that have become 'COVID normal' we will take into our ever-encroaching post-pandemic reality as the scars of extensive business closures, changing trade patterns and narrowed work and living possibilities indelibly shape the future. Being 'local', it turns out, can extend beyond UberEATS deliveries to encompass valuable and lasting bonds formed across newfound communities, creative trade systems that help us with our daily needs, and new work opportunities that demonstrate the value of thinking and operating closer to home on both a personal and global level. My mind is suddenly, and weirdly, drawn to recall the strange circumstances facing the children in Rick Moranis's 1989 classic *Honey, I Shrunk the Kids* as each blade of grass in their back yard became the stage for an epic new life lesson, and their journey was simply to make it to the safety and security of the back door.

●●●

Our homes, until recently, have largely been considered in their political and economic context, but not as constructions that shape or obstruct certain values or ideas. As design trends, land prices and monopolised development continue to constrict the average Australian home to even smaller outdoor spaces, the democracy of the urban dream is indelibly shifting in terms of open-space, and opportunities for DIY improvement. As dwindling resources start to be reflected in decision-making of governments and polity, the home has become the nexus through which the business-as-usual operation of our day-to-day lives can be disrupted and disturbed by more radical social, economic and cultural thinking.

In the years immediately after World War II, the home was often understood (particularly by women) as an active creation of place. With unprecedented affluence as disposable incomes rose and consumers had a dazzling array of products to buy, the creation of the modern dream home became a key means of strengthening the social fabric and economic vitality of Australia. In her appraisal of housewives in 1940s and 1950s Australia, feminist scholar Lesley Johnson argued that the home was not always opposed to or a place to retreat from the modern world but could represent a different vision of what modernity should be about. While the unfolding project of modernity continued to locate progress primarily in the public sphere, the domestic space emerged as a secondary site where wider aspirations could be explored, negotiated, (re)constructed and, ultimately, taken up in politically significant ways. Suburban affluence quickly became the defining image of the good life under capitalism, commonly held up as a model to which all humanity should aspire.

Throughout the 1970s and 1980s, and largely in response to the global oil crises and intense deliberations over nuclear power, the home front became a new battlefield for discourse on resources and consumerism. This shift was heavily influenced by E.F Schumacher's widely celebrated text *Small is Beautiful* (1973), in which he argued against excessive materialism and meaningless growth by promoting the use of small-scale technologies to benefit both humankind and the environment. With the rise of new, smaller, decentralised technologies such as solar and wind power, citizens began, slowly and tentatively, to resist the self-destructive chaos of modernity through an intrinsically satisfying pursuit of domestic self-sufficiency. According to human geographer Aidan Davison, this celebration of individual autonomy was not an expression of the liberal individualism of which environmentalism was so critical. Rather the technology choices of individuals were seen to form the 'straightest path to a truly post-materialistic political order'.[1]

The 1990s saw the politics of governance continue to move into the home. Shaped by new ideas of post-materialism that saw a strengthening of personal responsibilities in tandem with the rise of consumerism, came a small but determined movement for the devolution of power and resources away from central control, and towards local democratic structures, institutions and communities. This movement, broadly termed 'degrowth', was espoused by a small group of academics, radical environmentalists and political commentators across the globe who promoted an individual and collective transition towards what they called a 'conserver society'. This new brand of ecopolitics came to represent a broad movement of citizens engaging in a community-based process of self-government. This was built on the notion that ecology was more than an external system or space, as the Greek root *oikos* (meaning house) could also signify a ready form of green politics in the home.

It is important to note that this shiny new 'eco-conscious' home has long retained vestiges of a deeply divisive and exclusionary past. As historian Graeme Davison has observed, few words in the lexicon of colonialism are more resonant than the word

1
Aidan Davison,
'A Domestic Twist on
the Eco-Efficiency Turn:
Environmentalism,
Technology,
Home', in Andrew
Gorman-Murray (ed.),
*Material Geographies
of Household
Sustainability*,
pp. 35–50, Ashgate
Publishing, Surrey,
2011, p. 37.

home. As an idea and a place, it has been both mythic and traumatic. Notwithstanding a whitewashing of the landscape compounded by a long history of social and economic stratification, Australia's relationship to the home has long been vital to our social and cultural identity. As expressions of success and security, capitalist discourses and practices of home ownership are deeply implicated in the political, cultural and material boundaries of home in Australia. Emerging through the Howard years, the idea acquired a particular resonance in the face of ongoing social and economic transformations, with images of homes disappearing or being destroyed, being radically remade and made over, and being reclaimed and re-privatised as the primary site of care and security. The 1990s bearing witness to the *Bringing them Home* report that may have raised attention to the issue of dispossession and continued structures of inequality, the landmark report also reaffirmed foundational settler narratives of occupation and ownership.

In recent decades, and particularly through this new crisis that will shape the direction of modern civilisation for years to come, the home has become both a prison and a sanctuary, an unsteady amalgam of work and leisure, a political tool that has divided the haves and have-nots (the baby boomers from the rest of us who find ourselves on the wrong side of the 'housing crisis'), and for many, a vehicle or platform from which we can devise and execute plans for global economic and social salvation. As David Holmgren, one of the forefathers of permaculture, recently observed, with forced isolation as the only strategy we have come up with to control and contain the impact of the pandemic came a new reckoning with our dependence on centralised systems and resources, the limitations of living in debt, and a desire for greater independence from the means of production and systems of reproduction from unsustainable materials and lifestyle choices. Holmgren's latest book, *Retrosuburbia*, turns a largely rural gaze towards the suburbs, reframing the spiritual home of overconsumption as positive sites of production, community and economy. This new twenty-first-century 'home economy' is a far cry from the housewives of the 1950s as the average home once again transformed into a vehicle for challenging the central paradigm of growth, becomes a new imaginary of sustainability based on localised systems, economies and thinking.

• • •

In her 2020 article 'The pandemic is a portal', Arundhati Roy observed that historically pandemics have forced humans to break with the past and imagine their world anew. 'This one is no different,' Roy claims. 'It is a portal, a gateway between one world and the next.'[2] One of the many things this portal has revealed following the great toilet paper and spaghetti shortage of early 2020 is the perilousness of our supply chains with the demise of local manufacturing and localised distribution. Realising, often for the first time, that centralised food, medicine and basic sanitation have serious limitations as the world beings to panic, has led to discussions surrounding the oft-forgotten security provided by taking responsibility for our own basic needs at home. As Luke Gosling wrote

2
Arundhati Roy, 'The pandemic is a portal', *The Financial Times*, 4 April 2020.

in *Guardian Australia*, there emerged a national consensus from the double-barrelled bushfire and COVID-19 crises: Australia needs to be much more self-reliant than we have been. Such calls for national self-sufficiency have long been trotted out as political tools, but as hoarding emptied supermarket shelves, there came calls from the margins by those 'kooky' enough to believe in the apocalypse, and who had long believed in the values and mantras of self-sufficiency for exactly these reasons.

With little else to distract our attention, this crisis has brought what was previously a marginal consideration—what to do if the apocalypse comes—into sharper focus. *The New York Times* pointed out that whether by necessity or choice, many had begun adopting acts of 'frugal self-reliance like baking our own bread, teaching our own children—and fixing our own busted iPhone screens' in response to the realities of having to make more from what we have, and because 'we must, as we're more conscious of what we buy and do'.[3] We also started taking on home renovations and garden landscape improvements and looked at ways to make our homes more resilient, flexible and sustainable.

Such energy, born of a newfound capacity and spare time, for remodelling and reappraising the home as more than a site of consumption has also shifted outwards as we look to remake our community as an extension of these desires. A new politics of home as shaped by this pandemic has started to look at resources, supply chains and modalities of dependence, and led many of us to reimagine these links in the face of an unsettling future shaped by a looming recession and extended privations. Many of us turned away from supermarkets as they became chaotic and germ-filled, towards smaller stores and local vegetable boxes sourced through small-grower and direct-to-paddock networks.

Others started looking to local takeaway Facebook pages categorised by region to fill the gap (who wants to cook every night anyway?), to support the struggling restaurant and café industry. At first these links and causalities were framed on a global scale, but the discussion quickly pivoted from what the ineffectual leaders were and weren't doing to help us, to seeing our agency as consumers and realising the home, and its connection to land, food, economics and people, was the key to ensuring individual and collective security and prosperity.

In her 2015 book charting the rise of twentieth-century 'New Domesticity', journalist Emily Matchar observed that the return to home-based activities by modern women (and men) particularly in North America has emerged in response to a decline in public, communal solutions for essentials such as food production and childcare. The draw of 'nostalgic domesticity' through activities such as baking, knitting, canning and vegetable gardening, she notes, has also emerged as a fear response to unsettling sociopolitical situations, and to perceived failures by government institutions to deal adequately with environmental destruction and climate change. Alongside growing distrust in established systems such as healthcare and medicine, utilities, schooling and business, Matchar is not alone in her observation that the past decade has seen a considerable shift towards home-based environmentalism. The forging of 'modern environmentalism' in Australia

3
Shira Ovide, 'The Joys of Fixing Your Own Stuff', *The New York Times*, 14 May 2020.

may have occurred in the thick rainforests of Terania Creek near Nimbin, or the shores of Lake Pedder in Tasmania, but the mechanism through which most Australians in the twenty-first century view their activism is now firmly entrenched in individual and familial consumer choices.

Indeed, this pandemic has witnessed an unparalleled rise in edible gardening that has cascaded into the creation of new communities (largely digital) to support this newfound passion for growing, planting and harvesting our own food. As the findings of the 2020 Pandemic Gardening Survey by Sustain Australia (based on more than 9000 responses) indicates, more than 98% of respondents looked to their own food production in a new light since the start of the pandemic and are encouraged to grow more. This rise was triggered by a growing awareness of the fallibility of the mainstream urban food system as it is restricted by the supermarket duopoly, dependent on fossil fuels for production, packaging and transport, and highly vulnerable in the event of supply disruption.

This enthusiasm for vegetable seedlings was mirrored by a rush on back-yard chickens (and foster animals), and we can start to map out the deep-seated impulse towards security and personal responsibility that hasn't been witnessed on such a scale since the 1930s Depression and World War II. With so many people coming to small-scale back-yard self-sufficiency for the first time, the surge of interest has required new relationships and exchanges of knowledge and skill sharing, in many cases cutting across generation, class and ethnic boundaries. Much of these connections have been facilitated by social media networks, but neighbours have had to look to available resources as Bunnings largely shut its doors, and we've had to 'make do' with sharing equipment, experience and proceeds, in the spirit of tighter times.

In my neighbourhood, the older generation of Greek and Italian migrants are now more often shouting over the fence to younger cohorts of student share houses as we exchange tricks and details of our soils and conditions. As David Holmgren noted in his 2018 chapter in *Reclaiming the Urban Commons*, with more people sharing houses and spending more time at home there is a growing revitalisation of households that generates a 'critical mass of active and present residents in suburbia'. From this comes an increase in efficiency in use of costly infrastructure, reduces crime through casual surveillance and builds community connections. It also provides the economies of scale for efficient garden farming and a host of other self-reliance activities that are marginal in one- and two-person households. Larger households are already forming in a variety of ways including extended family consolidation, blended families and various forms of sharing and landlord–tenant arrangements.[4]

· · ·

While there is much to admire in this inspiring and surprising return to land-based self-sufficiency and domestic traditions and skills, the slow narrowing of vision to one's own home, property or family unit does come with disturbing implications. Where we may

4
David Holmgren, 'Garden Farming: the foundation for agriculturally productive cities and towns', in Andrea Gaynor and Nick Rose (eds), *Reclaiming the Urban Commons: The past, present and future of food growing in Australian towns and cities*, UWA Publishing, Crawley, WA, 2018, p. 5.

have once shown our care and concern for a wider concept of nature, its limited resources and landscapes by attending popular issue-based rallies, a forest lock-in or a petition to Parliament, the conversation around 'what are we doing to help save the environment' has nominally shifted to the relative benefits of buying copper straws and the latest electric bicycle as meaningful gestures towards responsible citizenry.

While the extensive lockdowns across Australia witnessed some reassuring trends, such as the dramatic demand for vegetable seedlings, sourdough starter and puzzles, these shifting behaviours and patterns of consumption also expose a troubling reality. Such pervasive exhortations to individual action, as noted by journalist Martin Lucaks in *The Guardian*, prolific across corporate ads, school textbooks and the campaigns of mainstream environmental groups, has come at the expense of collective public responses to the realities of climate change. While eco-consumerism may expiate one's guilt, most observers agree it is only public participation and intersectional, inter-class movements that have the power to alter the trajectory of the climate crisis. So, while sustainability remains hot on the lips of local if not state or federal governments, what has this extended lockdown and period of isolation taught us as many reconsider what the 'new normal' will look like and what will be available in terms of jobs, resources and public participation?

• • •

Amid the chaos of the past half year our landlord decided to send us a notice of eviction. Fighting off equal parts panic and exasperation, it forced me to think hard about my privilege and relative security, and the inequalities facing many who have been left destitute by the gaps in our government's protection plan, namely the homeless, the international students, the temporary visa holders, the travellers. As sad as I am to leave my veggie garden, my big back yard, my crumbling weatherboard with its stained-glass windows and cosy nooks, I will be able to find a new home. What has this year meant for the others who have found themselves truly 'homeless'? How have they navigated the fear, anxiety and insecurity that comes with every press conference, and every media grab spouting numbers, percentages and prognoses?

It makes me think of Christos Tsiolkas, who wrote of his response to the challenges of 2020 for *Guardian Australia*, comparing his family's displeasure at not being able to move around the globe freely to his migrant parents' 'decision' to move to Australia and stay put:

> In leaving their country at a time of war and poverty, in forging a new life in a new country in which they did not speak the language and which was on the other side of the earth, my mother and my father endured hardships that are inconceivable to a soft generation like my own. Their call is sacrifice. My response has to be gratitude.

His mother's mantra, 'We're not ill and we're not homeless. Let's be thankful for that' has become mine during the tougher moments of this lockdown. And I am reminded that we have so much to be grateful for, as much as we feel acutely all that we have already and will continue to lose through this crisis. What we have to remember, and which I try to remind myself as I enjoy my last few months sitting in the warm breeze on the porch, is to be grateful I have the chance to make a home and continue to build community.

• • •

Citronella

Ella
Ferris

Ella Ferris is a
Taribelang actor,
musician and writer
from far north
Queensland, now
living and working
on the lands of the
Boonwurrung and
Wurundjeri people
in Naarm.

I've got nowhere to be
and it's muggy this year
as if the house itself and the trees are panting
open mouthed and hot breathed

reptilian clouds look
to be sunning themselves
up there on the granite sky

down below we sun ourselves
on red pavement

the ferns quiver
golden in the rays
green in the shade
they seem to twiddle their fingers idly

among the fronds a citronella candle burns

the table is lopsided
but holds us well
sacred little table
it's heard all the pondering we've done
and would laugh along with our jokes if only it had lungs and
a mouth

we speak with looseness
the reek of beer on the tongue
the swoon of alcohol in the blood
I'm never drunk
just softer

the silence is gentle
stillness is only broken by the ripple of pages
or the promise of touch
sometimes a thing will be read aloud
we'll share words at the little table
as if they're part of our meal
I suppose it is nourishment
all the same
and we do serve them with the grace they deserve

the ashtray fills and the citronella flame wanes
the sun is soon to set behind the fence
so we shush and let it go by

Groundwater

Deborah
Wardle

Deborah Wardle
teaches creative
writing and
environmental
literatures at the
University of
Melbourne and
RMIT. Subterranean
imaginaries inspire her
writing and research
practice.

1
Robert Macfarlane's
*Underland: A Deep
Time Journey* (2019)
inspires some of
my reflections on
our journey to the
mound springs of
South Australia.

The water is the temperature of blood. Under a white-hot sky the swimming hole at Dalhousie Springs is fringed with thick reeds and creamy-flowered, paper-barked Melaleucas. Long-billed corellas on drooping branches watch me float.

Slightly saline, a whiff of sulphur suggests the decades, centuries, the millennia that this water has been seeping through aquifers of the Great Artesian Basin. After days of dusty driving the relief of bathing in silky warmth lulls me to thinking that there's plenty of water after all. Trickling emergences of water in the desert remind me of the importance of an inner life, something beyond the material. I muse on underland places, contemplating water oozing from deep below the surface.[1] Groundwater's place in localised water security is vital, yet often unrecognised. As weather events reach new extremes, groundwater is being pumped to its limits, pushed to the brink. I explore the narrative potency of groundwater, its links to the psyche of this continent, as it moves beneath my feet. What can this water story show? How are the effects of the Anthropocene being played out in subterranean ecosystems? I listen for groundwater's imagined voices. The mound springs inspire stories, they feed my soul.

As many travellers have before me, I have journeyed to the desert for a place to think. Inland South Australia is harsh and dry, open and sacred. It's a place where hearts and minds expand and shrink, like the daily cycle of heat and evening cool, like the coming and going of the moon. My partner and I and two long-time friends packed tents and a small gas cooker, food to last a fortnight. Remote townships are dots on our map. There are few options to purchase fuel or supplies, just enormous distances. Mound springs are dispersed like plot points on a graph across a broad arc from far northern parts of South Australia, through the Northern Territory and across to the western edges of Queensland. I imagine they emerge like full stops to many unfinished sentences.

Our journey to the mound springs aims to connect with hard-to-see places. This sojourn asks me to settle in places where I engage more deeply with groundwater's vitality. What stories can aquifers and springs tell about how we understand this country and about how I understand myself?

● ● ●

We drive the long straight roads towards the oozing edges of the Great Artesian Basin. We want to reach Dalhousie Springs, on the western side of the Simpson Desert, a place where paleo water finds its way to the light of day. Mound springs are not just endpoints to subterranean water flows. Their emergence is one small convolution in the water cycle.

Surface water transpires and evaporates, cycles as clouds, falls as rain or snow, fills rivers and oceans. Water also seeps underground, to nourish subterranean realms. Water moves me. The gradual disappearance of mound springs means that only about five hundred remain naturally active, from thousands. I want to see the mound springs before they're gone. What might come to light spending time on country where surface knowledge is not enough?

Clusters of spring-fed waterholes amid stony, gibber plains have been significant resting, hunting and ceremonial places for Indigenous people travelling on expansive inland trading routes. As custodians, they protected the naturally occurring mound springs for millennia. Aboriginal communities' survival was and is maintained by the steady rise of water from deep underground into desert pools. People traditionally met at the well, the spring, the source of water, the source of life.

Having been forced from their lands over the past 150 years, and after prolonged legal challenges, in 2012 the Arabana people were granted native title to 69,000 square kilometres in the north of South Australia, including Kati Thanda (Lake Eyre) and many of the mound springs. The Arabuna have worked to have the original Indigenous names

Photograph
by the author

of the low-lying salt lakes and the various clusters of springs acknowledged. The springs are highly important markers of connection to Country. Songlines and ancestral stories proclaim their ageless honouring of these watering holes.

• • •

Marree is a dusty township in South Australia on the southern end of the Oodnadatta Track. Its water supply comes from rainwater tanks that frequently dry out, and barely drinkable bore water. It's the stepping-off point from the bitumen. Heading north from Marree, many of the spring sites are dotted along the western rim of Kati Thanda. I am looking for places where dribbling water nourishes the desert, creating refuges for unique life forms. My thinking about groundwater starts predictably at the surface. Focusing on water's visible actions is illuminating, but I wonder how it obscures deeper understandings of Country and identity.

Providing the cellular fabric to millions of lives and cultures, groundwater is in many places indispensable. Appreciation of the significance of and limits to groundwater has been an imperative to sustainable life for eons. Civilisations worldwide and across epochs have devised ingenious ways to move groundwater from the underground realm to the surface for human consumption. From qanats of Mesopotamia to ornate stepwells in India, to underground wells and channels that cooled and watered the Alhambra palace of southern Spain, groundwater peekis and seeps until it leaks or flows though springs to exterior structures, revealing its ageless influence on human endeavour. Its invisibility, its ephemerality, its potency pique my curiosity. At times a shy player, at others a powerful protagonist, groundwater's many roles entice subtle readings. Where water is dragged from subterranean abodes through pumps and pipes, its pleas resound. I listen for high-pitched wails. I read landscape I'm imagining.

While hydrogeologists know an impressive array of extraordinary facts about groundwater, many aspects of groundwater flows are not yet fully understood. I swat hydrogeology to help me make sense of the springs. The watertable is the topmost level of an aquifer, the shifting, changing topmost level where rock is saturated with water. Groundwater occupies subterranean domains from just beneath shallow swamps to flows that are kilometres deep. Unobservable, deep aquifers' movements are difficult to measure. They are equally illusive in imaginings. Depths of the water table are measured through monitoring bores pinpricked around each state. As we drive towards the desert heartlands of the mound springs, the absence of surface water accentuates groundwater's shadowy concealment. I am wondering about groundwater's metaphoric reach.

Early white settlers took the lead from Indigenous people and followed the routes between the springs. Cameleers and traders watered thirsty stock, cattle herds camped at the delicate edges of springs, satiated. Colonial settlers showed little regard for sustainability of subterranean waters. Extraction and pollution of springs and aquifers persisted. Hard-hooved animals soon damaged these revered, sensitive sites.

Repeater stations along the Adelaide–to–Darwin Overland Telegraph Line were located where the water surfaced. Telegraph wires hung on gidgee saplings, linking spring to spring. Platforms, water tanks and stockyards for the Old Ghan train service were also built at the springs. The route became what is now known as the Oodnadatta Track. The springs have an illustrious history of supporting Indigenous and non-Indigenous life in an otherwise inhospitable region. Groundwater's emergence through the mound springs is a potent reminder of water's lifegiving capacity. The springs marked on the map became for me a string of pearls with fraught stories to tell.

•••

Underlying the driest inhabited continent on the planet, the Great Artesian Basin (GAB) is one of the largest networks of aquifers in the world. Water moves slowly, deeply, across vast distances. Mining, agricultural and industrial activities, as well as fast-growing inland communities, extract groundwater from across the GAB at rates that now outstrip the recharge. This is the term that refers to the ways water permeates into aquifers from rainfall, riverbeds, lakebeds and low-lying swamps. Rainwater enters the deep sedimentary layers of the Great Artesian Basin perhaps hundreds of kilometres away along the western slopes of the Great Dividing Range in Queensland and New South Wales and flows slowly through deep geological seams beneath Kati Thanda and towards their emergence in springs. Some underground geological folds have held water for thousands of years. Where does the water for BHP's Olympic Dam mining operation come from? The Basin. Where does much of the water for cotton growing in north-central NSW come from? The Basin. Recently approved coal-seam gas mining in the Pilliga Scrub sits squarely over the Great Artesian Basin, risking groundwater pollution from the chemicals used in fracking. The coal magnate Adani has been given unlimited access to groundwater from the Great Artesian Basin for the proposed Carmichael mine project in central Queensland. Groundwater is now mined, meaning that we know that the aquifers will not be replenished in any foreseeable future. Threats to the long-term future of unique mound-spring ecosystems proliferate. While the science behind known hazards remains ignored, economic opportunism tap-dances over the top of out-of-sight problems. Tap, tap, tapping.

Contemporary relationships with groundwater are based on an extractive history, derived from a seemly inherent belief that anything below the surface is for the taking. Interrelationality with lifegiving entities becomes stifled. Extracting groundwater for human consumption bleeds into new territory when we use it to water thirsty stock, irrigate crops and lubricate industries such as mining and forestry. Engineering technologies to enhance groundwater extraction and use have propped up the spread of white settler development, at the expense of acknowledging Indigenous sovereignty over Country and cultural Waters. Sustainable relationships with subterranean water sources beyond the whirring cogs of industry and agriculture means acknowledging Indigenous water rights. Sustaining an ecologically rich and flourishing future means changing the ways we think about groundwater, dismantling the extractive framework and replacing it with one that recognises groundwater's ecological connections to life and its place in Indigenous cultures.

As droughts increase in frequency and intensity and populations grow, demand for groundwater across this country escalates. Deeper bores barrel into the crust as drilling technologies evolve. Government efforts, particularly over the past 20 years, to monitor usage from agricultural and industrial bores, to cap free-flowing bore drains, and to buy and sell groundwater licences, have not slowed the increasing demands. Moves to preserve endangered groundwater-dependent ecosystems also remain insufficient, often unsuccessful. Inland towns are running out of water as groundwater reserves recede. Mound-spring flows are dwindling. The bores are drilling deeper. Will these losses of nationally significant and culturally and geologically extraordinary groundwater sites become a source of lamentation or a site of preservation?

• • •

Along the drive to Dalhousie I consider failure, I feel all that comes with that possibility. I could die out here. We might not make it. Australians have a knack for celebrating the most glorious, sorrowful and abysmal failures. The irony of this propensity to make ritual from calamity and collapse feels palpable as we cross increasingly brittle landscapes towards Kati Thanda and Witjira National Park. The land stretches long and low, 15 metres below sea level at Kati Thanda. It's as low as you can go on mainland Australia. The signs still say Lake Eyre, after Edward John Eyre, who 'explored' parts of South Australia. Failures to recognise Indigenous custodians in the rush for land, in the claims of ownership of property, linger shadow-like on the horizon. We drive onwards.

Burke and Wills' names appear on plinths and cairns along the route they took to their deaths. Innamincka and the Dig Tree are not far from the trail of springs that may have saved their expedition. From Melbourne to Innamincka their entourage scarred a trail across the land. Not knowing how to read the country, nor connect with the skills of Indigenous custodians, meant failure, their lives hung out to dry, bones pitted in the wind.

I don't share Charles Sturt's obsession to find an inland sea. Camels and horses loaded with food, tents and navigational gear had crossed these saltbush and gibber plains. Sturt's search for the surface-level catchment into which westward-flowing rivers must flow was ill-founded. The rivers mostly peter out, they evaporate or drain underground. Sienna-coloured corrugations leave billows of dust behind our wheels. The hanging, powdery plume eventually settles on ruby saltbush along the verges. It is as if the plants were going rusty, as they wait to be washed by that ever so intermittent rain. Cattle cluster around windmills and troughs in the distance. Deep red-brown and sleek, they thrive on the saltbush and spinifex. They are not affected by the dust.

I lose count of windmills standing solitary in bare paddocks, stark waving wings that evoke for me Don Quixote's madness. They pump groundwater. Every day many thousands of Australians drink and wash in groundwater pumped from bores or wells. Banjo Paterson's poem 'Song of the Artesian Water', written in 1896, narrates an early quest by a canny Scott to find groundwater. Deeper down, 'sinking down, deeper down', the steam-driven rig was knocking on 'Satan's dwelling'. Paterson was prescient in his descriptions of the desperation we humans muster to extract artesian water from a thousand, and now more than 5000, metres below. Paterson's water seekers would 'cave the roof of hell in' to reach the glistening, flowing salve to drought. We pump, we pump, we pump. As Banjo exclaims, 'How it glimmers in the shadow, how it flashes in the sun.' As we cross the miles my considerations of aquifers and groundwater shift towards imaginings of the microscopic pores in sandstones, the fractures in basalts, the dissolved clefts through limestone's depths. Banjo predicted that taking groundwater would not only provide relief for thirsty cattle. It risks encounters with deep, dark forces.

• • •

Four-wheel drives and campers pass us frequently along the Oodnadatta Track, almost a convoy rushing over this ancient route. Few take the side road across a glaring white plain that leads into the Wabma Kadarbu (Snake Head) Conservation Park. My first glimpse of a mound spring was the strangely named Blanche Cup. Original owners call it Thirrka, the oven, taken from a story of where the body of a snake is cooked. Sun-warmed timbers of a boardwalk curl over fragile terrain to the pool. The spring bleeds into a circular waterhole surrounded by bore-sedge, a tough, salt-tolerant desert reed. Beachscape smells are disorienting in the middle of nowhere. Scattered salt-loving plants survive the heat. Avocets in crisp black-and-white attire, with long beaks and bright-red, stilt-like legs, gather like formal waiters at the edge of a large tailings pool. They dip their beaks into brackish water. This is no oasis. I suddenly feel minute under an open sky, a tiny teardrop in an ocean. I bend to touch the ancient water, let it drip between my fingers, taste the salt. I have often been humbled by pressing my palm onto rock walls that may have been lifted and exposed millions of years ago. Touching spring water that has seeped and travelled imperceptibly slowly through aquifers, far underground for more than 2000 years, sends a shock through my body. I lick salt from my palm. Something intra-cellular connects me to deep times, to larger forces.

We take another track to the Bubbler. This spring is named Bidalinha or Pirdali-Nha in the Indigenous story of the serpent that was killed there, and which continues to writhe and convulse in the waters that pulsed in brown and creamy swirls. Concentric waves ripple as the spring belches, as the story comes to life. Water trickles out from the pool through the tail of the spring to spread and evaporate, leaving stark white streaks and watercolour washes across burnt-sienna sands.

We bathe in a timber tub of warm bore water at Coward Springs under a silken, starry sky. My hair feels straw-like for days. The metallic smell of bore water lingers on my skin. 'Hard water' describes its refusal to lather. I remember its sulphury smell, its bitter taste as we rattle over corrugations. I imagine its deep dwelling in my cells.

This region was once under the ocean. Sands and shells have been pressure-cooked and compressed underground for millions of years to form porous sandstone. The springs emerge through fissures and cracks in the layers of sediment. Accumulations of salts and windblown sands and dust over tens of thousands of years form the mounds. Some mound springs are the size of a dining table, others the dimensions of a house. Some, such as the extinct spring named Mount Hamilton, or Snake's Head to Arabana people, are indeed small mountains. Each mound spring, alive or extinct, has its own character, its own story to tell.

We search out other mound-spring sites along about 500 kilometres of rough dirt roads. The turn-off to the Strangways Mound Springs reveals rough scourings on wind-swept hillocks. Most of the mound springs at Strangways are extinct, their delicate venting systems having been plugged by cloven-hooved stock, and the ravages of wind and time. Some mounds sport tufts of tall, rustling reeds, phragmites, like quirky hairdos. The main homestead at Strangways is a pile of hand-hewn sandstone blocks and rubble where perky signs—blacksmith, baker, kitchen—evoke the sweat and labour that had built the now-collapsed walls. Sand collects along fallen stone fences, which had been bustling stockyards. An office of the Overland Telegraph Line had once buzzed and clicked. Now silence settles amid the dilapidated ruins. In a familiar story, white fella abuses, unmonitored bore-drilling and fouling of the springs predominantly by cattle and sheep grazing, mean that only a few springs dribble slowly into the sand. Brittle edges of extinct mound springs formed in the Pleistocene era are in some places high enough to walk into, like open-faced caves with scary dentata. Remnant stone fences surround a crumbling cemetery on a windswept hillock. Leaning gravestones tell tales of beginnings and endings, hopes and failures. Distant horizons lie flat against a pale blue sky.

William Creek is a tiny settlement consisting of a pub, a clutch of cabins in a gravelly camping area, an airstrip and a permanent population of three in the quiet season. In summer you can fry an egg on the bonnet of your car, the bartender tells me. It might rain, he adds. We buy fuel and head towards the edge of Kati Thanda. Lake Eyre settler signs are persistent. We pass a female dingo slinking along the roadside, lost-looking, furtive. Further on we see her mate, dead on the side of the track. Possibly shot.

Kati Thanda is an ephemeral lake. Predominantly an enormous saltpan, glistening with pinks, greys and silvers, *lake* is an optimistic euphemism describing when it boasts a shallow sheet of water that shifts and shimmers across the wide basin with the effects of the wind and the moon. The gibber turned to black clay. Not even saltbush survives. You can't get to the edge of Kati Thanda. Land and lake merge in wide, sticky swaths of mud. There are no beginnings and no ends. Boundaries evaporate as winds and moon cycles shift the sheets of water across the pan. Moonscape comes to mind. It rains, a light, sleeting shower, almost blown away by the wind. How much of this rain will seep and stay, how much will quickly evaporate into clouds? We wait and watch droplets on the windscreen.

Our boots clog with mud when we try a walk between showers. I find a rusted beer can. The ubiquitous VB green gleams, reminding me of throwaway lives. As if our rubbish is ever 'away'. As if our lives can ever be placed 'away'. Out there on the edge of nothingness I had wanted to feel that I had left behind the madness of a society that pollutes its water supply and creates waste and rubbish faster than it can be buried, decomposed or recycled. The can, even as I kick it, tied me to something I cannot yet escape. Returning to William Creek under ominous clouds, slippery black clay clogs the tyres. I throw the VB can and other litter we'd collected into the caged rubbish pits on the edge of the township. My boots are heavy with mud. I feel tied to Western detritus. Rain pounds the roof of the donga at the gravelled campground.

Next morning bristles hot and clear. We take the opportunity to see Kati Thanda from the air. An early-morning chartered flight lifts us over the lake. In the front seat of the small plane, the controls and tiny windscreen press close. The engine growls through earmuffs. We zoom over marbled-liquid patterning. The pallet is Impressionist. Low-lying, olive-green smudges, ochres blend to whites, pinks swirl towards umber browns. Flying over landscape-scale dot paintings I imagine ancient stories and the spirits that linger in the land. I feel we are invading sacred space from a higher dimension. My face is glued to the window. I snap images on my phone, hoping to remember the extraordinary patterns and colours unfolding where shallow water meets a non-existent shoreline, where salt crusts the sand in glistening white. Flying low, the pilot rattles off names of cattle stations that are larger than some European countries. Wandering cattle tracks and straight dirt roads draw a web design around waterholes. I am aching at the inexpressible beauty and artistry of the land. Views of Kati Thanda blur behind my tears.

Back on land, we push northwards to Peake Creek Station. Transitory images flash past the car window, leaving fragmented impressions. Peake Creek Station is another collection of springs that had attracted white settlement, now abandoned, in ruins. The Old Ghan railway had made a stop there, and a failed copper mine gapes from a terraced hillside. Before the journey I contacted the Friends of the Mound Springs, an intrepid group mostly from Adelaide, who are working for the restoration and preservation of damaged springs. They had a working bee coming up, perhaps we could join them to repair tracks, build fences, improve signage. We are meant to meet up with the work crew at Peake Creek. We wait for three days, camping, walking, sketching. Being in one place helps me see more details.

Here, silent stillness prevails. Fallen stone buildings echo stories from a long-folded cattle station. The low-lying flats are spongy, as they collect flows from the remnant springs. Mulgas and a local dwarfed variety of *Eucalyptus cameldulensis*, river red gum, grow along what might be called the creek line. Like most things in this desert landscape, where the creek begins and ends remains mysterious. I push through tall reeds, wary of snakes. One moment my feet sink through salt-crusted mud, then in the next I scrabble over stones and heat-baked sand. Boundaries are not neat, timeframes smear. We wait, without phone reception. We don't cross paths with the volunteers, maybe the dates are muddled. Eventually we drive on.

Further north, Witjira National Park unfolds with open grasslands and polished red-brown gibber plains that stretch for miles. Tough chenopods, silver spinifex grasses, grey saltbush and mauve-coloured samphire bushes hug endless, softly wrinkled plains. The sky is brilliant blue, fading to softer golden hues that shimmer on far, far away horizons. Purple hills glow. Saltpans glint. A sprawling tawny-coloured escarpment turns violet in the afternoon light. Raptors cruise on warm uplifts. A raven calls, a familiar descending caw, as we approach the spring country of the long-gone Dalhousie station.

Dalhousie Springs is the most northerly point to our journey, not far from the Northern Territory border. The campground is a launching place for intrepid drivers who cross the Simpson Desert in chunky four-wheel drives sporting orange flags on tall aerials. The flags signal the vehicle's approach to oncoming drivers on the narrow track that crosses endless sand-dune crests. Our ute was not properly equipped for such bone-crunching challenges.

We camp about five kilometres away from the bustling campground, choosing instead the sandy bed at Three O'clock Creek. Red mulga, a hardy acacia with distinctive maroon curls for bark, grows along the creek bed. Known locally as miniritchie, red mulga's strong limbs provided valuable hardwood for tools and weapons, later fence posts and stockyards. Companion species in the dry creek bed, the gidgee and coolabah trees, provide much-needed shade, as the bare land around is pulsing hot. I listen for the *maw-ww* of the waterbag frogs, who burrow in the river sands, waiting in semi-hibernation at times for years. They crawl out for breeding when the water flows. The twitter of honeyeaters and the rasp of crickets and cicadas rob the shimmering heat of its silence. I wonder about the water that dropped far beneath the gravelly sands of the dry creek bed. How deep did the water-bag frogs bury themselves with their cache of water stored in pockets of their skin? Dry spells are long. Mulga, gidgee and coolabah roots draw water from way beneath the waterbag frogs. Water cycles continue.

We return to Dalhousie Springs each afternoon to swim in the earth-warmed pool. Each day about four megalitres of tepid water rises naturally under artesian pressure from more than 600 metres below to fill and overflow from Dalhousie Springs. That's four Olympic-sized swimming pools of groundwater flowing upwards through hair-like pores in the crust. The jetty where you enter the main pool sports signage by Indigenous park managers welcoming visitors. Again, I feel like an intruder in someone's sacred place. A splash of colourful polystyrene noodles are supplied for floatation. A bright-orange life-saving ring decorates the decking. We climb down the wooden steps and flop into the reed-lined pool, relieved to wash away campfire smoke, sweat and dust. I float, torpid, motionless, watching with one eye the long-billed corellas who perch like sentinels on high. Unique to these springs, a tiny fish named the Dalhousie guppy nibbles at my skin, keeps me awake. In water at 37 degrees I soon melt, soporific. Ancient waters seep into my skin, bringing slow meanings to presence, to connections to place. I climb from the pool in only my undies as other travellers arrive for a dip. The warm water leaves me languid, calm, strengthened. As the earth absorbs waters through layers of skin-like sediments, I carry her waters in my skin. Waterbag me.

Weaving over sand tracks through the complex scattering of springs, we wander back to camp. A dingo in the distance pounces on prey in the long grass, trots away head high, successful. Sacred space embraces both the hunter and the prey. I understand something more of the land.

Leaving Dalhousie to begin the homeward journey reminds me of the wrench of leaving a terminally ill friend in a hospital bed, wondering if I might see her again. Would she die before my next visit? I have witnessed a failing link in the water cycle. Vulnerability and the beauty of springs in the desert collide. Despite the sense of plenitude of water at Dalhousie Springs, hydrogeological research shows that the mound springs of this region are slowly dying before their time. They have risen and receded over the past 12,000 years, as ice ages and their melts have dried and then flooded this continent. Ancient cavities, now extinct springs, are sun-baked testaments to the coming and going of water. Epochal fluctuations of groundwater's cycles do not match the relatively recent rapid receding of mound springs' flows. I grieve this premature loss. I leave Dalhousie feeling like I am being dragged away from a loved one.

We retrace our route southwards, remembering, revisiting campsites. Familiarity with the track reassures me. I try to imagine knowing this route as intimately as generations of Indigenous travellers before me knew these ways to water. Their wisdom grows from their attentive knowledge and from telling and retelling stories of the land. Profound stories emerge. The cycle is firm. Deep accountability to cultural Water and Country is enmeshed. Had we passed through, driven onwards, and crossed the Simpson Desert with a wobbling orange flag on a pole, to return by some other route, I would perhaps have missed this echo-like perspective that resounds. The return journey adds depth to what I'd found, enables iterative experiences to permeate, and lessens the transitory feel to the journey.

Potential failures had lurked, now they are nudged aside. We reached Dalhousie, we return. Fears dissipate. Swimming in warm spring water under open desert skies focuses my respect for the stories that stitch people to desert lands and waters. I drink spring water into my cells, imbibing a legacy of aquifers across millennia. The springs sojourn kindles my responsibilities to preserve groundwater. The waters that held me afloat inspire me to listen to the potency of subterranean stories. Voices of aquifers had called me on this odyssey, a journey with little-known cartographies. Rather than as a resource to be extracted whatever the cost, I learn of groundwater's place in the inherent psyche of this continent. Aquifers beneath our feet remind me of a watery life force beneath my skin.

In witnessing the wavering pulse of the mound springs, I lament the lost potency of subterranean realms. Only one of the multitudes of anthropogenic impacts on planetary geologies, losing groundwater is a little-known tragedy. Absence of water has fatal repercussions, imposing inconceivable consequences. I am enraged at the lack of political courage to address imperative questions that have national ecological and cultural impacts. Failures to consider the long-term effects of extracting and polluting groundwater for short-term profits are incomprehensible, inexcusable. Below the surface, ancient aquifers are bleeding. The lifeblood of futures ebbs. The unique ecologies of mound springs are gasping. Mound springs are on life support.

• • •

An Elegant Revenge: Language at Play

Lur
Alghurabi

Lur Alghurabi is an
Iraqi writer living
in Australia.

I try to interrogate my reader bias as often as I can; the questionable motives behind my rage or comfort when reading, how hard and how often I project my own life onto the protagonist, and sometimes even, to my own shame, onto the author. And I wonder how often I am so hungry to read something that does my feelings and my experience justice (knowing full well I'm the only one who can write that), that I start to be frustrated when a book fails to do so. I suppose I'm still working on my book, and a great way to procrastinate is to think about how other people are writing their own books, and all the things they should have done differently. It's been a safe and reliable distraction. I'm not above it.

One of my worst biases as a reader is that I think all good work is actually nonfiction and that only nonfiction makes for good work. Whenever I read good fiction, I do the mental gymnastics necessary to reframe it, for myself, as a real story, because I only believe in or know how to process real stories. I have no imagination. My mind does not travel far enough to invent anything, or perhaps I'm too occupied by my immediate reality, or perhaps my immediate reality has been too dominating, so I don't understand or compute invention when others do it. It's a limitation I become hyperconscious of when I read a good work of fiction and treat it with no distance; every comment, every abstract statement or flawed reaction draws radical and emotional responses from me as if it were all happening to me personally, or being sold to my very self.

I've advocated long and hard for the separation of author from protagonist, but I've not succeeded in similarly separating reader from protagonist, or reader from author. I take every book personally, I think about it too hard, and I find myself fixating on its shortcomings and successes, preaching to anyone who will listen, dragging my own uninterested friends and time-poor parents into the discourse with no sense of boundaries, with no ability to say, Relax, Lur, this is a book, and you're not a victim of it by any means. This is what stops me from reading fiction so often: I can't exercise a healthy separation, so I stick to memoir where at least my deep attachment has a connection to a real life, a real person. So when Omar Sakr acknowledged in his first novel *Son of Sin* that the protagonist Jamal is a distant avatar carrying the weight of Sakr's unreal life, an avatar shouldering a pain that is very much real, I thought to myself yes, yes, finally, a book of fiction I can hyperfixate on, justifiably.

Son of Sin, the accomplished poet's debut fiction work, traces Jamal Smith, a young Muslim man living in western Sydney who's learning of and coming to terms with his queerness, his faith, his roots and his greatest fears. In essence *Son of Sin* is about a boy then a man trying to reject an imposed sexuality, a demanding heritage and a harsh religion. His world is further restricted by language, where many of his confines come from an Arabic- (and at times Turkish-) speaking world, while he can barely catch a few loose words here and there, in either tongue. When he repeats these words, when he tries to say them, he presents a hybrid dialect that might make little sense to a native Arabic speaker, or might be worlds away from what has been colloquially standardised among diaspora Arabs in one country or another. The version of Arabic Jamal has ended up with might only carry meaning in his extremely specific circle, and it might even only carry meaning to him alone. It's a lonely place to be.

My hunger for 'adequate' (in the subjective, not objective, sense) storytelling makes me extremely curious about how other people receive a certain work, and with whom a work lands and with whom it fails to, so that I can better understand my proximity towards it and if this relationship I develop with the work will be successful. It helps me understand where I can situate myself in the audience: how close am I to the stage? What's my vantage point? Does my proximity allow me to dance to this music, or does the lack of it encourage me to judge and never participate? Where was I invited to sit? Who wasn't invited and who's not the target audience for this? Who's waiting outside with my same hunger yet no invitation? Who is this book trying to speak to, and who does it not care to speak to?

When French artist William Sami Étienne Grigahcine, known as DJ Snake, released his single 'Disco Maghreb', he wanted to get closer to his roots, or specifically the roots of his Oranian, West Algerian mother. 'Disco Maghreb' featured traditional Algerian instruments like the gallal and the ghaita, and the music video, directed by Elias Belkeddar, captured specific markers of Oranian life: Lacoste tracksuits, Adidas flip flops, steep terrains, modified Peugeot 103s, racers with covered faces, Allaoui dancing, a Tuareg party, *kahwiine* (the punks of West Algeria), and some redditors swear that one of the characters in the video is a traditional witch. The song is named after the Oranian record shop that gave birth to some of Algeria's greatest names of Rai, including the king of Rai himself, Cheb Khaled, whose vocals seal the track with a poetic finish. The track, dubbed a love letter to Algeria, had a moment of fame on TikTok and prompted a few written pieces with neutral acclaim. But Algerians on r/algeria, in comment sections and on Twitter, argued back and forth on whether this was an authentic representation of Oran, whether it was relatable to the common Oranian, and whether Grigahcine was ever a trusted authority on the disco of Algeria, let alone the disco of Maghreb or West Algeria, which he had hardly ever spent time in, if at all.

To create 'Disco Maghreb', Grigahcine made a personal and physical pilgrimage to a homeland that might have, until that point, been distant to him. But stylistically he didn't travel far outside the familiar. The lyrics don't stray from his first hit, 'Turn Down for What' (feat. Lil Jon), which featured only three iconic lines: 'Fire up the loud / Another round of shots / Turn down for what?' 'Disco Maghreb' is similar: 'Another one. Dance and stomp. One two three do it again.' Redditor fanbases didn't hesitate to call it a cringe caricature of their catchphrases, especially 'chta7 rda7' (dance and stomp), almost as if it were how a French person thought Algerians spoke, and once they did, this was all they said.

The reader and I will always, always, be distanced by language, unless I swim against the current to change that.

The burden of adequate representation didn't evade one of the world's most successful EDM producers. For as long as Grigahcine performed for a Western audience via 'Turn Down for What', 'Taki Taki' (with Selena Gomez, Cardi B and Ozuna) or 'Let Me Love You' (with Justin Bieber), he flew under the radar just fine; there was never a need to be authentic towards something that never related to the homeland, and who really cared when it was the perfect 1 am club track? These tracks earned him a Billboard Award, an MTV Video Music Award and even a Grammy nomination when he was on the brink of extreme poverty. But 'Disco Maghreb', a much more personal work, never quite landed the same with the very audience it tried to feature and celebrate.

I think about 'Disco Maghreb' a lot, because I'm aware that my greatest personal fear is for my work to be read in my own homeland. I've run away from this fear a fair bit but I think I'm getting too old and tired to sustain this avoidance. I wish it was a made-up fear of my own, but I am deeply aware of how diasporic writing can struggle to connect to the audiences that are also its protagonists, because it might be assessed with different criteria than in the new homeland. It often feels like setting oneself up for failure, to expect that the diaspora experience should ever resonate with our people living worlds away from us. I know I struggle to speak to my past self from the homeland because she was fighting entirely different battles and she could not care less what I think of DJ Snake. She just wants a passport and a safe bed with no need for weapons to be hidden under the mattress. If I were to go on to her about DJ Snake's physical departure from France yet commitment to the conventions of Western EDM, from where would we gain the tools to meet on the same page? And on top of all of that, in what language would we converse?

Awareness of how little language I had in common with my past self, and how my writing could fail to sustain the attention of my own flesh, has only fixated me further on learning how language can be manipulated for my own benefit. I spend a lot of time and energy learning how to perform to new audiences, what good performance looks like, how I can get my ideas across to them, and how I can build a bridge to them, so the people geographically closest to me would read me exactly how I wished. I have always been preoccupied with other people's perception of me, so thinking about the audience for a substantial amount of time is nothing tiring. If I ever get tired, the reception of 'Disco Maghreb' is all the cautionary tale I need, and it whips me right back into line.

This obsession is driven by the question of how language could become sufficiently transmittable: how could language give meaning? How could it be impactful and how could it compel a reader into a feeling? Could I only speak it the way other people understand it? Could I modify it so that it was understandable yet sincere? How well could I rehearse it? Could I plan it within an inch of its life, and could I then perform it with justice to the language and the audience? I need the audience to be engaged, so I need to tailor my speech accordingly. Whether to garner approval or the opposite, I need to make sure that I'm seen. I need to make sure they also feel seen, that they're not standing outside the theatre, hungry and with no invitation. The risk, otherwise, is to indulge in my own speech so deeply that my work stands lonely, inviting no engagement from anyone I care about.

The reader and I will always, always, be distanced by language, unless I swim against the current to change that. I might be a native speaker of both Arabic and English, but my speech is confined to the conventions I grew up with, and in Arabic-heritage diasporas, those conventions change at roughly every third door in the neighbourhood. I grew up in Iraq and lived in Arab countries and communities until I was eighteen; I am highly educated in classical Arabic and widely familiar with other dialects thanks to an obsession with Arabic-language television, music and film. My friends are from across the Middle East, and when they couldn't understand my Iraqi dialect, I had to learn and start speaking in theirs, which means I'm highly proficient in most of them.

Despite this, when I first heard the dialect of an Iraqi person who was born in Sydney, I was taken aback. I didn't recognise their cultural references; their enunciations were new to me, their body language different, their emphasis points in the sentence, their use of colloquial grammar and most of all their vocabulary: it was a separate world altogether that I felt I needed to learn from scratch just as I had learned to speak Palestinian Arabic before, like I had learned to speak Syrian and Lebanese and Emirati and Egyptian and Kuwaiti. There was no set of grammatical rules to guide me when it came to a hybrid tongue, so all I could do was listen and listen and listen until I could connect some dots, and then parrot.

I modify my language every time I want to connect with an audience. Sometimes I find myself, without conscious effort or awareness, even mimicking their accents. If I meet a person speaking in broken English, my Arab accent gets extremely thick to resemble my parents'. If they're English, I'm English. If their accent is intensely 'Aussie', I'm bringing up my inflections and turn up the ends of the sentence to match their music. Linguists call it the chameleon effect. I think it's empathy at best, or performativity at worst.

1
Hasib Hourani, 'I'm Not Hungry Anymore', *Liminal Review of Books*, October 2022, <https://www.liminalmag.com/liminal-review-of-books/not-hungry>.

In *Son of Sin*, Sakr's main character Jamal Smith makes no effort to warm up to the reader's Arabic. Jamal's dialect, spelling and grammar seem to make sense at least to himself and his immediate community, but I can't say if it does carry logic to other Arabs outside that community, and definitely not for Lebanese-Palestinian critic Hasib Hourani. In their essay for *Liminal Review of Books* 'I'm Not Hungry Anymore',[1] Hourani picks up on the unusual grammar and spelling and classifies them 'reckless'; Turkish characters say 'Astugfirullah' instead of the 'Estagfirulah' we might expect; name spellings seem to stray from convention; transliteration is harder to identify. To me it is a common thread in Sakr's transliteration of Arabic words in and outside *Son of Sin*: it usually takes me a few tries to figure out how the sound of these transliterations should be making up a word; so I read a word like *soyam* and stare at it for a while wondering what I'm looking at, before realising it's what I'd pronounce as *sayem*, but I'm from Baghdad, not Tripoli, and I've learnt Beirut's Lebanese dialect, not Sakr's Lebanese dialect.

I read *khiri tukhti* and realise I'd have written it as *kharrit tahti* and that's why it took me a few seconds to realise what I was reading. I knew *khiri* was a derivative of *shit*, but with this transliteration it could be a noun or an imperative verb, and *tukhti* could mean 'my bed' but that wouldn't sit right in the context of this sentence. *Khirit* on the other hand means 'I shit' (the 't' at the end is the first-person pronoun, so it needs to stick to the first word because verb and first person noun are actually always just one word), and *tuhti*, which I understand others might pronounce as *tukhti* depending on where they're from, means 'under me' or 'I shit myself'. When Sakr writes *hatha subbi hon*, I wonder, 'There is a Sabian in here'? 'There is a [random] boy in here'? No, it's what I would have written as *hatha-ss-ubby hon*, or 'this boy is here'. These instances of different language use in *Son of Sin* are too numerous to list, where Jamal and I (and Jamal and Hourani) are fundamentally different people with different speech, and we don't see eye to eye on language even for a moment: on spelling, on pronunciation or on grammar.

One historic crisis point in the life of Arabic grammar is when al-Farazdaq, renowned poet, deliberately used a grammatically inappropriate diacritical mark at the end of a stanza, leading to a different pronunciation and, not coincidentally, improving the stanza's rhythm. When Ibn Abi Is'haq (who was no lightweight: Ibn Abi Is'haq is widely considered the first Arabic-language grammarian) called him out on it, al-Farazdaq snarkishly said, 'My job is to speak and yours is to grammarise what I have said' (or, in other words: you'll always live in my shadow, son, or sounds like a *you* problem, or: grammar was built upon poetry, not the other way around). Arabic language grammar was established on two foundations: the Quran and Bedouin poetry, because god makes no mistakes, and Bedouins are too isolated from trade routes to have their language tarnished by foreign style—both of these foundations lending themselves to a mostly consistent grammar structure.

But the thing about retrospective grammar, what came second cannot possibly contain what had come first, and god, in consequence, is often found to be breaking these rules, because when the Quran was written these rules simply did not exist.

So for purist grammarians to explain these 'errors' in god's grammar (remembering god is meant to be perfect and he makes no errors), they often resort to mental gymnastics to make it appear that god wasn't wrong, he just meant something different, or the grammar isn't wrong, but every now and then there's an exception to the rule. While these gymnastics can be quite entertaining to me, they've resulted in varying (and sometimes opposite) interpretations of the Quran to justify the scripture's lack of conformity to grammatical rules. There are specific instances where these different interpretations have resulted in the formation of new sects within Islam, and this is how fundamental and drastic these differences can be.

> I read *khiri tukhti* and realise I'd have written it as *kharrit tahti* and that's why it took me a few seconds to realise what I was reading.

While classical grammar was created to be as strict as it is, and when the rules became as complex as Ibn Abi Is'haq, al-Farahidi or Sibawayh had laid them out, non-standardised Arabic has allowed for a freer expression that moves with the people's usage, evolving and expanding until we ended up with a dialect per country, and within that country a dialect per region, per province, per city, per neighbourhood, per economic class, with as many variables as an identity could hold. These dialects of Arabic, the ones we use at home, the ones we use to talk to each other, have not been contained by formal grammar because formal grammar simply never cared to acknowledge them. Their very existence is an ongoing protest to grammarian dictatorship: they say, My job is to speak, and I don't care what yours is.

When diasporas move into new homelands with new styles of speech and new communities, these dialects take a step further away from what's conventional or widely accepted, creating new 'local' dialects as opposed to the general or 'universal' non-formal dialects, and here we might end up with Sakr's creation of the Jamal dialect, specific to this man who is half-Tripolian, half-Turkish, living in a specific community in a specific side of Sydney, influenced by X, Y and Z, dialect shared with families A, B and C. We might encounter an extremely and radically localised version of language that only makes sense to a small group of people, creating a block for readers like myself and Hourani to whom this language simply does not conform.

How much does diaspora writing or expression owe it to the reader to be communicable? And if it isn't communicable, how can it be impactful? Before I engage with this question I feel I first have to ask myself if the diaspora can do any differently. How much is in the hands of a character who is specifically half-Tripolian, half-Turkish, living in a specific community in a particular part of Sydney, influenced by X, Y and Z, dialect shared with families A, B and C? At what point in Jamal's life could he have been exposed to Egyptian comedies, Lebanese pop or Palestinian slam poetry? Where would Khaleeji drama have slotted into his lifestyle, and where would Bedouin poetry have presented itself as a teacher? Could Jamal have spoken any differently? Could he have had a less localised dialect, as limited as his vocabulary was? Could his vocabulary have been any wider given the data we have about how his life has turned out?

Jamal spends very little time thinking about whether his limited vocabulary or his localised dialect will engage the reader. As a people pleaser and a person perpetually in performance, I can't relate. It almost makes me uncomfortable that he is speaking purely to himself and to the handful of people (they might be a family of 320 cousins if they're anything like mine) who understand his language style. But I believe, if I can put Jamal aside for a moment and turn my attention towards the author, that a narrator's ability to speak to a wide audience, to an audience with different localised dialects, to a homeland audience, can only stem from the author's education in, or exposure to, these different dialects and worlds of language outside the local. If Sakr never offered himself this exposure, if Sakr never sought this wide vocabulary, then how could he have written this book any differently? And how much should we as writers be learning about wider uses of language, before we create the hyper-localised character?

On the opposite end of the spectrum to Sakr, Polish-Australian poet Ania Walwicz intensely trained herself in the conventions of language in order to create localised dialects that were elegant and deliberately designed. In 'Cut Tongue and the Mechanism of Defence', she writes:

> i'm army in army arm me defence i'm defence now my father marshall general zhukov he is my leader i am soldier my father big guns hero of russian army now he leads me here i am soldier and i march now and i march left right left right i obey now i march i polish shoe polish bright i obey now i say yes yes yes sir yes sir yes sir now i do what i'm told to do i do what i'm told i am told here i do what i have to do i defend the defender i obey now i do what i'm told to now i am dog now i dog dog dog i train army left and right now i march and i march i obey i do what i tell now i do what i'm told now i do yes.[2]

2
Ania Walwicz, 'Cut Tongue and the Mechanism of Defence', *Southerly* 73, no. 1 (2013): 89–95, p. 93.

In her fragmented and dismembered style, Walwicz takes the reader into the heart of her language so much so they could adopt it: its absurdity oddly effective, its service to the subject matter obvious, and its voice one that's easy to trust as sincere. One of the reasons behind Walwicz's choice of voice is that we, as readers, often do not think in paragraphs in a linear fashion. So in reading fragmented or dismembered language, the reader can position themselves in the text and completely absorb it; it is the language closest to the process of thinking. Interviewed by Jenny Digby, Walwicz says:

> I am reworking language and taking it apart, slicing the top layer off it, peeling it away and revealing the subconscious and unconscious levels of language. And this is done quite deliberately, because obviously I don't speak like this. I am producing this language, reworking and rearranging it until it comes closer to the actual process of feeling.[3]

3
Jenny Digby, 'The Politics of Experience', *Meanjin* 51, no. 4 (1992), 819–38, p. 819.

Walwicz here manufactures the localised and specific language with full intent; unlike Sakr, her deliberately difficult language can never be credited to her not knowing differently, or not having adequate exposure. It can never be credited to her language being taken away in diaspora: she's given herself a new one that, while artificial, is no less compelling than her native tongue (yes, it makes sense that she was first and foremost a theatrist). Jamal might be doing as much as he can with the tools he has, but Walwicz, unlike Sakr, has chosen to create more sophisticated tools.

> But perhaps it is for this reason that I see mastering language as an elegant revenge against every person and every ethno-state that has wronged me

Walwicz, just like Janet Frame, Zeina Hashem Beck, Marwa Helal, Caroline Bird or Lamia Abbas Amara, feeds my belief that the language we bastardise (and I use this term affectionately; I love to see language manipulated and shifted and twisted) carries impact because it is bastardised with purpose rather than out of helplessness. This is where impact comes from: rehearsal. There is a risk, otherwise, that the diaspora author, without the knowledge of how to dive deep into language, only gives their protagonist breadcrumbs of Arabic phrases to see them through their narrative, a means to no worthwhile end. These scattered Arabic phrases, a group of habibs and khiris and wulahs and ahwes and soyams and inshallahs and bismillahs and yallahs, become no more than superfluous punctuation serving only to remind the reader that a character carries an Arab identity, and nothing will be explored further. George Szirtes writes:

> Sometimes language seems no more than a piece of tissue paper carried
> on the wind: flimsy, semi-transparent, endlessly vulnerable, like a deflated
> talks-bubble, almost weightless. At other times it is a brick wall, or worse still a
> room with dense walls and no exit, with only the sense of voices beyond the
> wall, faintly audible and never clear enough, everything they say immediately
> becoming part of the wall.[4]

I understand, I do, I really do, that diaspora language has often felt like a brick wall that lets no sentiment through, nor sincerity, nor fluidity of expression, nor room for a complex or sophisticated emotion, because those in the diaspora have lost an abundant and plentiful language with their migration, be that migration forced or chosen. It's a cruel fate. I wish it upon no-one. But perhaps it is for this reason that I see mastering language as an elegant revenge against every person and every ethno-state that has wronged me and forced me out of the place where my language lived. And perhaps this is the reason *Son of Sin* left me starving, almost angry—the book fails to protest against this loneliness. It simply waves its hands in the air and gestures vaguely, 'What can I do? This is the world I grew up in. This is the tongue I've been dealt.' Szirtes writes on, 'Always provisional, language appears this or that way to us according to our own disposition and relation to it.'

We might agree that the Arabic language is overly complex. We might see that as a problem (hostile and unwelcoming, too many rules) and we might see it as a tool to

4
George Szirtes, 'What being bilingual means for my writing and identity', *Guardian*, May 2014, <https://www.theguardian.com/education/2014/may/03/george-szirtes-bilingual-poetry-translation>.

escape the prison (this complexity was designed by mortals like us, so we can redesign it whenever; poetry will always, always come before its grammar, it will always defeat its grammar). I have found Arabic to be at its most exciting when it exits academia and precedes grammar, once it farewells Ibn Abi Is'haq and enters our streets, where education and its complexities are redundant in the presence of the breadth and the experience of the poet. I refer to the poet because I believe, just as al-Farazdaq did, that the poem is the building block of Arabic language, and the poet, imaginative and intelligent, takes these building blocks to create new limits for this language. This poet, irrespective of their academic education (and good Arab poetry is rarely ever made inside the academy), can break these rules of Arabic into something ... fun.

But Jamal's relationship with Arabic is that of a fleeting tourist, only visiting language (and at times in the novel, only visiting country) for a moment. But it is Sakr, not Jamal, who refrains from diving into language further. So Jamal, his character, doesn't play, because he hasn't seen enough of these games in the first place to know how to kick the ball and definitely not how to smash a window.

In its essence, this is an argument for a true and genuine performance of a flashy, flamboyant and attention-seeking language that demands we stay on its level by playing with all its variables. By performance, I don't mean to imply a lack of sincerity or a centralisation of the audience above all else. By performance, I mean doing something well and doing it justice.

Jamal remains trapped in his own world. Similar to Grigahcine, his physical voyage to his 'homeland' never expands this world, sadly enough, and only closes in these walls further. Until its last pages, *Son of Sin* makes no effort to lend itself to a profound study of what language can do, in its beautiful brokenness, in its hybridity, in its 'error' and its deconstruction. The language refuses to move in the way of literary play to advance Jamal's story or to give him new ways of existing in a liminal space. *Son of Sin*'s reluctance to explore language makes for one of the tallest walls in Jamal's prison, and it stands for the real language cringe of the 'in between two worlds' coming-of-age story. The novel, just like its protagonist, becomes a wandering boy trying to scramble together what or who he is and to find a place or a person to accept it in return. *Son of Sin*, just like Jamal, has left me hungry for a fervorous push of spirit, and for something a little more brave, a little more experimental, a little more fun.

Maybe in 20 years, once he's found his tongue, we can meet again. Maybe then, we'll have a common language to speak in.

• • •

–ZOOM–a talking mirror

```
Z OO OO OO OO OO OO OO OO OO OO OO OO OO OO OO M
   Z OO OO OO OO OO OO OO OO OO OO OO OO OO OO OO OO M
Z OO OO OO OO OO OO OO OO OO OO OO OO OO OO OO OO M
   Z OO OO OO OO OO OO OO OO OO OO OO OO OO OO OO OO M
Z OO OO OO OO OO OO OO OO OO OO OO OO OO OO OO OO M
   Z OO OO OO OO OO OO OO OO OO OO OO OO OO OO OO OO M
Z OO OO OO OO OO OO OO OO OO OO OO OO OO OO OO M
   Z OO OO OO OO OO OO OO OO OO OO OO OO OO OO OO OO M
Z OO OO OO OO OO OO OO OO OO OO OO OO OO OO OO M
   Z OO OO OO OO OO OO OO OO OO OO OO OO OO OO OO OO M
Z OO OO OO OO OO OO OO OO OO OO OO OO OO OO OO M
   Z OO OO OO OO OO OO OO OO OO OO OO OO OO OO OO OO M
Z OO OO OO OO OO OO OO OO OO OO OO OO OO OO OO M
   Z OO OO OO OO OO OO OO OO OO OO OO OO OO OO OO OO M
Z OO OO OO OO OO OO OO OO OO OO OO OO OO OO OO M
   Z OO OO OO OO OO OO OO OO OO OO OO OO OO OO OO OO M
Z OO OO OO OO OO OO OO OO OO OO OO OO OO OO OO M
   Z OO OO OO OO OO OO OO OO OO OO OO OO OO OO OO OO M
Z OO OO OO OO OO OO OO OO OO OO OO OO OO OO OO M
   Z OO OO OO OO OO OO OO OO OO OO OO OO OO OO OO OO M
Z OO OO OO OO OO OO OO OO OO OO OO OO OO OO OO M
   Z OO OO OO OO OO OO OO OO OO OO OO OO OO OO OO OO M
Z OO OO OO OO OO OO OO OO OO OO OO OO OO OO OO M
   Z OO OO OO OO OO OO OO OO OO OO OO OO OO OO OO OO M
Z OO OO OO OO OO OO OO OO OO OO OO OO OO OO OO M
   Z OO OO OO OO OO OO OO OO OO OO OO OO OO OO OO OO M
Z OO OO OO OO OO OO OO OO OO OO OO OO OO OO OO OO M
   Z OO OO OO OO OO OO OO OO OO OO OO OO OO OO OO OO M
```

Alex
Selenitsch

Alex Selenitsch is
a poet, artist and
architect. His most
recent solo exhibition
was *The Language
Factory* at the MSD
in the University of
Melbourne, installed
during the 2021
lockdown.

Why does Elon Musk, the largest clown in the clown car, simply not eat the other clowns?

Patrick
Lenton

Patrick Lenton is an
author and journalist
from Melbourne. His
recent book of short
stories is *Sexy Tales of
Paleontology*.

Twitter, when you simmer it down to its base premise, like some kind of unholy stock, is essentially a super-fast way to spread little sentences all around the world. If you like writing and using writing to say things, chances are you'll thrive on Twitter, which remains stubbornly word-based, a storm of textual sound and fury that is as ferocious as it is brief and transitory.

As a result, Twitter more than any other social media app tends to create its own shared language, a series of phrases and references that pass into common parlance. Sometimes they originate outside the app, but become so enthusiastically used on the platform that they become a part of the communal speech. Often they grow, flower and die entirely in the closed Twitter ecosystem. It's always been my favourite part of the contentious app, the way language and jokes and written memes mutate and spread, fungal and mysterious. It's code-switching, but for the incurably online. There are obviously other places where this happens too: Tumblr and Reddit each have their own dialogues, for example, and often there's bleed between them all. You can track many famous catchphrases and words and terms to things like AAVE (African American Vernacular English), queer ballroom jargon or even popular stand-up comedy sets, but like floating seeds, they settle down and sprout weird and mutated new life on Twitter.

One of the better examples of an influential term from Twitter language is the 'milkshake duck', a widespread, useful and uncomfortably apt term that has become so ubiquitous and necessary on Twitter that it's spread into the real world, with the *Macquarie Dictionary* naming 'milkshake duck' its 2017 word of the year.

'The whole internet loves Milkshake Duck, a lovely duck that drinks milkshakes! *5 seconds later* We regret to inform you the duck is racist,' tweeted Ben Ward, an Australian cartoonist using the handle @pixelatedboat. It became shorthand for a person who gains popularity on social media for some positive or charming trait but is later revealed to have a distasteful history or to engage in offensive behaviour. Since the term's invention in 2016, it has become a defining way to explain the way the internet engages with celebrities and famous figures.

These language trends don't all last forever—they can have seasons, or disappear after a small peak. You can sometimes carbon date the age of a person based on where their online terminology paused: if something is a 'major fail' or 'roflcopter', there's a good chance they are an elder millennial who went offline and found a peaceful life for themselves.

You can learn a lot about minimalism from Twitter—a milkshake duck is a complicated and nuanced phenomenon with a comedic tone, referenced entirely with two words. Now, without having ever seen the original tweet, you might understand everything about the danger of being mikshake ducked.

In 2019, Twitter user @maplecocaine tweeted: 'Each day on twitter there is one main character. The goal is to never be it.' The concept of the main character of the day never took off outside Twitter, but that's because it's inherently about Twitter. Like milkshake duck, it's a perfect capture of a widespread trend, that when captured in a sentence was immediately recognisable by a huge portion of the site.

The main character of the day is someone on Twitter who somehow, usually through a terrible mistake when tweeting, becomes the main topic of conversation on the app. A person who, seemingly independent of planning, becomes all anyone on the site can talk about for 12 to 24 hours or even longer. They capture the attention of so much of the platform that it feels like everyone is talking about them, as impossible as that may be. It's negative virality on a grand scope.

It's when you can't get away from three or four days of constant references to the Cinnamon Toast Crunch Shrimp Guy scandal, a guy who began by tweeting a picture of what appeared to be shrimp tails in his box of Cinnamon Toast Crunch cereal. It ended with him publicly accused of multiple acts of misconduct and going completely radio silent, a common resolution to the lifespan of the main character of the day types, that draws back to the milkshake duck term.

If a main character had a trait to differentiate them from simply a viral figure, a brief moment of online celebrity, it's the instinct to keep 'posting through' the situation, sending more and more tweets, inevitably making everything worse. Often posting through will be continuing to tweet, to double down, to half-retract, to get defensive, to defend themselves. It's digging their own grave, despite all the people yelling for them to stop. It's using fire to try and put out a fire.

The main character of the day is a quintessential Twitter concept, and one worth exploring more, because it utilises this inherent idea of shared language and exemplifies the horrible potential of the social media community in one of the funniest and worst ways possible.

And it also helps explain what's going on in 2023, when Elon Musk, one of Twitter's most infamous main characters, has done something completely new and unexpected—he bought the entire site. Is this a case of a main character fighting back? Or is it more a case of inevitable escalation, an apocalyptic end-game scenario, the climactic moment of absurdity in the dying days of a website? I've never been the main character of Twitter, and you can tell because my life hasn't been utterly ruined by a social media app. I am thankful for that.

There's something about Twitter that is hard to explain to anyone who doesn't use it regularly, an allure drawn from somewhere other than logic. When you explain the app, it almost seems to just be the basic platonic ideal of social media, people online talking to each other about various things and stuff. Nothing really more than that. In fact one of the more enduring notions about Twitter is that it has mostly failed to bedeck itself in functions and adornments like other social media, stubbornly holding true to its idiosyncratic core use—a silly little word machine.

It's addictive in a way—but I always think of Twitter as having some kind of thrall, especially when I see the latest main character, someone who has managed to tweet themselves into a twisted, corrupted version of their earlier life—and who, even if they do manage to stop tweeting, will never truly be the same again, like the ring bearers from *Lord of the Rings*, simple hobbit folk who become ruined by something dark and compulsive.

I've felt the merest echoes of what this sensation is like. A beloved former boss of mine once asked me, 'Patrick, are you okay? You're tweeting a lot and that's usually a good or a bad sign.' I get that sensation of being unable to tear my eyes away or stop feeding the beast.

I've gone viral before—articles and tweets that I've written bouncing around the internet and seen by more eyes than I can comprehend, sometimes even resulting in brief bursts of fame or notoriety. But that's not what creates main-character syndrome either—there is an element of virality to being the main character, it's a crucial vehicle for becoming the main character—but it doesn't define it.

I think I've even had days when in certain circles I was a Twitter character—it doesn't take much for a subsection of the app to have their own dramas, their own glossary of heroes and villains. I've been reviled for an article I wrote by the ivory- tower dwellers of what's known as 'film' Twitter' (people who love films, not movies). I've been piled on and have received waves of homophobia by the TERF and transphobe movements. I once even got doxxed and had my address shared by right-wing Men's Rights Activists. A particularly strange experience was waking up to one of my tweets being taken out of context by the massive Korean boyband BTS 'standom', and having close to a million new mentions and notifications, mostly in a language I didn't understand. Often these situations were horrible, or consuming, or even just very funny—but they were still only an echo of what being the main character of Twitter must be like.

Nobody wants to be the main character

Elon Musk, Twitter's new owner, has consistently described Twitter as a 'town square', mostly as a way to try to validate bigoted opinions and flagrant misinformation as 'free speech'—but it's actually not a bad description for the culture of gossip-mongering, bickering and shared humour that has the potential to dominate the site. On its best and worst days, it does resemble a town square, but more the cartoonishly judgemental fishmongers and small-minded town folk from *Beauty and the Beast*, ready to pivot at any moment from harmless gossip and group singing, to picking up the pitchforks and flaming torches.

This must be what being the main character is like, going about your regular day, mongering your fish, and suddenly turning around and finding that your simple provincial life has become an object of ridicule and hatred and consequences from an overwhelmingly huge mob. A good example is the 2021 'bean dad', when John Roderick, the very mildly famous lead singer of an indie band from the 2000s, decided to share a story on Twitter where in a mixture of laziness and confusing parenting choices, he decided to let his nine-year-old daughter learn how to open and cook a can of beans on her own, with no help. According to his thread, she spent six hours being hungry. Obviously people not only accused him of unnecessary cruelty towards his daughter, they also questioned the decision to broadcast this so confidently and publicly. There was something inherently funny about a multi-tweet thread where a guy waxed lyrical about denying his daughter beans, which propelled him into an app-wide joke, a readily accessible meme. To this day, you can short-hand reference 'bean dad'.

The story doesn't end there, unfortunately. Before long, old tweets of Roderick's were dredged up, showing an affinity with racist, anti-Semitic and transphobic language and jokes, prompting people to pile on more criticism. He quickly deleted his Twitter account, and has never returned. The whole process—from virality, to memedom, to cancellation, to deletion—took about eighteen hours in total, during which you could safely call him the main character.

There have been more main characters than you could possibly document, ranging from actual celebrities to complete random nobodies. There are people who become jokes, such as the guy who weighed in on gun control in the United States, asking how he's going to defend his children from 35 to 40 feral hogs without guns, or the guy whose wife couldn't eat fajitas without shredded cheese. There are people who shoot themselves in the foot, like the Twitter user who engaged in radical leftist politics who let slip that they work for LockheedMartin, a huge weapons maker. And then there are people who manage to create a moment of main-character joy, without particularly suffering themselves, such as the guy who tried to bulk-buy rice for frugality and accidentally ended up with an entire truckload of it, or the Ariana Grande fan whose mum confiscated her phone and who tweeted through her smart fridge instead.

There is a lot of diversity in main-character syndrome, but at the end of the day it's someone who for better or worse preoccupies a good portion of a famously scattered app, who manages to be on the tip of the tongue of the townsfolk. One of the earliest documented main characters of the day was Justine Sacco, 30 years old and the senior director of corporate communications at digital services company IAC, who back in 2013 began tweeting some little 'jokes' about the indignities of travel to her handful (170) of followers while travelling from the United States to Africa. 'Going to Africa. Hope I don't get AIDS. Just kidding. I'm white!'

The racist tweet quickly went viral, with her name becoming the number-one worldwide trend. On its own, it seems like an appalling but not that exciting example of early Twitter virality (back when going viral meant something, goddamnit), and was often used as an example of 'cancel culture' in action. But what turned her into the main character of the day was one part of the story: she went viral while she was on an eleven-hour flight. Anticipation turned to a fever pitch when people realised how incredibly funny it was that she would get off the plane and discover she'd ruined her life with one tweet, that she was on the fast track to being fired.

Her employer, IAC, tweeted: 'This is an outrageous, offensive comment. Employee in question currently unreachable on an intl flight.' The hashtag #HasJustineLandedYet began trending. Schadenfreude united the app, escalating an unknown racist into an event. A Twitter main character of the day is an event, a sugar-fuelled public holiday where all the fireworks go off at once, like a once-in-a-lifetime comet made out of flaming shit, drawing all eyes to the sky.

Some people manage to hold a kind of recurring position in this role, often the already famous. Author Joyce Carol Oates has had several famous moments of incoherent Twitter stardom, such as the time she posted her leprous-looking foot to the site. Chrissy Teigen has managed to be the main character so often it essentially became a part of her brand. Former US president Donald Trump was such a prolific user, he became known as the first Twitter president, and was later banned from the site.

There's almost a begrudging respect for the people so incorrigibly terrible that they have a main character moment and continue simply to post through it, giving themselves an almost sitcom special guest role. When something goes down, when discourse is firing, it's not surprising for one of Twitter's recurring main characters to lumber out of the woodwork and get involved.

That is why Twitter, for the past couple of months, has lived in an unnaturally extended state of main-character excitement, because one of the app's most committed failsons, a recurring main character, actually went and bought the app itself. One of the main characters has taken over the mad house, and like all main-character moments, it's horrible and hilarious. And he won't stop posting through it all.

Congratulations on your internet success

In 2016, incredibly hungover, I procrastinated on an article I was writing by playing the Xbox game Skyrim, an open-world game where an element of chaos and individual experience come into it. Blearily, and with the kind of pain-filled hysteria that a true hangover can bring out, I shared my experiences on Twitter, focusing on the strange narrative detour I took as I tried to protect a dog I found in the game. If that makes no sense, that's fine—the tweet thread took off and went viral.

A true viral thread is mostly just overwhelming, a storm of notifications and retweets that you tend to just mute after a while to achieve some form of peace. But this one didn't die off after a day, it kept growing. Soon I had reporters from *BuzzFeed* and *Kotaku* and *LadBible* reaching out to me, which I happily answered. I was in an interesting position of just finding the whole situation mildly funny and interesting. I decided simply to lean into it—it was so harmless and silly that I decided I might as well see where it took me. After another day, it was reporters from *The New York Times* and the BBC. I was staying up until 2 am to chat on British morning radio about a computer game I once played, and the funny things I wrote about it.

Imagine driving your car from Leeds to Manchester, drinking tea out of a thermos, listening to a strange Australian boy explain why he loves his computer dog so much. I adored how stupid the whole situation was. I have a much-loved text from my mother, who after reading about it in *The New York Times*, still had no clue what the hell was going on, but wanted to be supportive and wrote 'congratulations on your internet success'.

After explaining the feverish lynch-mob intensity of Twitter, it feels like most people would want to be involved in literally anything else. Have a nice cup of tea and read a book, rather than join the tomato-throwing mob, the mean-spirited horde of gossips and idiots. And this isn't entirely incorrect. While Twitter as a site has the power to destroy you, it's like all social media—a double-edged tool that can build and connect just as well.

My first paid commission came indirectly from Twitter—I was writing a comedy blog, back in the blog era, and an editor saw one of my articles and thought it was funny. They offered me $50 to write something else for their site. That was the slippery slope to becoming a journalist for me, but also one of the primary ways that I use the site: it's the perfect breeding ground for writers and writing, ideas, and opinions.

This kind of narrative sits hand in hand with the main character of Twitter—a factory of wild and weird unexpected dreams, where every second box is a nightmare. It is also a tool, a networking opportunity, a creative outlet. But focusing on the utilitarian aspects of the site is one of the quickest ways to destroy yourself. Twitter, above all, hates it when people try to turn it into LinkedIn. There has to be an element of coincidence and fluke, happenstance and serendipity to everything—successes and failures.

The main characters are moments, they are events—but they couldn't occur without everyone having their own private worlds on the app, using it for work, socialising, or in my case, accidentally meeting the love of my life on it, playing out the first months of our courtship via the direct message function.

But that's part of the joy of creating a shared narrative like this—the fact that connection comes from something strangely organic but also contrived. We delight in the process of turning happenstance, chaos and miscellany into a story we can engage with. The fact that tropes and archetypes recur over and over helps make this happen. The main characters keep generating, creating something like an oral history, a legacy of idiots and fools.

Divorced-man-in-chief

What kind of story are we telling that consistently has this kind of main character? I think it's simple—we're telling a story of absurd tragedy. The main character of a narrative is usually the audience's point of reference, of engagement. They are usually the hero, the protagonist—the story is about them. We are watching them grow, triumph, take down the bad guy, get the girl. Rooting for them.

The main character of the day on Twitter has all the narrative power, but a complete inverse of this format. They are not so much an anti-hero as a comedic, tragic figure. They are a figure of buffoonery and schadenfreude, who hang themselves by their own petard. They are deeply indicative of the story we are collectively trying to tell—they represent it.

Twitter, it seems, loves to tell a story of grand failure and stupidity. It has permeated so much of the experience—we refer to it as 'the hellsite', and actively engage in a semi-gleeful way with how bad it is for us. 'This website is free', we say, when we see another example of a terrible tweet, another example of an opinion so full of brainworms that it should never have been broadcast. We collectively tell a story of spiralling chaos on this app, and gleefully reflect on the days we all went mad together, like when Donald Trump got COVID, and the site devolved into a churning maelstrom of jokes and opinions. Our own existence on the app is part of the joke.

Of course the main character of this story would be a clown, who became a clown by their own persistent clowning. In this narrative, in the Twitter story, we collectively see ourselves as almost the antagonist, damned and blighted for being on the app, existing to rise up the protagonist and then make fun of them. It's a strange story we're telling.

That's why I think Elon Musk buying the site fits in with this narrative so well. There's nothing more main character than strenuously digging your own grave, making your bed and refusing to stop lying in it. By buying the site and committing himself to a dizzying series of failures, he seems to be pushing the narrative of Twitter towards some form of climax. We, the Twitter storytellers, can sense an ending coming, like blood in the water.

Musk exemplifies the energy of a sub-category of main character called 'deeply divorced'. When he finalised the sale in October 2022, he arrived at Twitter HQ carrying a sink in his arms, and tweeted a picture saying 'let that sink in'. It was just the beginning of a spree of clownery that persists to this day.

He has bounced around from scheme to scheme, doing things like rolling out a Twitter Blue subscription service, which allows people to purchase verification, which was immediately used by comedy accounts to impersonate celebrities and brands—complete with an official 'Verified' stamp. It was bedlam, with 'George W Bush' tweeting that he 'misses killing Iraqis' and pharmaceutical company Eli Lilly announcing, 'We are excited to announce insulin is free now.' Even Musk himself got parodied, with a verified Elon Musk account offering 'free nightly dinners' and family vacations to anyone whose name happened to be that of his ex, Grimes. It was such a delicious failure that he immediately rolled the subscription service back, but not before losing the majority of Twitter's top 100 advertisers.

The buffoonery never seems to rest—from viral videos of him going on stage and being booed at a Dave Chapelle comedy show, to the day he put up a poll asking whether he should quit as the CEO of Twitter and promising to commit to the result— and overwhelmingly being told to go.

But he still remains, still actively making the site worse, still posting through it. It's an escalation of main-character theory, an ability for the main character to not just have a moment in the horrific limelight of ridicule, but nestle into it, keep bodily pulling the spotlight back onto him. He will not stop hitting himself, and nobody is holding his hands. It's a litany of failures, his personal wealth and his Tesla stock plummeting every day.

Twitter these days still has the feeling of moving towards a climax, but it's almost apocalyptic, dystopian. The site is barely usable, with various functions breaking every day. Musk has fired most of the employees, and continues to knee-jerk sabotage things. Recently, he tried to work out why he wasn't getting much engagement on his tweets, only to be told by an employee that there were no software reasons for it, he just wasn't tweeting very good stuff. Musk fired him. Shortly after, the site basically shut down for a day, broken and unusable.

There's even something reminiscent of the final series of long-running television shows that went for too long, an escalation of absurdity, a lack of narrative pacing, a feeling like perhaps it's just time to wrap this all up. People are talking about other platforms to migrate to. Old, long-forgotten villains and main characters are being spun up again (mostly due to Musk deliberately bringing back long-banned far-right figures, alleged sex traffickers like Andrew Tate, and super-divorced transphobes like British anti-trans activist Graham Linehan), making it feel almost like a nostalgia tour. A greatest hits of absolute dipshits.

I don't know whether Musk will bring about the end of Twitter—but as someone who has been thoroughly poisoned by this cursed group-storytelling project, I almost want it to implode in this way, to finally be destroyed by the main character.

• • •

Maxine Beneba Clarke

Welcome, Maxine! Wonderful to have you here. So much to discuss... One of the abiding principles that motivated Clem Christesen to found *Meanjin* was, in his words: 'to make clear the connection between literature and politics'. So let's start there. What does that mean to you? What is the connection between literature and politics?

For me—for my writing, at least—writing is a political act. For me, that means that I don't generally create something unless I have an impetus to create it. You know—unless I feel like there is a need for *this* story to be told. Perhaps it hasn't been told before. Perhaps it's the *right* time to tell it in terms of doing the work it needs to do to start conversations. But I don't think it necessarily means that for every writer. I think, for some, the political act is choosing not to make political work. And that could also be a kind of avoidance: it could be a commercial consideration, or it could be an avoidance of wanting to get into Politics with a capital P.

For me, it can mean *choosing* to create. You know, I think often writers of colour are pushed into making political work. So for me, sometimes the choice *not* to make political work can be like... well, because everyone is expecting me! Because I'm Black and #BlackLivesMatter means they're all expecting me to make a particular work. So ok my next book is just going to be... a fairy tale! So it might be that I'm pushing against the political in that way.

I feel as if the recognition that writing itself is a political act needs a bigger context—in terms of, Who actually *can* read and write? Who has the power to put the written word on the page? The fact that it is the *written* word. I think, when I write, I'm really cognisant of that—because *of* my family history, because of colonisation. My family is part of the trans-Atlantic slave trade in the West Indies, which means that, for many generations, we weren't allowed to read or write. You know, having lost whatever language was spoken in the part of West Africa where my family was taken from, and then not being able to learn English properly. And being forbidden to—for generations. This means I'm very aware now of the privilege of not only *having* a pen, but actually the *power* to get what I'm writing published. And so part of the political decision is, well, what do I do with that? What's my responsibility when there are people who don't actually have that? So maybe that's what the founder was talking about—this exploration of: What does it mean

Maxine Beneba Clarke

Maxine Beneba Clarke is the author of twelve books for children and adults, including the short-fiction collection *Foreign Soil*, the memoir *The Hate Race*, and the poetry collections *Carrying the World*, *How Decent Folk Behave* and *It's the Sound of the Thing: 100 new poems for young people*. She is Poet in Residence at the University of Melbourne.

Photograph: *Meanjin*

to write? What does that mean politically? Both in terms of what you choose to write, and the actual act of writing.

MEANJIN   That's such an important distinction: that power to *choose* to write or not to write, or to *choose* to be political or not political. Because as you say, that's not a choice that's available to everybody—and as a Black woman, it's an expectation that's imposed on you. The flip side of that, of course, is how power and white power in particular can often seem invisible and neutral. Some people can blithely exercise a choice without having to consider the political dimensions of that choice.

MAXINE   Yeah, absolutely. And obviously the more power you have, the more choice you have. Both in terms of whether somebody facilitates writing and makes decisions about what should be published, or about what to write. You know, I don't think many people would necessarily question a white writer: Why aren't you writing about climate change? Or why aren't you writing about racism? Yeah, that idea of what you're expected to produce— and challenging that.

MEANJIN   It has struck me as long as I've known your writing that you kind of announce that connection between literature and politics the moment you walk onto a stage. Across the full scope of your work—for children and for adults—I see a real orientation to a public in that civic sense: to an Australia that your work is bringing into being. The politics of something complex that is also a kind of everydayness.

MAXINE   Well, I started out at university—but really I started out in spoken word. And part of that was because I'd done a law degree and a creative writing degree, then came out of that working entry-level legal jobs, which I sort of found enjoyable but wasn't really in love with them. And I didn't really know how to go about getting my work published, even though I had done a creative writing degree! So I started submitting things to literary journals, and getting rejections—and then I discovered that there's this thing called spoken word where you can just turn up, there's a microphone there, and you were guaranteed to get airtime. There's a democracy about that. There's no-one to say, 'I don't like this, therefore you don't get to have an audience.'

When you're delivering your work in person, you are a Black female body at a microphone. So even if I were to read a poem about roses, there is no getting away from the fact that it's a Black female body at a microphone in a room full of people. You know that you're holding that space. And I think that is where that orientation of my work comes from. For my first six-seven-eight years of making work, it was only spoken word. You have to turn up and take a chair. To some extent, it's also about making someone sit in that chair! And who else can I get up on stage with me? Working on *Growing Up African in Australia*, I'm like, Who else is going to be at the microphone? I very rarely perform spoken word now, but I am so shaped by that democratic space of having a seat at the table, and spending time at the microphone. I'm really interested in what you do with the two minutes that you have.

MEANJIN   There's a real immediacy around spoken word: the preparation, the performance, and then also, the response of the audience. There's also a really fun immediacy to your Twitter presence! Writing can be quite solitary... is that what Twitter is for you? Is it more honing the craft, or being with people, in the communities you're helping to create?

MAXINE   I think for me, Twitter has never been about craft; my primary focus is just to talk to people. It's funny because, being a writer, the only time that people get to see you is when you're on the promotion track. But that's such a small part of being a writer. Often you're alone, in a room, at a table working. When I'm doing that for a six- or eight-hour day, I love that ability to go, 'So what's everyone else doing?' and have that funny conversation.

It's also been a really interesting way to get work out fast. And I think that was a precursor to my work with the *Saturday Paper*. I actually pitched that to them: 'Look at these poems I posted on Twitter!' Poetry can happen fast. It can respond to current events. It can hold that space of discussion in a very different way. And in a sense, my work had always been doing that, even when I was doing slam poetry, it was responding to things that were happening in Australia, and how I was processing them.

It's interesting, that sense of responsiveness... A library approached me last year about creating a living archive of my work, my notes and correspondence. Part of me was thinking: I'm not dead yet! What are they trying to say?!? but the idea is that we gather things as we go along. One of the interesting things they asked was would I consent to them archiving my Twitter? This was at the time of Elon Musk and the risk of losing it all, and I was just really shocked—I mean I tweet about lunchboxes being emptied—

MEANJIN   Hey now that is a national service!

MAXINE   And it really is the place where I have fun. I'm talking to people about things that I wouldn't necessarily talk about on a writers' festival panel. You're not talking to people about, you know, having to force your kids to wear the school uniform. You're sort of kept in this highbrow space, a literary space, where we talk about craft. So Twitter is a space to *actually* have those real conversations with people while they're working or they're on their lunch break. It feels like the water cooler.

MEANJIN   And I really hope it can remain that way! Because I love that we get to encounter poets and poetry on social media, in that extreme contingency of whatever your timeline is today. It's not as democratic a space as the spoken word mic, but then it also makes me think of what it means to encounter poetry in a newspaper. It's the publication saying to us, 'Yes, we're presenting news—and we're not going to pretend that it's from the view from nowhere, an apolitical perspective—and there's also going to be a cartoon that pushes you to think differently—and now here is a poem.' So what did that mean for you: being in the news cycle, as a poet?

MAXINE   I think part of the reason that worked was because the audience was, by and large, left leaning. There are some criticisms of the *Saturday Paper* around their position on Palestine (which is part of the reason I haven't written for them for a couple years now), but by and large, you know that you're not necessarily going to have a massive blowback, even though you know that people might not necessarily have the same opinion as you. If you had to classify them in terms of the sections of a newspaper, the poems would probably go under commentary or opinion, because they weren't pretending to be neutral.

And some were quite anthemic. There's a poem I wrote about polling day: sausages and people trying to give you pamphlets. That was just a kind of 'this is us on this particular day'. Obviously I'm talking about democracy in the process of voting as a value in itself, and that in itself is political. And yeah, there were other poems where I was really gonna push my opinion! The idea of making space for poetry wherever there's *any* other type of writing published is really important to me. That's something we should be making a case for.

MEANJIN   Why is that? What does poetry do for us?

MAXINE   I think it allows us to think differently. I think people approach poetry differently to the way they approach nonfiction, even though a poem may be nonfiction. They approach it with a sense of, you know, the idea that it doesn't necessarily have to be explaining something or simply giving facts. It can evoke a feeling. The thing about news is that it's often devoid of feeling. You know, you can be describing a massacre and it's literally just the facts. This many people were killed. This is how it unfolded, these are the different groups involved. The reaction of the reader depends on their life experiences, on where they stand politically. But with a poem you can evoke a feeling, you can probe that. What do I agree with? What do I feel and why do I feel uncomfortable about it?

And the condensation of language in poetry—that you can use language in a way that actually evokes emotion—that you can use it to make people respond in a different way. Probably the most interesting thing about that job is that there were a lot of letters to the editor about poems! Almost like that Twitter thing, where it was a conversation between myself and the readers. The most correspondence I got was about a poem titled 'Communion', which was about the Catholic Church. It was when Pell was under investigation, and it was about clergy abuse. I had quite a few survivors write into the paper and say, 'We never thought we'd see this kind of thing published, and thank you for writing this.' I think it's because it *did* express an opinion *and* evoke emotion. It asked people to consider the survivors and said, 'We believe you.' You can't do that in a news article.

MEANJIN   I also see, in what you describe there, a real power in the dignity that a poem presents. A poem can arrest you, make you think differently, make time move differently. There's a respect and an awe that a poem attracts... from the immediacy of slam poetry, through to hip hop, to the epic and the lyrical. There's an extraordinary way in which poetry offers the dignity of an understanding.

MAXINE   I think the space that poetry creates is a contemplative space. Same with children's books. All of my children's picture books are poems. I've recently finished writing a book of poetry for children, and that came about partly from conversations with teachers who said there's no contemporary children's poetry! But that's because most of the contemporary children's poetry is in picture books! When you read picture books, they're written in rhyme! If you took two hundred of the best picture books and turned them into a book, there you would have the collection. Poetry is very much that same bedtime space that picture books occupy: it's the end of the day, everything else is done, and now it's just about sitting with something, reading together, having that quiet time. If you give the right poem to the right person, it can have that effect as well.

MEANJIN   That contemplative space of poetry and picture books sits within a world of increasing clutter—an increasingly divided public space. That question of where our public conversations happen, within an increasingly concentrated media ownership with social media near collapse... When you look for today's news and critical perspectives, how do you and your family negotiate all that pre-structured, pre-politicised media?

MAXINE   I look to the people who are working in a similar way to me. I read the work of other poets, or people who might be writing in long form, like in *The New York Times* or whatever publication. It's an increasing realisation for me, looking beyond the 24-hour news cycle for the voices outside of that, maybe from podcasting. An increasing realisation of the sound-bite packaging that comes from the news cycle and from social media. Parallel to that are the spaces operating *against* that—so where are they? With my kids, if I see that they gravitate to one particular source, I ask them to look at this other person who's doing this as well, and then, let's critique that person!

There's an incredible energy in the people creating climate change dialogue, or in the Black Lives Matter movement. The energy of keeping up with that is huge! Being someone who creates that kind of material, often altruistically—can it be sustained? I think that's part of my worries. Can the voices of critique actually be sustained? In a situation where there is no financial—I mean people need to eat.

MEANJIN   You know, I think this is one of the biggest questions of our times. How are the voices of critique going to be sustained? And it brings us back to our first question about the connection between literature and politics—because that space to critique and respond, whether it's opinion pieces or book reviews or poetry, that's how we create the future. So we can change the question now. It's not so much about an abstract relationship, but about where and how is the connection between literature and politics happening?

MAXINE   I think it's happening at *every* level. There's that kind of mantra: who controls the means of production. And I think, increasingly for me, I realise how much of a financial question it is. Not just in terms of who has the time to write, but publishing is one of those jobs where it's not necessarily well paid, and yet you generally need to be tertiary educated—or most people in that area are tertiary educated, highly literate. A lot of people have middle-class upbringings. If you look at the writing world as well, where a lot of people are underpaid, and a lot of people have partners who are in a well-paid job so they're able to do it. So we need to look at who can actually dedicate that time. And then in the publishing industry, looking at who makes decisions, right down to the readers of the slush pile! I have no doubt that if I walked into a publishing house and read the entire slush pile and picked out three manuscripts, they would be completely different to whoever's sitting in the editor's chair!

It's at every level and even down to education. I've had two books on the English syllabus in the past few years, so it's also a matter of who is teaching those texts? Who is booklisting them? Who's on the panel that decides VCE English? Who's in the libraries? Who's stocking the texts? Who's ordering them?

And it's not as simple as being someone who has published so widely across genres. It's actually not as simple as just making the work, or even just awarding the work. You get this sense that we've had a few winners of colour in this particular prize, so everything's fine now.

I think it's all of those things, so deeply embedded in the politics of those who have their hand in making the work. And then when you get past all of that, it's about the booksellers, it's about the parents who walk into the shop, what they're prepared to buy for their kid and how open they are to someone suggesting something they might not have thought of. I think it's an entire ecosystem that is part of—essentially, in Australia—a colonial enterprise, no different from the schooling system or sports or any other system.

Australia is a country founded on stolen Black land. How do you undo that—even bit by bit—when there are people working to keep it as it is? And although I think literature is a field that is largely left leaning—where people are open to those kinds of conversations more than, say, 50 years ago—it's systemic. It's not just about the work that is created at the artist's table.

MEANJIN   Every one of those moments you describe is a small but highly politicised intervention in how literature happens—and when we zoom out beyond all those systems within systems, there's a systematic entrenchment of different kinds of advantage and disadvantage, a real reluctance to consider what is essentially intersectional about that disadvantage. Thus the power of your poem 'My Feminism', after Flavia Dzodan. To be able to do that requires a kind of circuit breaker, a moment to stop or opt out, to reflect on intention, to find that contemplative space. Because too easily that apparatus just recomposes itself with everyone too busy playing their part. Can poetry be that circuit breaker?

MAXINE I think it can be, you know. I think it is. It's one of those places that people still go to with an open heart. Given a poem, and the choice to read a poem—so I'm not necessarily talking about kids in school who are forced to read certain work! They won't necessarily find that contemplative space. So I guess the question is, 'How do we make people more open to that space?' So that they're not all, 'Ugh, I don't do poetry.' That space is really important, and once you make that choice to read a poem, essentially you're saying, 'I'm open to what this person is giving me.' You're saying, 'I'm open to emotion, and I'm open to a different way of thinking, and I'm open to connection'—these are all the things you come to a poem with, which are so counter to so many of the ways that we communicate with each other.

MEANJIN When I was first reading your poetry in the *Saturday Paper*, what first came to mind for me was the encounter with public art. You don't choose to encounter art in the public space, you don't necessarily choose or encounter poetry among news and political analysis, but then here you are. And here inside you is this open heart that you didn't even realise you had before encountering it.

MAXINE Ok that's really interesting. The first picture book I wrote was illustrated by a street artist—Van T Rudd—and that's how I found him! Walking around the neighbourhood and going, oh wow, there's a mural there, or there's a hand just here on the wall with the word 'refugee'. Here was someone just putting art out where people *have* to confront it. So I guess that's the flip side to my description of how you have to come to poetry. How do we make people come to it with an open heart? And I guess part of that might be to surprise them with it. To put poetry in unexpected places. Put it on cereal boxes!

MEANJIN Yes! And you could collect them! Make your own little cut-up!

MAXINE No we have to stop! Someone will say, 'You're a philistine! Don't put it on cereal boxes!' And we've had poetry on trams in Melbourne, and on scrolling displays at Federation Square. Maybe some haiku or eight-word poems on billboards...
    I think that's part of the irony of how do you open people's minds to poetry: you just give them poetry, and show them what it can do.

MEANJIN I love that. Thank you so much, Maxine—you've opened my heart.

•••

The *Meanjin* Interviews honour Founding Editor Clem Christesen's commitment 'to make clear the connection between literature and politics'.

Beyond the Governance Gaps

Kate
Larsen

Kate Larsen (she/
her) is a writer and
arts leader based
on Kaurna Yerta in
Tarntanya/Adelaide.
See <larsenkeys.
com.au> and
@KateLarsenKeys

Past and present board members and those who support our boards—I want to thank you. In the machine of arts, cultural and not-for-profit governance you are one of our most necessary cogs: legislated, expected and required. From statutory authorities to volunteer-run collectives, you underpin all of our work.

The skills you must wield are varied and plentiful, yet your presence, consideration and time receive little or no remuneration—and often little thanks. But your work is a literal gift, an extraordinary, mandated generosity—without which our organisations would not be allowed to exist.

It's not you, it's ~~me~~ the system

Bad boards have made for even worse headlines over the past couple of years. In Boorloo/Perth, the boards of Black Swan State Theatre Company and Barking Gecko Theatre controversially ended their CEOs' contracts in 2019 and 2021 respectively. In a move condemned by the company's founders and peers, Black Swan's CEO was replaced with one of their own board members—with no experience of running a comparable arts organisation.[1] Sponsors and stakeholders expressed concerns over both decisions, including fears of board overreach, conflicts of interest and potential use of public funding for unnecessary HR processes.[2]

In a surprise announcement at the end of 2021, the Circus Oz board in Naarm/Melbourne announced its plan to wind up the organisation after being unable to convince its membership to change its governance structure, which would have involved members giving up their decision-making power.[3] After years of governance issues, the company's funding was already under review by state and federal governments, which were assumed to be behind the recommended 'corporatisation' that the proudly artist-led organisation dismissed.[4] The members quickly appointed an entirely new board, which hasn't made any further public announcements in more than a year since—except about their 2023 Melbourne Comedy Festival show.

Greenwashing is starting to cause governance headaches too, with high-profile board members stepping down to protest unethical corporate sponsorships—such as Benjamin Law's departure from the Sydney Festival Board in 2022.[5] In New Zealand, ongoing governance concerns were blamed for the vote of no confidence that saw the entire

1
Richard Watts, 'Black
Swan drama continues
as executive director
leaves early', ArtsHub,
2019.

2
Richard Watts,
'Sector speaks out
over Barking Gecko
concerns', ArtsHub,
2021.

3
Richard Watts,
'Circus Oz to wind up',
ArtsHub, 2021.

4
Tully Barnett, Julian
Meyrick and Justin
O'Connor, 'Circus Oz:
a crisis in a crisis',
ArtsHub, 2021.

5
Kelly Burke, 'Benjamin
Law resigns from
Sydney festival board
over Israeli embassy
sponsorship', Guardian
Australia, 2022.

board of Museums Aotearoa step down in 2021.[6] Similarly, the board of Seattle's ACT Theatre voluntarily stepped down in 2022, other than the three position-holders required by US law—the chair, secretary and treasurer. It seems, though, that their ambition to rethink their governance radically has resulted in the reintroduction of a remarkably similar model.

Meanwhile, new research has revealed boards' poor track record in most of their responsible areas. Notably, this includes: lack of diversity, limited or non-existent introspection and review, limited or negligent CEO oversight and regular failures of duty of care, not to mention the lack of inductions, training, financial literacy or direct board involvement in financial sustainability.[7]

Even our successes have been damned with faint praise and lower-than-low expectations. While, on average, board members are 'strongest' when acting as ambassadors, in no way does this equate to 'strong'. Only 40% attend their organisation's events; less than half understand their organisation or are able to speak on its behalf; and less than 20% are seen to carry out their roles appropriately and contribute to positive and productive workplace cultures most of the time.

I'm sure some of you are shocked by these stories. I'm sure others are not at all surprised. As the author of some of those studies, I acknowledge I may have contributed to you feeling attacked, under-appreciated, overwhelmed or misunderstood. In which case, I'm sorry. It was never about you. It was always about a system I believe is setting you, your organisations and our sector up to fail.

It's not about #NotAllBoards

I hope we can take this as read: boards and board members can do good work. I am in awe of you and the work you're asked to do. Let's also acknowledge the opposite is equally true: boards and board members can damage their organisations, teams and peers. This is not about blame. This is about data. Of course, it's #NotAllBoards and #NotAllBoardMembers. But the evidence suggests it's a lot—at least enough to acknowledge the issues and the actions that need to come next. We need to have a genuine conversation, not defend against defensiveness or bolster board fragility. We need to do what board members should do best: be allies for our organisations—even when that means taking an uncomfortable look at ourselves.

The information gap

In 2020 the Arts and Culture Governance Report from Australia Council for the Arts, Institute of Community Directors Australia (ICDA) and Our Community began to shine the spotlight on Australian arts sector governance.[8] My 2022 survey did the same, recording nearly double the number of responses from serving and former board members, CEOs and other sector leaders, employees, artists, contractors and more.[9] All over the world, colleagues, researchers and cultural organisations are also approaching this issue from a range of different angles. So while it's true, as Algonquin playwright Yvette Nolan writes, 'every dysfunctional board is dysfunctional in its own way',[10] this research has articulated

6
Mark Amery, 'Not on Board', the *Big Idea*, 2021.

7
Kate Larsen, 'Bad news Boards', *ArtsHub*, 2022.

8
ICDA Spotlight Report: Arts and Culture Governance, Institute of Company Directors Australia (ICDA), Our Community and Australia Council for the Arts, 2020.

9
Kate Larsen, Art of Governance survey, 2020.

10
Yvette Nolan, 'Governance structures for theatres, by theatres: what I wish existed', *Mass Culture*, 2020 (quoted with permission).

significant consensus governance issues that we've all had to muddle through for years. Our poor-performing boards, however, are symptoms of a bigger system problem. Our governance model is the cause.

With a few tiny variations, our national *Corporations Act* and each state and territory's incorporated association laws impose a hierarchical and corporate structure on not-for-profit governance that attempts to be all things for all organisations. Statutory authorities, public companies and other incorporated structures aren't much different either. The statistics show this approach isn't working. 'One-size-fits-all does not fit anyone,' Nolan writes. 'And has created a culture that allows dysfunction to hide behind a structure that gives the appearance of legitimacy, the illusion of oversight.'

Meanwhile, the governance traditions and training that have evolved around this legislation have reinforced our understanding of unquestioned 'best practice' governance. However, these familiar, 'business as usual' recommendations are based on colonial, military and patriarchal structures that are often antithetical to contemporary not-for-profit or community-engaged work, and are not keeping pace with the ways in which the sector continues to evolve.

'Organisations are facing unprecedented changes in their environments and, as a result, are transforming how they operate and fulfil their mission,' the Ontario Nonprofit Network (ONN) notes in their newly launched Reimagining Governance Lab.[11] 'However, the fundamentals of governance design in nonprofit organisations haven't changed a lot from decades ago when boards were put in place to create more accountability.'

11
Reimagining
Governance Lab,
Ontario Nonprofit
Network.

If everything else in the world is changing, surely our governance practices need to change too. Not doing so will perpetuate the unreasonable, unfair and unnecessary burden of expectation that it's no wonder boards are often unable to meet.

The awareness gap

We know the problems. We can even prove the problems. The information and evidence gap has closed. I believe what we're experiencing now is a gap between acknowledgement and self-awareness. I speak to a lot of boards and board members who nod in vigorous agreement at every grim revelation and research finding, but who are much less likely to realise the statistics apply to them too.

One aspect of this is practical. Finding the time and energy to reflect on (let alone reimagine) our organisations' governance is a big ask when many of us are already struggling with the current model's requirements, and mostly doing so in our own, limited time as volunteers.

But if the research shows that *most* Australian arts and cultural boards are experiencing some or all of these issues, why would we think ours exempt? And if our boards are resistant to comparing our performance to the sector's shared experience, what are we trying to hide—even (or especially) from ourselves? 'Five, ten years ago, we had a lot of pushback,' ONN's Erin Kang says. 'Over time, we noticed a shift in appetite. Part of this was finding arguments that were outside the individual and shifting to making things better for board members.'

We need to bridge the awareness gap by making board members allies for the change that needs to come, and equip them with the confidence that they're meeting their legal and fiduciary obligations and duties of care. We need to bring bold, rigorous and uncomfortable discussions into our boardrooms—not just about our performance but also about how we're expected to perform, and whether those expectations are necessary, efficacious or fair.

The imagination and implementation gap

Looking at arts governance as a systems issue, not a people issue, is hugely empowering. It makes it something we can review and improve, rather than resigning ourselves to expecting too much or throwing money at training that won't stick.

It does, however, create another gap: between knowing change is needed and knowing what and how to change (including dedicating the time and resources we need to find out). This will always be a challenge in an under-resourced sector. Two-thirds of Australian not-for-profits turn over less than $250,000 each year. Our underpaid and overworked teams and boards are used to exceeding minimum requirements on perpetually dwindling resources. Now, amid our 'post'-COVID burnout, many are trying to move from this 'less is more' to a 'less is necessary' mindset—making governance one of the most problematic *and* most overlooked parts of our work.[12]

Meanwhile, the world is a bin fire of multiple, ongoing crises that have put systemic change at the bottom of our ever-growing to-do lists—while simultaneously bringing the challenges of our governance model into very sharp relief. 'The model has failed,' Nolan says. 'In these COVID times, these #MeToo times, these Black Lives Matter times, this new civil rights movement time, the failures become even more obvious.'

Those with greater capacity will need to lead the way. Kang talks about the importance of 'early wave riders' in implementing governance innovations. 'The bigger organisations are key because they have the capacity to do the work and thinking involved,' she says. 'Doing so gives the rest of the sector permission and provides case studies others can work towards.'

We also need to support one another while we wait for the r/evolution to happen. Self-care and duty of care are the pointiest ends of most sectors right now, and the things we'll need to address before we can think about doing things differently longer term. This means we don't only need to be allies for change, but also for the ongoing challenges of navigating our flawed system while waiting for the change we need to come.

Make the best of it

Our legislation requires us to have boards. Our funders, members and stakeholders expect them. We're used to them being around. For most of us, boards are the way that business has always been done. We can acknowledge, I hope, that our governance model is broken. We're not yet in a position to throw it out and start again, but that doesn't mean we can't make the best of our imperfect situation. We are used to applying training and other governance resources to this task, but the research suggests this investment

12
Kate Larsen,
'Post-COVID or
post-burnout: less is
necessary', *Artshub*,
2022.

is neither particularly effective nor something that lasts beyond each trained board member's term.

This never-ending investment cycle generates fantastic business for governance-training providers. In spite of the COVID downturn, the Governance Institute of Australia turned over $9.9 million in 2021, dwarfed by the $72.4 million turnover of the Australian Institute of Company Directors (with nearly $1 million in surplus, equivalent to two to four small-to-medium arts organisations' entire operating budgets). In the name of full disclosure, I should note that I too make part of my income from governance consultancy, albeit nothing on that scale.

This isn't, however, such good business for the organisations we train. Board members move on and usually take their learning with them—ideally to another board in a sort of sector karma in which we'd benefit from another organisation's investment, though the evidence suggests that's not the case. As allies, governance trainers and service providers need to acknowledge the irony at the heart of this business model—supporting sustainability while asking organisations to make an unsustainable investment to train each new generation of board members who come through.

Bend the rules

Until we can imagine and implement something new, we've got to make the best of what we've got. So, if training isn't answer enough, we need to find ways and work-arounds to create better conditions for governance that still technically comply with the rules.

We need to know what those rules are to bend them, so some of this starts with unlearning. While we *think* we know why things have always been done, we find there's more room for innovation than we've been told. 'Most practices we've associated with boards over the decades are completely optional,' Vu Le writes for *Nonprofit AF*.[13] 'They are traditions we've just passed down to the point where we think they're legally required, but they're not. The board hires the ED. Who says? The board meets once a month. Why? The board approves the budget. Not necessarily!'

Organisations all over the world are beginning to experiment with micro or 'minimally viable' board models that reduce governance structures to the minimum size and remit needed to satisfy legislative, funding and other requirements. This usually involves fewer board members, office holders, responsibilities and meetings than we've come to think of as 'normal' operating procedures. In Australia, for example, it's generally perceived as 'best practice' to have eight to twelve board members on a not-for-profit board. However, the *Corporations Act* only requires companies limited by guarantee to have at least three directors, including one nominated office holder (the secretary).

As incorporated associations should only operate in their respective regions, their legislation varies slightly between states and territories. However, most similarly require only a single nominated office holder (usually the public officer, who often doesn't need to be a member of the board at all).

Technically speaking, the Northern Territory has the most stringent legislation, but still only requires incorporated associations to have at least five board members.

13
Vu Le, 'The default nonprofit board model is archaic and toxic; let's try some new models', *Nonprofit AF*, 2020 (quoted with permission).

The Australian Capital Territory, New South Wales, Queensland and South Australia only require three. Even more surprisingly, while Tasmania, Victoria and Western Australia require a minimum number of organisational members in order to incorporate in the first place, they don't specify a minimum number of board members. This information is not common knowledge, and some of it is really hard to find. I spoke to someone at Consumer Affairs Victoria to verify their requirements, who acknowledged the only place they could find them written down was on a third-party information sheet that was more than five years old.

While the recommendations of each state or territory's model rules may differ, they are just that: *recommendations*. Big boards aren't required. Monthly or even bimonthly board meetings aren't required, nor pages and pages of board reporting that takes staff away from their work.

Chairs, vice-chairs and treasurers aren't required either. There is absolutely nothing that says boards need to be hierarchical or—aside from a few requirements about obligations to members and government—to operate in the way ours usually do.

The familiar nominating and seconding motions of Robert's Rules of Order are based on military and parliamentary procedures that date back to 1876—but the world has changed an awful lot since then.[14] Eradicating what US arts leader Michael J. Bobbitt calls these 'archaic, pointless and extremely white' agendas could be a good starting point to 'investigate new forms of decision-making: emergent strategy, consensus voting, or decision-making processes as they have long been practised [in] non-white cultures'.[15]

Many of the other policies and procedures we use around governance are also of our own making. Working out what's required and what's optional could be a simple yet revolutionary first step in realising we have more choice and control than we thought. 'Many practices are ensconced in by-laws,' Le writes. 'But by-laws are easily changed.'

Find your own way

Needing boards and knowing that boards are the best way to achieve what we need are two different things. This is not to suggest that minimally viable boards will fix all our governance woes. It's fair to assume, however, that reducing the roles and expectations of what we know as boards would make them more likely to succeed. Reducing the number of board members we need would also make it easier to recruit and retain them.

If we were designing the system from scratch, I suspect we'd think it unreasonable to task unpaid or low-paid board members with everything we do. At present that requires board members to have a disparate mix of skills and expertise in order to provide oversight and compliance; strategic direction; decision-making; stewardship; risk and crisis management; and the recruitment, management and duty of care of our CEOs or equivalent. Let alone providing free access to relevant sector skills and experience; being public-facing ambassadors; and directly supporting our organisations' finances through fundraising, soliciting donations, sharing their personal contacts or becoming individual donors themselves.

14
Robert's Rules of Order.

15
Michael J. Bobbitt, 'Boards are broken, so let's break and remake them', *American Theatre*, 2021 (quoted with permission).

The minimally viable board provocation reminds us we don't need a single entity that does all of these things. Allocating fewer people to our legislatively required tasks could free up resources to meet the other 'board' responsibilities in more creative, representative and effective ways. 'I honestly think we can come up with a better way to do the accountability, cheerleading, support, and advising that boards at their best should and could be doing,' Bobbitt says. 'The way we are currently operating isn't working. I triple dog dare us all to use our imaginative skills to redesign it.'

Blow it all up and start again

'We've been having this discussion on repeat for years, emphasising the systemic white supremacy and patriarchy that plagues the non-profit Board of Directors model,' Brendan McMurtry-Howlett wrote as part of *Generator*'s Governance Reimaginings blog. 'But we haven't really had a clear alternative to point to.'[16]

16
Brendan McMurtry-Howlett, 'Governance reimaginings (or, there's got to be a better way)', *Generator*, 2021 (with permission).

We might not be able to parachute into our future governance utopia, but we need to start imagining what it could look like when we're there—particularly as this imagining will fuel the legislative revolution we'll need. If starting again, how would we articulate what organisations really need and how best we could provide it? How could we embed equity, diversity and anti-oppression into postcolonial, post-patriarchal and decolonised governance structures? How could we all be better allies for the organisations we love?

As board members (or whatever we call ourselves in our newly bendy structures), we can begin this process by asking big, foundational questions about why we think what we think; why we do what we do; and how we can do things differently, particularly in terms of how decisions are made—and by whom. 'The whole ecosystem of your organisation should be part of governance decision-making,' Bobbitt says. If our expertise primarily lies in our staff, artists, audiences and communities: 'Boards should be players in a partnership, not the ones in charge'.

Tweaking the existing system isn't going to cut it. We can't just ask who's not in the room, we need to ask if we need a room at all. We need to train ourselves to think beyond boards in order to open our minds to something new—whether that's a single model or a pick-and-mix range of options our organisations can choose from. McMurtry-Howlett argues that:

> Governance is no one thing for any one person. It is about a practice of decision making that is undertaken in community. There is no magic wand, or perfect structure that will solve all the problems. Anything we create must be engaged with, nourished, and sustained by those impacted by and connected to the organisation.

That includes arts funders, whose expectations and funding agreements drive govern-ance practices as much as legislation. In this, the Canada Council has led the way in recent years, Nolan says, by allowing ad hoc groups with ad hoc governance models to access funding. In this way, funders are in the unique and exciting position to be able to lead this charge, rather than reiterating existing best practice that the sector has already surpassed.

Keep governance in the spotlight

Governance is not an academic exercise. Volunteerism was decreasing even before the pandemic. Bad boards making the news have made governance even less attractive, as have workforce issues and sector-wide exhaustion. Many organisations are too busy struggling with compliance (number of board members, attendance at meetings, etc.) even to think about the system in which we perform. This means we need to fix the system that requires us to have boards before we run out of board members in it, not the other way around.

We also need to provide safe and anonymous ways for our peers and teams to contribute to this discussion. The innate power dynamics of arts governance make it difficult for many of us to speak out, in fear of our current or future work, board roles or relationships.

In pulling together this research over the past several years, I feel I've become an unofficial sector therapist—collating and sharing governance horror stories that board members, artists and arts workers are unable, uncomfortable or scared to share. There is strength and solidarity in hearing and sharing these types of experiences, and huge value in strategic venting to our similarly affected peers. But we need to be able to critique our boards, colleagues and governance culture without fear of making that culture even worse. We need to put and keep this discussion in the spotlight, where it belongs.

This means being allies for our own sakes, as well as for the work our teams and artists do. We need to be brave and open and focused on our purpose: being the best stewards of our organisations we can be. Board members, I know you have it in you. I can't wait to see what you can do.

•••

Aim Happy

Ken
Bolton

Ken Bolton, a long-time employee of Adelaide's Experimental Art Foundation, has recently published *A Pirate Life* (Cordite) and *Fantastic Day* (Puncher & Wattmann).

I chop
some wood, to
get warm,
& listen to a bit
of *Radio Italia*,
Cath gone for a walk—

after photographing
her favourite bird

a tiny, impossibly
spherical
red robin, chest
brilliant against
the greens that
surround it
(vine & leaves
on the fence—

deep olive green &
'spinach'—the pale

yellowed green
of the hay

in the barn across the road).

Tho the bird
is gone
in a moment.

Others appear—
a jay, a finch—
                    seem to say
gulp! when they see us,

& depart.

The Italians, *to my
surprise*, are discussing
sex-change therapies
—hormones, & procedures—

fairly calmly

(family support groups,
decision factors, etcetera),

then 'Kevin
Rudd'—

in whom one
(the male voice)

detects
'a certain narcissism'.

The other speaker agrees,
leaders need it etcetera

(a woman's voice).

Of course with him
it was a problem,
                    says the
male voice. Had *been*
a problem.
                    'Tell me,
as a psychologist,' he asks

'Can he change?'

There is a pause. 'No.'

It is very definite
& faintly amused. 'The
spots will re-emerge?'

(leopards, & their spots,
were mentioned earlier)

It seems funny,
after the acceptance
of gender change.

'People do *not* change.'

The voice is low, hushed,
regretful—on humanity's behalf,
nothing to do with politicians.

•

(One can't see Rudd
on humble pills.)

•

I like this particular woman's
voice. ('Aim happy,'
she says,
contentedly
at one point

when asked about herself.)

(The accent.)

•

Cath returns.

'The guy says he'll fix
the car up'—(I phone)—

'or have a look if we
bring it in.' *He* has
a place on Bruny too, he says,
& describes where it is.

I take
some photos
of Cath—for use
on her internet
'hangout spot'
—a chat site for
her & the kids
Gabe started.
                          His
signature photo—*Goose*
among the flowers.

Cath's will be
Rube among roses.

Small bush-roses
hover behind her in
the picture—near where
the bird went to,
after its first fright.

Cath said, *Oh boy,*
my favourite, & it
took off
at her approach—
went that-a-way,
to the right.

Cath followed, a
measured pursuit.

•

Bright sun, approaching cloud,
the sound of wind.
Small birds come & go.

I went for a walk and saw my own dystopian art

A reflection on the policing and control of public health responses to the pandemic

Catherine
Ryan

Catherine Ryan is
an artist and writer
living on Wurundjeri
Country. She makes
video work, sound
work and performance
lectures. She is a PhD
candidate at RMIT's
School of Art.

I

All we were allowed to do was to go for walks. 'Stupid little walks for our mental health', as one meme put it. So that is what we did. Whether in the period of lockdown when I was single and living by myself, or the one when I had a girlfriend, walks were what we did, because that is all we could do. I joked to friends that once the pandemic was over, I would never walk anywhere ever again. It was an extremely monotonous period of life, confined to the concrete streets within 30 minutes of my home: going for a daily stroll, simply to get out of the house; walks without a real destination or reason, walking for walking's sake.

As I charged along the pavement day after day, I noticed small changes. Little fashions that had swept through. There was the week where disused cheap office furniture suddenly appeared everywhere, signalling that each of us had accepted that working from home was not going away anytime soon, which meant that our initial makeshift arrangements with laptops on kitchen tables were not going to cut it, lest we pay with our necks and backs in aches and physiotherapy appointments (a price many of us would end up paying regardless).

During these first panicked months, it seemed that after living for many years in a time in which not much happened (one of those periods opposite from the proverb 'may you live in interesting times'), History was suddenly happening. I had a sense that I was now living in an important era, a bit like the Blitz or the Great Depression.

So I started keeping notes and photos of the small, quotidian ways in which the big global event of the pandemic affected the fabric of the everyday. One day, I thought, I will tell my grandchildren about these things, just as my Grandma once told me about what her social life was like in a small country town during World War II.

This impulse to record neglected one key fact: the iron law of pandemics is forgetting. As I write these words, nearly three years after the first images of collapsing hospital systems in Italy appeared alongside graphs exhorting us to 'flatten the curve', it is clear that many parts of our society wish to deem the pandemic a thing of the past. This urge to forget accompanies all plagues. The Spanish Flu, as science journalist Laura Spinney observes, caused more deaths than either the first or second world wars, yet no cenotaph or memorial commemorates it.[1] The narrator of Albert Camus's *The Plague*, writing of the fictional pestilence that sealed the Algerian town of Oran off from the world, records how afterwards the townspeople, against all evidence, 'calmly denied that we had ever known this senseless world, [...] the calculated delirium and the imprisonment that brought with it a terrible freedom from everything that was not the immediate present'.[2] The urge to forget comes from many sources, and perhaps it is a healthy one: the will to continue with life after a trauma. Unless you have been under a Sleeping Beauty-like spell, locked in a castle in a deep, magical slumber for the past three years, my descriptions of toilet paper panic buying and the humdrum acceptance of working from home will not be news to you. We were all there and we all suffered, to varying extents, over this strange period.

At the time, however, I was gripped by an urge to record. I photographed the enormous roll of toilet paper that the local $2 shop had price gouged me for ($6!). I reported to my family about the absence and return of stocks of tissues to supermarket shelves.

Perhaps the saddest phenomenon I recorded was the sudden roping-off of the playgrounds. One of the uncountable edicts proclaimed from the Victorian Government's press conference podium, when the virus was explained to us as a thing spread through touch rather than through the air, declared children's playgrounds to be a site of risk.

1
Laura Spinney, *The Pale Rider: The Spanish Flu of 1918 and how it Changed the World*, New York: Random House, 2017.

2
Albert Camus, *The Plague*, trans. Sandra Smith, London: Penguin, 2020, p. 229.

A playground in Essendon during the Melbourne lockdown. Photo: Catherine Ryan.

Children might touch each other, or touch surfaces and leave fomites behind for another child to touch. So they were closed.

It's hard to say whether we really knew why we were doing this, what scientific purpose lay behind forbidding access to public play equipment. This was a phase of the pandemic where decisions seemed driven by sheer panic. Like a reflex, this panic wanted just to *shut things down*. As if everything outside the house should simply be stopped— dog parks shut, golf courses closed, as if by stopping outdoor fun and revelry, we might stop the virus too. An all-encompassing wowserism, not of alcohol and drinking, but of public recreation.

On one of the sad little walks I'd take for my mental health, I encountered a sign hastily erected at my local playground, declaring this area to be closed for public health reasons. Improvised ingenuity had been used to render the different apparatus of the playground unusable. Swings had been wound over and over their supporting steel frames, their chains wrapped up tight so the seats were unreachable. At a local skate park, a large plastic traffic barrier was plonked in the middle of a run, obstructing prospective skaters. I was reminded of minimalist sculptures I had encountered in galleries.

I started to notice painted lines on the ground everywhere, be it in the queue for the supermarket checkout, the bottle shop or the local café. In parks all over Melbourne, following a similar trend in New York, white circles were painted on the grass using the sort of paint usually used to mark out centre circles and 50-metre lines on a football field. Council workers had diligently measured out safe zones in which you could have your picnic or sit and talk with a friend, following health advice that told us to keep two metres between ourselves and others. Public health orders mandated that only small groups of people could gather—at one point, as few as two, and then at others as many as five, providing you followed myriad sub-rules about how many people could be from a different household, or needed to be vaccinated.

Immobilised swings and skate parks in Brunswick, 2020. Photos: Catherine Ryan.

In some ways, the picnic circles were a compromise. If all of the people living in this state didn't have the pesky need to socialise and see other people, then the whole

pandemic health management thing would have been much easier. For reasons that are hard to remember now, beaches and national parks were closed. Newspapers published photos of beaches heaving with people, confected to stir outrage about how *flagrantly* some people were *flouting* the rules, disrespecting the sacrifice made by others ('flagrant' and 'flouting' being words that emerge when people want to adopt the moral stance of the principal chastising the school at assembly). The painted lines in urban parks were a concession towards this unstoppable desire for people physically to be together. If we couldn't stop people doing activities as 'dangerous' as talking to one another, then perhaps we could make it safe. And, in what I am inclined to call a very Australian mode, it was assumed that people couldn't be trusted to judge the safe socialising distance themselves. A friendly government hand was needed to guide them, to show them the right way to sit near each other on a grassy lawn.

As I walked around observing these changes, I experienced an uncanny sense of deja vu. These extemporised urban interventions—the tape cordoning off swings and slides, the painted lines—were images I had seen before. I had seen them before because they resembled artworks that I had made myself.

II

For a number of years prior to the pandemic, I had worked with another artist, Amy Spiers, to create a series of artworks in which we confected strange situations using the mediums of performance and installation. These works mimicked the activities of security guards and the police, as well as the banal markings and objects often found in public areas which demarcate what is permissible and impermissible. Our art practice examined the policing and control of public space. Sometimes our pieces were enacted by performers we had trained in aestheticised versions of techniques of crowd control and protest management that Amy and I had researched obsessively. In other works, we would hire security guards to perform for us, an approach known as delegated performance.

In 2014 we executed a complicated performance work, belonging to a genre called 'live art', entitled *Nothing to See Here (Dispersal)*. The majority of the people who had come to see this piece at the Festival of Live Art were told, upon entering a large performance space, that it couldn't be guaranteed that they would be able to see a performance, though they were free to wait. While they waited, our ensemble of performers, dressed in yellow uniforms, divided up the crowd into different groups and corralled them into various groups, encircled by bollards and chains.

One by one, over the course of an hour, most of the audience members were kicked out of the performance space: it was our aim to make as many leave as possible. Some of our ensemble became more menacing, putting on sunglasses and rubber gloves before performing a choreography based on the heavy-handed tactics that police had used to break up the Occupy Melbourne protest in 2011. The small remaining group of audience members were gathered into a small group and then encircled by temporary fencing. As each group of people was kicked out of the room, the spaces they had occupied were tied up with specially printed caution tape that read 'NOTHING TO SEE HERE'.

Documentation
of Amy Spiers and
Catherine Ryan,
*Nothing to See Here
(Dispersal)*, Festival
of Live Art, Arts
House, 2014. Photos:
John Possemato.

Though *Dispersal* took place in a performance venue, most of our works occurred as interventions in public spaces, in streets and public squares. In our most frequently performed piece, *Closed to the Public*, we would mark out the perimeter of a small square of space on the ground, usually two metres by two metres. We would then get the institution presenting the work to hire a disproportionately large number of security guards in relation to those tiny dimensions, to keep the square empty. Over the following hours, passers-by would react to the sight of the over-guarded empty space in a disparate range of ways.

The first occasion we presented the work was at a large commercial art fair in Melbourne. We taped off a neat square in one of the walkways between the cubicles that had been hired out at exorbitant rates by prominent commercial Australian art dealers. Subsequent iterations of the piece were performed in the streets of Freiburg, Germany and at a festival in Corinth, Greece.

Often people wouldn't initially notice the diminutive, taped-off space, and so would react apologetically when our security guards indicated towards the lines on the ground and asked that they be kept empty. Others would engage our guards in conversation, asking about the space, or who they were working for. Our guards had been directed to be evasive in their answers.

At the Melbourne Art Fair, our guards were tested as if they were guards at Buckingham Palace: fairgoers tossed coins into the square and waited for a reaction. Others became irate at not being allowed into the space, even though it was plainly empty. We were informed that one lady, after complaining to everyone standing near the work about the fact that she hadn't been allowed into the square, had continued to exclaim about this injustice for the rest of the afternoon. She was still complaining when she went to pick up her belongings from the cloak room hours later.

The reaction that fascinated me the most was when people noticed the square on the ground and the security guards surrounding it, and then swerved to avoid it without thinking. The mere suggestion of something resembling public order was enough to make them change their path, to react on autopilot. Moments later, after they had walked past, they would suddenly look puzzled and turn their heads to look back. I liked to imagine that they had noticed how *automatically* they had changed their behaviour when encountering our guards, despite the diminutive size of this over-surveilled empty space.

III

Although we had not worked together in years, Amy and I began messaging each other at the start of the pandemic with photos of the caution tape and extemporised crowd-management signage we were seeing around us in our neighbourhoods and on the news. The conclusion was unavoidable: versions of our own work were appearing in reality.

Documentation of Amy Spiers and Catherine Ryan, *Closed to the Public (Protecting Space)*, Melbourne Art Fair, 2014 and Museum für neue Kunst, Freiburg, 2016. Photos: Tom X Teutenberg, Marc Doradzillo.

3
'Ads needed to stop boat people: Bowen', SBS, <https://www.sbs.com.au/news/article/ads-needed-to-stop-boat-people-bowen/c1nrjam4h>.

4
Slavoj Žižek, in Judith Butler, Ernesto Laclau and Slavoj Žižek, *Contingency, Hegemony, Universality: Contemporary Dialogues on the Left*, London: Verso, 2000, p. 220.

This was not the first time this sort of thing had happened. In 2013, when Amy and I were building an installation work in Sydney about how Australia prefers to keep refugees out of sight and out of mind, the Rudd Labor government announced that all refugees arriving by boat would henceforth be settled in Papua New Guinea and Nauru rather than Australia. They took out large adverts in newspapers and on billboards overseas, informing prospective asylum seekers that 'If you come here by boat without a visa you won't be settled in Australia.'[3] The echoes with our work were uncanny, suggesting that we had observed something essential about the contemporary political zeitgeist. It is the desire of many artists to make work that is relevant to the present moment, but Amy and I used to joke that because we made art about the policing of borders and erosion of democratic rights, it was usually better for the world if our art was irrelevant.

And now in 2020, our work was, alas, more relevant than ever. Images and interventions resembling our practice were not only on the news, but in every one of the few shops we were allowed to go into, wrapped around every piece of public exercise equipment we walked past on our interminable walks in our allotted hour of exercise.

This was not a case of life mimicking art by accident. Amy and I had made the works in our Public Order series by deliberately using techniques focused on copying and imitating the real world. We were drawn to a philosophy of making called 'overidentification', in which an artwork aims not simply to criticise elements of the present social order from an external position, but rather to change people's habitual relationship to it by mimicking the apparatuses of power, taking them more seriously than they take themselves. One source for this approach was the philosopher Slavoj Žižek, who writes that sometimes 'overidentifying with the explicit power discourse—ignoring this inherent obscene underside and simply taking the power discourse at its (public) word, acting as if it really means what it explicitly says (and promises)—can be the most effective way of disturbing its smooth functioning'.[4]

Often, as was the case with *Closed to the Public*, our works were not announced as artworks to the members of the public who experienced them. We believed that if our interventions in public space were framed too obviously as artworks, those

Taped-off exercise equipment in Brunswick, 2020. Photo: Catherine Ryan

who encountered them would feel let off the hook. We wanted our security guard performances to blend in with their environments, chameleon-like. We took a leaf from an approach to art described by art historian Carrie Lambert-Beatty as 'parafiction', a type of artistic performance or presentation that depicts fiction as fact.[5]

For both overidentification and the parafictional approach, what is essential is stylistic imitation. Our works, though exaggerated versions of policing, needed to be plausible. To achieve this, we became diligent students of the securitised urban environment and the way it is utilised to direct the movements of people and to make many types of public gathering (gathering for anything except commerce) impossible. Scenarios usually boring and frustrating became fascinating sites for research. If we were at airports being subjected to endless security theatre or funnelled through spirals of never-ending luxury gift shops instead of being allowed to walk directly to our gate, we did not complain, but took notes. Bollards and safety-cone deployment became our inspiration. We absorbed with delight the poetics of passive-aggressive language on public signage. We made character studies of the imposing stances of security guards and aesthetic observations about the livery of their uniforms.

We undertook all this observation in order that we might better simulate the apparatus of security. We wanted our works to look like things you had seen before, but weirder and worse. We made plans for Escher-like mazes of bollards. We would stop and take photos of temporary fencing, improvised traffic-calming measures and absurdly long cordoned-off queues. We emailed articles to each other about hostile architecture, the mean-spirited spikes used to keep homeless people and teenagers from resting in malls and on public benches.

All this was devoted to creating works that responded to the question, what if the rationales for policing public space and enforcing rules were removed, leaving only the rules themselves? What if these techniques of urban control were emptied out, such that we could observe the forms of rules themselves, distilled to their essence?

And that is what had returned to haunt us in the pandemic—a concentrated tangle of purified regulation. The rhetoric surrounding the pandemic presented it as an aberration, the word 'unprecedented' being so overused that it moved into the realm of cliché. And yet, years before those fateful events at the Wuhan market upended the globe, by exaggerating the logic of policing that we observed in public spaces, Amy and I managed to create spectacles of control eerily reminiscent of those that would later spring up around us in lockdown.

IV

The resemblance really was uncanny. In 2015 in Austria, we made a piece for the Vienna Biennale called *Ordering the Public*. The Festival for Performing Art hired performers, playing the role of unspecified security personnel in uniforms and hi-vis vests, to patrol public areas in the centre of Vienna and enforce a series of absurd rules that we had made about behaviours that we had decided were no longer permitted. There was no announcement made about what had been forbidden.

5
Carrie Lambert-Beatty, 'Make-Believe: Parafiction and Plausibility', *October*, vol. 129 (Summer, 2009), pp. 51–84.

On one day of the performance, our 'security guards' were deployed near a large cathedral that is a popular tourist destination in Vienna. For the several hours' duration of that performance, we decided that it was no longer permitted to point with your finger. So our guards intervened every time someone indicated something with their finger to their family or friends. Being a tourist spot, pointing with the finger happened quite often. Each time it did, our guards would politely censure the offending pointer, informing them that this gesture was not permitted at this time, with no explanation given as to why.

On other days of the performance, different activities were forbidden in various places. In a manicured garden in a popular nearby park, we enforced an interdiction against talking. In another pleasant green space, people were told that lying down on the grass was not permitted. In a busy shopping strip, people were halted when they walked too fast.

Our rationale for choosing the activities we forbade was that they should be completely innocuous. They were to be gestures and actions that posed no risk to anyone. Our reference points were things such as the security theatre that you had to perform every time you went through an airport: how shoes or bottles of water were treated as dangerous objects on aeroplanes. We also had in mind—naively, perhaps, in a time before the Black Lives Matter protests rose to such international prominence—the racial profiling and undue suspicion that many people of colour experience when going about their daily lives; suspicion that all too often has consequences incompatible with life. We wanted to extend this experience out to everyone, to people who did not necessarily consider themselves the likely targets of suspicion. And so we constructed a work that treated innocent ways of spending time in a public place as dangerous acts that required policing.

V

In 2016 we were commissioned to make a work for an exhibition at the Royal College of Art in London. This was a rule-based participatory piece called *The Public is Touching (The Iron Fist in the Rubber Glove)*. For the duration of the show's opening gala, every person in attendance at the gallery was required to wear purple nitrile gloves. Purple was the most lurid and unflattering colour that we could find of the gloves that were available. We wanted to reflect on the state's horror at the prospect of people gathering together and being close. A text we wrote about the work at the time read:

> Nitrile gloves are worn to prevent contamination in many lines of work, including by the police and security when they undertake bag checks, pat-downs or in situations of potential violence. *The Public is Touching* produces the spectacle of a paranoid, overly germ-phobic art audience, protected against contamination or direct contact.

We mocked up signage that parroted the aesthetic of the public safety signage that could already be found around the campus of the college. Our new signs, replete with

Documentation of Amy Spiers and Catherine Ryan, *The Public is Touching (The Iron Fist in the Rubber Glove)*, performance, 2016. *Sorry You Missed Me*, Royal College of Art, London.

clip art images of gloves, informed visitors that wearing gloves was now required in the gallery. We wrote a script for the people invigilating the show, which suggested language they could use to inform gallery patrons of the new situation:

> Invigilators are to wear a pair of nitrile gloves while they are in the gallery, provided they are happy to do so. Ideally all invigilators in the gallery will wear the gloves.
>
> **Breaks:** it is fine to take gloves off when there are no patrons but it is important gloves are put back on when people enter the gallery.
>
> Some invigilators will be stationed near each of the entrances. As members of the public enter the gallery, these invigilators are to tell them that protective gloves must be worn in the gallery. This could be phrased in a number of ways, e.g. 'The RCA gallery is a gloved space. You will need to wear a pair of protective gloves while you are in the gallery.' The precise phrasing of this is up to the individual invigilator. They must remain polite and courteous whenever instructing the public.

6
Victorian Ombudsman, *Investigation into the detention and treatment of public housing residents arising from a COVID-19 'hard lockdown' in July 2020*, December 2020, <https://www.ombudsman.vic.gov.au/our-impact/investigation-reports/investigation-into-the-detention-and-treatment-of-public-housing-residents-arising-from-a-covid-19-hard-lockdown-in-july-2020/>.

The photographs of the show's opening event were almost indistinguishable from those of any other, but the usual images of sociable people holding beers and glasses of wine and having cheerful, erudite conversations in front of artworks now had an addition: the saggy purple nitrile gloves. They were rudely present on every hand in the space, undercutting the glamour of an evening at an invite-only art soiree.

Amy and I spoke at the time about how absurd these images seemed. Wasn't it funny that personal protective equipment was so ubiquitous, that there had been such an uptake of the spectacle of hygiene neurosis? We were innocently unaware of how commonplace directives to use personal protective equipment would become years later. Instead, we focused on the insinuation that the state, or other powers that be, might find the prospect of people being together in an unmediated way, rubbing up against one another in close quarters, disgusting. To us, this piece was about a discomfort that arose from people gathering together spontaneously. This was the reasoning behind the part of this work's title in parentheses, *The Iron Fist in the Rubber Glove*, a riff on the phrase 'the iron fist in the velvet glove', which evokes the menacing force that lies behind even so-called soft power.

VI

It could be argued that our works conflated things that were unconnected. Are nitrile gloves, empty lines on the ground, unannounced rules about pointing and the violent quashing of protest really the same thing? In fact, of course they are not. The intention of our work was to find broad formal similarities that ran like a thread through all interventions in public space, regardless of the good reasons given for their enactment. Our pieces avoided taking a moral position or clarifying what we thought was right or wrong in the treatment of public space. They simply traced a regulatory logic. The conceit of our work was to regard it all as the same: as if everything was about rules, policing and control.

Perhaps this treatment of everything as an object that is best dealt with by police intervention was the worst of the uncanny echoes of our work in the events of Victoria's lockdown. In July of 2020, thousands of vulnerable residents of public commission housing in North Melbourne and Flemington were summarily locked in their homes, in an attempt to halt an outbreak of COVID-19. Many of these residents were from backgrounds that made them vulnerable, with terrible experiences of the military and police. It was not nursing staff or health officials who enforced this summary lockdown, but police. In the words of a later report by Victorian Ombudsman Deborah Glass, 'Many residents knew nothing of the lockdown or the reason for it when large numbers of police appeared on their estate that afternoon [...] The rushed lockdown was not compatible with the residents' human rights, including their right to humane treatment when deprived of liberty.'[6]

Months later, my news feed was full of testimony by public servants at the inquiry into the Victorian hotel quarantine outbreak, about how casualised security staff with very little training were put in charge of supervising people staying in their rooms, leading to an outbreak of COVID-19. This outbreak would lead to an extension of the 2020 Victorian lockdown by several months. The discussion during the inquiry about the lack of training received by the guards reminded me of the many conversations Amy and I had with our security guards as we tried to make them do our strange bidding.

To a hammer, everything looks like a nail. To a state that has systematically underfunded its health system for decades yet increased spending on the police, everything looks like something to be solved and enforced by the police or privatised security.

7
Michel Foucault, 'On the Genealogy of Ethics: an Overview of a Work in Progress', in Paul Rabinow (ed.), *Essential Works of Foucault 1954–1984: Ethics*, London: Penguin, 2000, p. 256.

VII

My point is not that everything is bad, but that everything is dangerous, which is not exactly the same as bad. If everything is dangerous then we always have something to do.[7]

—Michel Foucault

There is a will to regard the pandemic as an unprecedented, unique blip, as if there were no continuity between what came before and what came after. Like anyone, I long to forget those unpleasant, restless days, oscillating between extreme anxiety and humongous boredom. But the fact that assemblages that looked so much like my artwork could appear in the real world implies that certain logics of regulation that were activated in the pandemic were lying dormant before the events of 2020 kicked off.

Presumably this means that they remain still, to be activated in the future. There is a need for vigilance. Not every epidemiological intervention is anti-democratic or a harbinger of state violence; I wouldn't place myself on the same side of politics as the anti-vaxxers and conspiracy theorists who protested the Victorian Government's lockdowns. But many of the conditions our works responded to have not changed, even though they were made almost a decade ago. Most of what we said in interviews about the privatisation of public space and the restriction of the right to protest in Australia remains relevant now—particularly as state and federal governments have introduced many climate change–related anti-protest laws.

Despite my uncomfortable sense that Amy and I somehow manifested the more absurd spectacles of the public order responses to the pandemic, we were not prophets or oracles. Our only power lay in a sensitivity towards techniques of regulation and control, and an openness to questioning the conditions that determine access to public space.

•••

The Cleaner

Lisa Nan Joo

Lisa Nan Joo is an emerging writer of fiction, non-fiction and poetry. Her work has appeared in *Overland*, *Kill Your Darlings*, *Mascara Literary Review* and *Strange Horizons*.

A cleaner was called to an urgent job in a large house in an unfashionable suburb. She was to prepare the house for sale; at the end of the week, a photographer would come to take pictures for the newspaper ads. The cleaner knew only the most basic facts: that the house belonged to a woman who had died and, although she was survived by children and grandchildren, they wanted no keepsakes or hand-me-downs. Nothing at all to remember her by.

The cleaner approved of this approach. Why waste time sorting through heirlooms with no value, only to box them up and store them in a garage, burdening the next generation? The cleaner did not believe in phrases like 'One day I might ...' or 'It could come in handy if ...' Uncertainty was terrible, but sentimentality even worse. Better to purge it all and move on.

The dead woman's house was secluded, separated from its neighbours by a clutch of weary ironbarks. It was a large two-storey federation affair, red brick with white eaves, but sagging towards decrepitude. The roof was a jigsaw puzzle of missing tiles, the windows veiled with decades of dirt. Starved agapanthuses lingered in the garden beds, the dry heads like old wedding veils.

The cleaner approached the entrance warily, avoiding the steps that had rotted through, and unlocked the front door. In the entryway she could smell years of sickness, unwashed carpets, mildewy drains. Donning face mask and gloves, she proceeded to survey the work that lay ahead.

First, she went from room to room and opened all the windows. Most were resolved to their swollen sashes but all yielded, in the end, to her single-mindedness. The cartography of the house was predictable: downstairs were the sitting room, living room, dining room, kitchen, laundry; upstairs were three bedrooms, two bathrooms and a storage space with a narrow set of steps leading up to what the cleaner presumed was the attic.

The dead woman did not appear to be a hoarder; however, she had neglected to maintain adequate oversight of her possessions in the way the cleaner deemed necessary. She had not, for example, re-evaluated the use of the second and third bedrooms after her children had moved out. Those rooms were still cluttered with the possessions of a teenage boy and girl: single beds with faded doonas, video-game consoles stacked among swimming trophies in the bottom of wardrobes. Why had the woman not turned these rooms to new purposes—for crafts, for meditation, for renting to itinerant university students—after her children left? Similarly, in the master bedroom, the cleaner found clothes from four decades clogging the walk-in wardrobe. The dead woman had seen fit to keep her bell-bottom jeans, her velour tracksuits, her power suits with shoulder pads, her polyester wedding dress draped in black plastic. Judging by her wardrobe and dresser, the woman had not bought any new clothing after the 1980s, resorting to dressing gowns and orthopaedic slippers in her later years.

The cleaner wondered what the woman had done once her children grew up and moved out. Had she gone back to work? Had she separated from her husband? Had she taken ill, of pancreatic cancer or coronary artery disease or some sort of neurodegenerative condition? There were no signs of an ex-husband, other than the wedding dress. No signs of a more recent partner. There weren't even family photos on the mantelpiece. What had the woman done, if anything, to deserve her solitude, before and after death?

The cleaner began her work. She was methodical. She did not switch on a television or radio, working only to the rasp of her scrubbing brush on grout, the whoosh of her steam cleaner. She threw away everything, filling the large skip left for her in the front yard. There was no impediment to her ruthless exterminations. The broken furniture, the good china, the wedding dress: all were discarded.

It grew late. The cleaner emerged from the master bedroom, where she had been bagging the medications in the dead woman's bedside table (antidepressants, pain killers, beta blockers, antibiotics, blood thinners—suggesting a range of possible causes of death, but no definitive answers) to the sudden realisation that, outside, it was almost dark. She pulled off her gloves and washed her hands and face in the dead woman's bathroom.

As she was leaving, she paused at the double doors that led to the attic at the top of the stairs. It was dark and musty inside. The space seemed to go back a long way, but she couldn't clearly discern its contours. To her right, there were shelves lined with boxes and crates. She groped for a switch or a cord, but found none. She frowned, deeply. Was the house resisting her, despite her day's work wresting it from the disregard of its dead owner? It was not right for the house to oppose her like this. She resolved to tackle the attic first thing in the morning.

On her way out, she locked all the windows and doors. She drove home and slept a very still, uninterrupted sleep, corpse-like in her serenity, oblivious to the soft noises of the night.

When she was a child, the cleaner had constantly been on the move, accompanying her mother—a country-music singer of minor fame—across the country. Her mother sang the national anthem at sporting events and performed on weekends at sports clubs or private functions. Although the caravan was small, it was a complete world, a closed system, in which the cleaner was content. Her mother's costumes and guitars and vinyl records were strewn across the narrow, fold-out beds. There were a few books around—a set of primary school readers, her mother's biology textbook from high school, and an English–French dictionary—so they could pretend the cleaner was home-schooled to anyone who asked. Mostly, there were tins of hairspray, instant noodle packets, discarded water bottles, supermarket catalogues and old takeaway containers cluttering all available surfaces. When she was twelve, the cleaner learned to drink double espresso and drive the caravan, sitting on the very edge of the seat atop two street directories. She and her mother took turns at the wheel on interstate trips.

The only stable thing in their weekly routine was the Sunday cleaning. Though she wasn't religious, the cleaner's mother insisted that they never travel on Sundays. Sundays were reserved for tidying the caravan, washing clothes at the coin laundry, and getting a three-course meal from a drive-through restaurant. Chicken nuggets for entrée, burgers and fries for main, soft-serve ice-cream cones for dessert. They would sit on the steps of the caravan to eat, wiping their fingers on their jeans and letting ribbons of lettuce fall into the dirt to be carried away by ants. Afterwards, when the ice in their drinks had melted, the cleaner's mother might strum her guitar, improvising a new song, or they would sit in the cabin and put their feet up on the dash to paint their toenails red.

They would fall asleep tangled up in one bed, forgetting to brush their teeth but ready to start their week again, shining and new.

The cleaner returned to the house on the second day, ready to tackle the room at the top of the stairs. But when she opened the front door, she found yesterday's work undone.

The untidiness had, somehow, reasserted itself. The mouldy shower curtains had reattached themselves to the hooks hanging from the railing. The piles of clothes had stuffed themselves back into lopsided drawers. Rotten food had restocked the fridge, dead plants had resumed their morbid poses in dank corners of the living room. The hanging pictures were again wayward in their tacky frames, the mirrors unpolished, the floor uneven with years of dust and grime.

It was as though the cleaner had never been.

She didn't know what to do. She considered calling her agency and telling them what had happened. But would they believe her? Perhaps they would assume she had lied and was trying to wrangle another day's pay out of them. That wouldn't do. The cleaner prided herself on her reputation.

No, the only thing she could do was start over. She began again, first by opening the windows, and then donning her gloves, mask and hairnet. This time she laboured without pause, filling the bins, scrubbing at the hard surfaces, scraping away decades of the dead woman's life. She was faster but even more thorough than she had been the day before, determined to make her work stick.

It wasn't until the end of the day that she thought to return to the attic upstairs. This time, she found a switch embedded in a timber beam. A bare bulb hissed as it came to life. The shelves were lined with boxes of various sizes, all with their lids taped shut. She didn't bother opening them but began to stack them in piles to carry down to the skip. But then she paused. Her fingers fluttered over the lid of one particular box. It felt as light as air. She tried to peel off the tape, but it wouldn't budge. She turned to another, then another, but all were equally impenetrable. She could not open a single one.

Frustrated, she began to shake the boxes, demanding they reveal their contents. She found herself throwing them on the ground, attempting to tear through the cardboard with her fingernails. She failed to make even a single dent.

At last, surrounded by the untroubled boxes, she realised how futile this was. The house deemed her an unwilling proprietor of its secrets. If it refused to give up all its contents, willingly and absolutely, then the fault was hers.

The cleaner suspected it was to do with her mindset. She had not brought the necessary mental rigour to her work. Other people—other cleaners, even—underestimated the tenacity this job required. Not just physical fortitude, but emotional strength as well. To clean someone's house was to become attuned to their most intimate selves. The stains on their carpets, their bedsheets, their underwear—all were acknowledgement that life was never pristine, no matter how it looked from the outside. Everyone had rubbish. Everyone had shame. The cleaner's job was to remove these burdens and create the illusion that there was no mess here; that her clients lived without mess, did not make mess, that they existed in a state of spiritual purification that left no mark at all.

The cleaner took a deep breath, then picked up the boxes and stacked them away on the shelves. She would return in a more appropriate state of mind in the morning and, she was sure, the items in this cupboard would not only bend to her will but, in their submission, be glad of her authority.

When the cleaner turned fourteen, her mother found a regular gig singing at a gentlemen's club four nights a week. The club's manager let her park the caravan out back, near the dumpsters. Soon the cleaner found herself spending her Sundays alone while her mother and the manager went to restaurants, bars, movies, mini-golf. When they came back to the caravan, they would ask the cleaner to go to the corner store and pick up something they needed. But by the time the cleaner returned, she'd find herself locked out and she would have to sit outside on a crate near the dumpsters, waiting for the manager to emerge. As he left, he would nod to her and bid her good night, as though he were a patron and she the bouncer at closing time.

One night, when her mother returned to the caravan after her show, the cleaner saw her wearing a new sterling silver bracelet with a heart-shaped locket. The week after, the club manager suggested to her mother that she send the cleaner to school.

'She shouldn't be hanging around the club all the time,' he said. 'Plus, shouldn't she have some friends?'

Although she disliked the manager—who, by clipping a cheap promise to her mother's wrist, had inserted himself irreversibly into their family—the cleaner welcomed the opportunity to escape the caravan.

The manager paid for the cleaner's school uniform and books. He let her pick out a pencil case that held a dozen gel pens, a protractor, a miniature stapler. The cleaner's mother walked with her into the front office on the first day and assured the enrolment adviser that the cleaner had completed eighth grade and was even so bright that perhaps she should skip a year.

Despite the enthusiastic endorsements from her mother, the cleaner soon found herself trailing behind the rest of her class. At first she did her best to catch up. She would concentrate intently on the words of her teachers, matching them with the ones she recognised from her books. But the letters kinked on the page, forming nonsensical strings. She hid the letters the teachers sent home at the bottom of her bag, and lied to her mother, telling her she enjoyed school, that she was doing well. The girls she had thought might be her friends were aloof, holding sleepovers and pool parties to which she never received invitations.

The cleaner began to skip classes, then to cut school altogether. She would wander the shopping centre or slip into the cinema without a ticket. Soon after, she began to steal. The thrift store was the easiest target. There weren't any cameras inside and the old ladies who volunteered there took pity on her, letting her keep small trinkets she fancied: an ashtray shaped like a goldfish, a set of coasters with pictures of the queen's corgis, a necklace she thought would match her mother's bracelet. The supermarket was another good option; she became adept at slipping chocolate bars, tampons and lip gloss into the pockets of her culottes.

She hid these things in an old pillowcase under her mattress, trusting the caravan to keep them quiet.

That night, the cleaner couldn't sleep. With her eyes closed, she saw dirty plates amassing in kitchens, bedclothes pooling on floors, drains clogging with grease, pantries inviting moths into open bags of flour.

She was forced from her bed and paced her apartment, sensing the malice of all the objects around her: the coffee cups, the TV remote, the keys on the bench. She checked, several times, that the tea towels in the second drawer were folded in the exact order she remembered. White, blue, white, blue. She returned to bed, lying absolutely still under her quilt, and ran through a mental checklist of household goods that might exhibit disorderly intent. Socks that could be unpaired. Pens that could leak ink. Teapots that could crack, shoes that could wear thin at the soles, books that could harbour mould, plants that could fail to bloom.

The list was ceaseless, unfurling in front of her eyes until she was compelled to get up and check the tea towels again, make sure the creak was a floorboard settling, a window sighing, and not her belongings choreographing mayhem behind her back.

One afternoon, a few weeks after she had begun to play truant, the cleaner came home to find her mother holding an empty pillow case with all the stolen items lined up in front of her on the fold-out table. There they were: the goldfish ashtray, the corgi coasters, the lip gloss. Curled in her mother's hand was the necklace the cleaner had thought would match the silver bracelet. It had already started to tarnish, and looked green under the caravan's claustrophobic light.

'Where did you get all this from?' said the cleaner's mother. The cleaner knew there was no point in denying what she had done.

'You stole it, didn't you?'

There, with the manager sitting on the fold-out bed less than an arm's length away, her mother threw the necklace so hard that, when it hit the cleaner's lip, the skin split and she tasted silver plating.

'Didn't I teach you better than that?' screamed the cleaner's mother. 'Don't we give you everything you need?'

The cleaner backed away as her mother began to throw each item on the table at her, harder and harder: the coasters, an ashtray, an apple, a spatula. She turned her back and covered her head with her arms, pressed into a corner of the kitchenette.

The manager said nothing, but seemed to cringe from the wildness of the mother's rhetoric, which swung abruptly from accusation to lament.

'I'm sorry,' said the cleaner, her voice muffled, her tongue dabbing at the blood on her lip. 'I won't do it again.'

The cleaner's mother flung the pillowcase to the floor and stomped on it. The cleaner didn't know what to say. She was embarrassed for her mother, for her wild display in front of the manager. She was angry, too, but unsure who to direct it towards. The manager? Their world had been perfect until he came along, but it couldn't have lasted forever. The cleaner saw that now. At some point, she was always going to grow out of the caravan.

When the manager announced he would be taking the cleaner's mother on a national tour, he did not invite the cleaner along with them. There was no longer room in her mother's life for her. The cleaner bought two mobile phones, so they could still talk every Sunday, but the phones only seemed to increase the distance between them; the line would crackle and unspool between them, until one or the other finally chose to disconnect.

When the cleaner returned to the dead woman's house the next morning, she found it exactly as it had been the first day, before she began work. All the items were in their original situations, all the dirt and grime and mould returned in force. The cleaner did not know what to make of it. She pulled out her phone to call her agency.

'Hello,' she said. 'This is Grace.'

'Grace? Where have you been?' said the receptionist.

'At the deceased estate, of course.'

'What deceased estate?'

'The dead woman's house. I've been here for three days now. I think there's a problem.'

'You said you were on leave. You said you'd call when you got back. Are you back now? We need someone this afternoon to do a preschool...'

'I never said that.'

'You did. You said you were going to visit your mother.'

The cleaner ended the call.

She went straight up the stairs and opened the closet doors. She felt sure that the house's treacherous intent would become clear if only she could see everything inside.

She flung the attic doors open and began pulling the boxes down off the shelves. This time, the lids came off easily. She plucked the items out, one by one, until they were all arrayed before her, dazzling in the gloom.

She knew each of the items stored in the boxes in that attic. All of them hers: the ashtray, the corgi coasters, the silver bracelet. Even the lip gloss, the chocolates and the tampons she'd stolen from the supermarket. Deeper still, in a shoe box taped shut, was the phone she'd given her mother, its plastic casing good as new.

When the cleaner had moved into her own apartment, she'd never bothered decorating. She had lived sparingly, shunning material things. Through cleaning others' homes, she realised that they were not what she once thought they were. Objects were worthless. Depreciating by the year, the month, the second. To own a beautiful thing was to draw a glossy curtain across the blight of each day's passing: the cereal crusted in the breakfast bowl, the flowers wilting in the vase, the cracked dish, the broken spine on the book, the laundry that needs folding, the bills that are overdue, the tyres going bald, the dental cavities that need filling, the unanswered phone calls and the long silences between where there is nothing, just the terrible quiet, pregnant with decay.

The only thing the cleaner had truly yearned for was a home of her own. Not the caravan, but something like it—the sense of belonging she'd known as a girl. She wanted somewhere that would possess her, as surely as she possessed it.

She set the boxes aside. Seeking room to think, she climbed up further, past the shelves and into the attic proper.

Here, there was clear space. A thick layer of dust lay on the floor, like a fleece comforter. A light came in from the north-facing windows. She walked over and peered down at the garden beds. She could see her car parked in the driveway and, beyond that, the road, the place where it twisted, cutting off the world beyond. No-one could see her up here.

No real estate agent arrived that afternoon. The cleaner supposed that if a woman could die and her family abandon her house, then it wasn't too hard to imagine a cleaning contract falling through the cracks. Perhaps it had never been, or came and went like a singer passing through town.

The cleaner moved into the attic. She left the house as it had been, touching nothing. She knew better than to violate the sanctity of the objects living there. She continued to work as a cleaner, switching to a different agency that paid a higher hourly rate. When she saw an ad for a country-music night at the local club, her mother's name under the headline act, she thought about buying a ticket, or waiting outside the stage door after the gig ended.

She would bring her mother back to the house. They would climb up to the attic and eat soft-serve ice-cream cones that dripped onto the floorboards. They would paint their toenails red. They would fall asleep and wake up feeling out of place, wondering what time it was and where they were supposed to drive next. And, while they slept, they would ignore the symphony of the objects downstairs, busily orchestrating their own private resistance.

• • •

'The Graceful Incoming of a Revolution'

The story of how Australia came to have a woman on the bench of its highest court has an unlikely first chapter. It starts with a young girl in northern New South Wales, dawdling to avoid chores from her mother.

Tom
McIlroy

Tom McIlroy is federal political correspondent with the *Australian Financial Review*.

It was the middle of 1951 and Mary Gaudron had seen her father among a group gathered around a blue Holden ute in Moree's Jellicoe Park, on the banks of the Mehi River. They were listening to an impassioned speech delivered by a man standing on the vehicle's tray. The subject was the looming referendum on constitutional powers to ban communism in Australia. The speaker was barnstorming opposition leader H.V. Evatt.

After wandering over, Gaudron, eight years old and enrolled at the local primary school, raised her hand, asking, 'Please sir, what's a constitution?' Evatt, a former justice of the High Court and Labor leader since Ben Chifley's death a few months earlier, told the child that constitutions were the laws that bind democracies together.

Campaigning against the referendum question put by the Menzies government—which had been rolled by the court on its bid to ban the Communist Party in March in 1951—Evatt promised to send the young Gaudron a copy of the Australian Constitution if she wrote to him in Canberra.

The small document arrived not long after from Parliament House, in a brown envelope marked 'OHMS'. When Gaudron showed the pamphlet to another child in the schoolyard, the boy dismissively said a book wasn't of much use to anyone. 'It's a lot of use to lawyers,' she told him. When he pointed out she was not a lawyer, Gaudron shot back: 'Well, I'm going to be one.'

Mary Gaudron did become a lawyer, specialising in industrial and defamation law, and serving on the Commonwealth Conciliation and Arbitration Commission and as solicitor-general of New South Wales. She made history in 1987 as the first woman appointed to the High Court of Australia, joining nearly six decades after Doc Evatt himself.

More than 35 years later, and since the appointment of former Federal Court judge

Photo by
Andrew Meares

Jayne Jagot in October last year, women make up the majority on the seven-person court for the first time. Under Chief Justice Susan Kiefel—the first woman to lead the court—are justices Jagot, Jacqueline Gleeson and Michelle Gordon. They follow in the footsteps of Gaudron, Susan Crennan and Virginia Bell.

The court's female majority puts the judicial branch well ahead of parliament, and Australia ahead of many comparable countries. But what significance does it have for the court's role of applying the laws of Australia, hearing appeals and deciding cases of constitutional significance, and to the institution itself? Should the composition of the High Court reflect the nation it serves? Susan Kiefel has some thoughts. When the future chief justice was first admitted to the Queensland Bar in 1975, just 4% of practising barristers in the state were women. It wasn't until 1982 that women entering law schools around the country passed the 50% mark. A year earlier, the New South Wales Bar was 95% male.

In public speeches, Kiefel, appointed to the court in 2007 by the Howard government and promoted to chief a decade later by Malcolm Turnbull, likes to point to data from the *National Profile of Solicitors*, published annually by the Law Society of New South Wales. The latest report, from June 2022, shows women make up 54% of solicitors in Australia, having first outnumbered men in the profession in 2018. It follows a four-fold increase in the number of female solicitors since 1997, growing to nearly 20,000 last year. Women make up about one-third of partners in Australian law firms, and in the first half of 2022 a survey by the *Australian Financial Review* found 46% of new partners were women.

Kiefel commissioned the High Court's legal research officer, Rebecca Lucas, to track the number of women appearing in the court since 2007. The pair found a 'bleak' picture fifteen years ago, with women comprising an average 14.9% of barristers appearing. In the period 2019 to 2021, the figure increased to more than 24%. The number of female senior counsel appearing at the court has risen from 5.6% in 2007 to a bit less than 13% in recent years. Among silk, of the 47 appearances by women senior counsel in the period reviewed, Kiefel and Lucas found more than 20% included appearances by solicitors-general for Victoria and the Northern Territory, both of whom were women.

The court's thirteenth chief justice, Kiefel—who left school at fifteen, worked as a receptionist at a law firm and eventually became Queensland's first female Queen's Counsel in 1987—used a speech to the Australian Women Lawyers Conference last year to remark that she had expected better figures. 'I had perhaps assumed that female representation on the bench and a female chief justice would have had a greater impact,' she told delegates. 'But at least they appear to be improving.'

Kiefel highlights one reason for the slow progress in the number of female silks: federal and state attorneys-general keep snapping up outstanding women for judicial appointments. 'This may be good for the courts and society more generally, but the Bar and the women in question pay a price. The Bar loses female mentors and examples to younger women lawyers of senior women appearing in the highest courts and assuming leadership positions at the Bar,' Kiefel said. 'The female silks who quickly accept appointment may also lose the experience of leading a litigation team and the responsibility of being the principal advisor and decision-maker. Such experience is very important to the confidence which is necessary to carry out the office of a judge.'

When she was sworn in to the top job, in a ceremony conducted by Virginia Bell in January 2017, Kiefel reflected on the fact that women were given the right to vote in Australian federal elections in 1902, a year before the High Court opened. 'It was then that they truly became part of "the people" to whom our Constitution refers,' she told the packed courtroom.

'Women are men's equals in every way and they are quite competent to hold their own in all spheres of life'

But that year, and despite receiving a degree from Sydney University in 1902, Ada Evans, Australia's first female law graduate, was blocked from admission to the New South Wales Bar on the basis of her sex. Under the *Legal Practitioners Act* of 1898, it was thought a woman was not 'a person'. Newspaper reports of Evans from the time say 'every judge in Sydney is opposed to her admission'. It wasn't until 1918 that Evans and her supporters convinced state parliament of the need for change, prompting passage of the *Women's Legal Status Act.* In May 1921, she became the first woman admitted to practise as a barrister in the state. She was reported to have been followed by 'a flight of press photographers and cinema-men' once at work.

In Victoria in 1903, Flos Greig, the first woman to enrol in law at the University of Melbourne, graduated second in her class. Six years after commencing her study, Greig and her supporters secured passage in the Victorian Parliament of the *Women's Disabilities Removal Bill.* Designed to excise 'some anomalies in the law relating to women', it was also known as the 'Flos Greig Enabling Bill'. Enable it did. Greig was admitted in August 1905, the first woman to enter the legal profession in Australia.

'Women are men's equals in every way and they are quite competent to hold their own in all spheres of life,' she said at the time. On the day of her admission, Victoria's chief justice, John Madden, called Greig 'the graceful incoming of a revolution'. In a more dispiriting foretelling of women's future progress, a newspaper reporter soon asked Greig what she was wearing for the occasion.

Madden also took a dim view of Greig's prospects of success. 'Women are more sympathetic than judicial, more emotional than logical,' he said. 'In the legal profession knowledge of the world is almost if not quite as essential as knowledge of the law, and knowledge of the world, women, even if they possess it, would lie loth to assert.'

His pessimism was misplaced. When Greig enrolled in 1903, the woman who would become the first female appointed as Queen's Counsel in Victoria was seven years old. Born in Ballarat, Joan Rosanove was the daughter of a prominent barrister. She was formally admitted to practice in June 1919, after having had her registration delayed to enable returned servicemen from World War I to complete their degrees, to add 'gravitas' to the ceremony. When she took silk in November 1965, her colleagues admitted she had been treated 'shabbily' by the system. Rosanove's experience influenced her style. Standing a little over five feet (153 cm), she is remembered as pugnacious, penetrating in cross-examination and prepared to challenge any ruling against her.

Since Evans, Greig and Rosanove, as well as countless other trailblazers, women have served on major courts around Australia, including at the highest levels. Elizabeth Evatt, the niece of Bert Evatt, became the first chief justice of the Family Court in 1976, making her the first female judge on the federal bench. Deirdre O'Connor followed in 1990, as the first woman appointed to the bench of the Federal Court of Australia, and in 2000 Diana Bryant was named as the first female chief federal magistrate of Australia. Women including Marilyn Warren, Anne Ferguson, Julie Ward, Debra Mullins, Helen Bowskill and Lucy McCallum have led state and territory supreme courts and courts of appeal around the country.

With an eye to the future, Kiefel, who will reach 70 in January 2024, the age of compulsory retirement for High Court justices, said there was no reason to think the situation for women at the court would not be maintained or improved. But the road to the court's female majority has been long. When she became the second woman on the court, appointed by the Howard government in 2005, Susan Crennan had appeared before exactly one female judge in her entire career: Mary Gaudron in the High Court.

Headlines called her a 'legal dynamo' and 'the High Court's anti-feminist', citing a 1992 interview in which Crennan said it was wrong for women to seek an accelerated rite of passage to the top of the professions in compensation for previous exclusion. Barrister Fiona McLeod wrote that Crennan was eminently qualified, had excelled at the highest levels, while supporting and inspiring young women in the law. Businesswoman Eve Mahlab said Crennan's success was simple: 'She thinks like a man and works like a dog.'

Crennan said in a 2014 speech that establishing truth in a courtroom calls upon 'human capacities for perspicacity, constancy, empathy and fairness', as applied to the particular set of facts at hand. Asked to reflect on women in the law, she recalled the story of Roma Mitchell, the first woman made Queen's Counsel in Australia, in 1962. She went on to become the first female justice of a state supreme court in 1965 and was asked by a journalist if she was married. 'No,' she told the man. 'Do you drive a car?' he asked next. 'No' was the response again. Noting that the chief justice at the time was also unmarried, the reporter asked if the pair might 'get together'. 'No,' Mitchell said a third time. 'That wouldn't work, he doesn't drive either.'

Crennan said that during her long legal career, which continues at the Victorian Bar, she had witnessed palpable change. 'The success today of women in the law is undoubtedly a reflection of great social, cultural and institutional change,' she told an event hosted by Foley's List in Melbourne. Progress wasn't always easy. Crennan said that admitting to balancing motherhood and a busy legal practice sometimes prompted 'rather cross visits' from women barristers, who regardedadmitting to it as somewhat unimaginative.

Crennan said changing social attitudes gave all women the opportunity to aspire to demanding jobs, such as surgery or the law. 'Practical liberation, changing ideas of justice and greater access to education freed women, who so chose, to take a place in the professions and the academy, commensurate with their talents and energies and reflecting their perspectives,' she said.

If the talents and energies of potential high court justices are not in question, what then of their perspectives? Do men and women bring different outlooks to the court? Helen Irving believes they do. Professor Emerita at Sydney Law School, she has studied constitutional law and gender in Australia and the United States. She says some superior courts in eastern Europe and in countries including Rwanda reached gender balance well ahead of Australia, describing the appointment of qualified women to the High Court as recognition of genuine merit.

The Supreme Court of the United Kingdom has eleven men and one woman on the bench, while in Washington, DC, there are six men and three women on the US Supreme Court. Canada has a 5–4 split, while New Zealand's Supreme Court has three women and three men. The Federal Court of Malaysia has a majority of women, with eight on a bench of fourteen judges.

Irving says she noticed the relatively small amount of attention paid in Australia to the new female majority when Jagot's appointment was announced in Canberra last October. 'The lack of notability is notable,' she said. 'I think it's also a good thing to celebrate, but what we celebrate is what it represents, which is, while not necessarily stable, the normalisation of gender diversity on the High Court.'

She has tracked research in the United States and Canada showing a noticeable difference in the legal reasoning between male and female judges in particular areas of the law, including criminal and family law cases:

> Women judges were more inclined in their reasoning to refer to and take into account the context or the conduct in the question brought before the court. It is a larger sort of contextual reasoning, rather than focusing narrowly on the law itself. A larger, broader understanding of the way the law works in those cases. I don't doubt that women reason differently as judges from their male colleagues, and I think, just intuitively, that would make sense because women do have different experiences as women than men.

But at the High Court, Irving does not see much evidence of a difference in reasoning or approach to thinking between female and male judges. Irving believes the questions before other courts—such as in the United States, where high-profile cases relate to hot-button social issues such as abortion, race or gay rights—may show up other differences.

But like other close watchers of the High Court, she points to the 2013 case *Monis v The Queen* as a rare split along gender lines. The case, dealing with Australia's implied freedom of political communication, was about the conduct of Man Haron Monis, the Iranian-born refugee turned Australian citizen who would go on to carry out the 2014 siege at Sydney's Lindt Café. Long before he caused the deaths of two people, Monis had sent offensive letters and other material to the families of Australian soldiers killed while serving in the Afghanistan War.

Monis came to the court from the New South Wales Court of Appeal. He had been charged under federal laws that prohibit the use of a postal service for sending offensive material. Along with his girlfriend, Amirah Droudis, Monis sent fake expressions of sympathy to the parents and partners of dead diggers, followed by abuse and invective, calling them 'murderers', 'pigs' and morally inferior to Adolf Hitler. Lawyers for the couple argued the offence under which they were indicted breached the Constitution's implied freedom of political communication. Critical to the case was the styling of the letters as a form of political protest, against Australia's military involvement in Afghanistan.

Only six justices heard the Monis case, because the seventh, William Gummow, had retired from the court before the case began. It allowed the possibility of a 3–3 split. Each of the judges agreed the content of Monis's letters was political and the law in question had the legal effect of restricting the freedom of political communication.

'Unbelievably, the floor I was leaving refused to accept her as a member,' McHugh said. 'I had to sell the chambers to a male barrister, selected by the floor.'

But, in a result Irving calls striking, the court split evenly along gender lines, with the justices disagreeing on the law's legitimacy. The three men all found the law invalid, while the women found it valid. Without a majority, the decision of the lower court was allowed to stand. Monis and Droudis lost their appeal.

Irving says the case's subject matter is critical. The deepest loss known to a parent or spouse, tragedy borne down on families, the unbearable pain of abusive messages arriving in the letterbox. The female justices found the law's purpose of protection against offensive material being sent in the post was legitimate and the conduct objectively offensive. Abusing people whose children had died was not a reasonable form of political communication, and the pair had any number of other outlets to make their point of view known.

While the three female justices wrote their judgment together, the males wrote separately. Hayne wrote 'abuses and invective are an inevitable part of political discourse'. Justice Dyson Heydon, in his judgment, also wrote about the pain parents suffer when they outlive a child, quoting a poem, 'My Boy Jack', written by Rudyard Kipling, describing the grief of a father losing his son in war.

Irving says accounts of a 'feminine judicial voice' often hinge on attention to context and experience:

> It was remarkable that the three women voted together. It seemed fairly evident from that case that the women had thought more broadly about the experience of the soldiers' families, and about what it meant to be offensive. They had a wider understanding of offence, in such a way as they could accept that it might limit the freedom of political communication.

> I did feel at the time, and I do think it is so retrospectively as well, there
> was something in it about the difference between the way the women judges
> reasoned and the way that male judges reason. I don't think that it's evident, at
> least from my reading of the constitutional cases on the High Court currently,
> that the female and the male judges reason differently.

Michael McHugh, who served on the High Court from 1989 until 2005, used a speech before his retirement to call out the discrimination against female lawyers he said had been 'rife' throughout his 43 years in the law. Moving to another floor of barristers before becoming a judge, he tried to sell his chambers to a rising star of the profession, a woman named Mary Gaudron. 'Unbelievably, the floor I was leaving refused to accept her as a member,' McHugh said. 'I had to sell the chambers to a male barrister, selected by the floor.'

He said academics seeking to explain the differences that a woman brings to judicial office sometimes refer to 'an ethic of care' informing their adjudication, as well as the idea of a more consensual, less adversarial approach. McHugh dismissed what he described as the persistent notion that female judges could recognise and correct gendered aspects of the substantive law and the argument that having been on the receiving end of stereotypes and prejudice, women were more likely to spot such biases.

He told a Western Australia Law Society event that social scientists and lawyers had failed to verify the hypothesis of difference, emerging only with inconclusive results:

> If there is a possibility that female judges may reach different decisions in
> some cases, it is then but a short step to wondering whether an all-male
> final appeal court can deliver justice in a truly impartial fashion in those cases.
> At all events, if that possibility exists, there are grounds for thinking that the
> decisions of such a court may be improved by the presence of female judges.

But unless the gender imbalance in judicial appointments was addressed, McHugh warned, there was an ever-increasing risk that the public support on which the legitimacy of the judiciary rests would erode.

Now the court's female majority was locked in, Kcasey McLoughlin, a legal expert at the University of Newcastle, says Jagot's appointment and the gender shift were viewed by commentators as something of a happy, if politically expedient, coincidence. She says the presence of four women is significant, but not because there is a distinctive women's judicial voice:

> Certainly, a lot of women judges have rejected the idea that there's a women's
> judicial voice, in part because they thought it would exclude them from being
> judges, or would make them seem less qualified. Although I don't think there's
> a women's judicial voice, I think having women in positions of authority
> changes institutions.

Both McLoughlin and Irving point to Ruth Bader Ginsburg. Asked when there would be 'enough' women on the US Supreme Court, the late liberal icon was blunt. 'I say when there are nine,' she told an audience. 'There'd been nine men, and nobody's ever raised a question about that.'

McLoughlin, whose doctoral thesis was about women on the High Court, argues the exchange demonstrates how comfortable we remain with the idea that courts are the domain of men. 'The thing that is so stinging or fabulous about that quote is that it reveals how normalised the idea of an all-male bench was. The idea that these are positions that are for men is absolutely entrenched. And that lingers.'

She cites American lawyer Carrie Menkel-Meadow, who asked, 'What would our legal system look like if women had not been excluded from its creation?' McLoughlin says it is impossible to know the answer, because it is impossible to remake institutions without 'masculinist origins'.

For the High Court of Australia, one step towards a kind of remaking was the 2020 investigation into sexual harassment of six young female associates by Dyson Heydon when he was on the bench, between 2003 and 2013. Expressing shame for what happened at the court, Kiefel said an independent investigation had been ordered once reports of allegations were received.

Heydon's predatory behaviour was described as an 'open secret' in legal and judicial circles, but the former justice and royal commissioner denied any wrongdoing when the story broke in *The Sydney Morning Herald*. An unnamed judge reportedly told the investigation: 'Mr Heydon slid his hand between her thighs at a professional law dinner not long after he joined the High Court bench.' She was a barrister at the time and decided Heydon was too powerful to complain about.

Kiefel said the court had done everything in its power to ensure the women's experience could never be repeated. A supplementary human resources policy was drafted for the personal staff of the justices, induction activities were reviewed and new reporting lines created. Even in the #MeToo era, the deft response was not guaranteed. Kiefel's investigation and disclosure, based in transparency and honesty, were the opposite of many other powerful institutions faced with similar crimes over recent decades.

McLoughlin says the response might have been different under a male chief justice. 'I don't think that it's irrelevant that it was under a woman chief justice that complainants felt safe to come forward. The way that she acknowledged the difficulty in coming forward and apologised to the complainant was a really powerful thing.'

George Williams, the University of New South Wales law professor, wrote the book on the nation's highest court. *The Oxford Companion to the High Court of Australia* was published in 2001. A regular commentator on the law, and having appeared as a barrister in the court over two decades, Williams praises Kiefel's tenure as chief justice, describing the court as collegial and effective under her leadership. 'You can see many areas in which she's had an impact, including how the court has run, through to areas of law, where she's made a distinctive contribution.'

But Irving says the success and diversity of the Kiefel court cannot be taken for granted or be expected to maintain itself. She believes a woman should replace the chief justice next year, an appointment due to be considered by Attorney-General Mark Dreyfus soon.

The Albanese government has sought to achieve a gender balance in appointments since coming to office last year, and, at ten of 23 members, the federal Cabinet has more women than any of its predecessors. Albanese is fond of noting that his is the first government in Australian history with a majority of women members—54 out of 103 MPs. Dreyfus consulted widely before naming Jagot to the court, including speaking to all state and territory attorneys-general, senior judges, bar associations, law societies, law school deans and the Australian Women Lawyers Association.

> Kiefel's investigation and disclosure, based in transparency and honesty, were the opposite of many other powerful institutions faced with similar crimes over recent decades.

'It will be a shame if a man is chosen to replace the chief justice, because in some respects, it would show this type of diversity isn't necessarily secure or stable,' Irving said. Some court watchers say a middle ground is possible: a male justice, possibly Stephen Gageler, could become chief justice and a woman appointed to the vacant position. Gageler was appointed by Labor in 2012 and could serve until he is due to retire in 2028. The new appointment could come from Kiefel's home state of Queensland, or from South Australia or Tasmania—the two states never to send a judge to the court.

Williams sees speedy change on the court, from Gaudron's appointment in 1987 to 2005, when after her retirement the court again only had male justices, to today:

> For an institution which tends to move at a very slow pace, that's a rapid turnaround. It speaks well of the Australian legal profession that we've had so many talented women appointed to the court. It also speaks well of past governments, Labor and Coalition, that have looked for talent and found talented women to be appointed.

When Heydon was sworn in, and there was no woman on the court following Gaudron's retirement, a protester stood outside the court with a sign that read: 'Mum, can women be High Court judges?' When Crennan was appointed by attorney-general Philip Ruddock in 2005, two young girls held similar signs. 'Thank you, Mr Ruddock, can we have some more?'

Williams agrees with Kiefel's argument about the eagerness of governments to name the best female lawyers to the bench, but says gender inequity in the law is a deeper problem. 'We've seen that male senior counsel have been more likely to brief male junior counsel, who then in turn become the senior counsel who do the appointments. There's still a sort of underrepresentation in senior barristers and that's something that should be focused on.'

Williams says Australians have less visibility of the court than other branches of government, with decision-making happening in private, and the resulting judgments usually too long and complex for many people to understand. 'I think the appointment of women does make a difference,' he says.

> Merit is, of course, the primary consideration. We want great people on the court. But women can bring different life experience, they can also provide greater confidence in judicial decision-making. If you've got a court entirely of men, or for that matter, women, that doesn't give you confidence that the court has the best people on it, or is well placed to deal with the sort of complex issues of life experience, and matters that often intersect with issues of gender, that the court has to decide.

Announcing Jagot's appointment, Mark Dreyfus was asked by the Canberra press corps about the new female majority he was helping usher in, and whether it would remain intact after Kiefel's retirement. He dodged the second part of the question. 'This was an appointment of the best possible person to the High Court of Australia,' Dreyfus said in the Blue Room at Parliament House.

For her part, Mary Gaudron argued in 2005 that the law was critical to the struggle for equality in the law, even suggesting it challenged Australia's boast of being a country of egalitarianism. The trailblazing former justice remembered the saga of trying to buy Michael McHugh's chambers as a problem wider than just that floor. Other barristers had insisted their decisions not to allow her in were neither discriminatory nor personal; 'it was just that I was a woman'.

Eventually one silk told Gaudron that a certain clerk had threatened to resign if a woman were allowed onto their floor. The man explained they'd been trying to get rid of 'that so-and-so' for years. 'This is our big opportunity,' he said.

Accepted as the lesser of two evils, Gaudron moved in. The clerk didn't resign and the pair became friends. He later helped secure industrial law work in an area Gaudron had not previously practised. For Gaudron, and the High Court, perhaps it truly was the graceful incoming of a revolution.

•••

Overflow

Today, everything seems to be spilling over,
the acanthus that grew from wind-blown seed,
its glossy roman leaves reaching over the
terraced wall, the chooks patrolling the fence line,
searching for a way out, the pond fish surfacing
in a pond brimming with last night's rain,
existing in one world, but needing another,
and then there's me, standing in unkempt grass
in a rippling breeze, my basket heavy
with the week's damp clothes, as I peg
sock   after sock   after sock.

Vanessa
Proctor

Vanessa Proctor is a
Sydney-based poet.
She is immediate
past president of
the Australian Haiku
Society. Her poetry
appears in print and
on permanent art
installations in New
Zealand and Australia.
She writes on the
traditional land of the
Gu-ring-gai people.

Justine & Jacquie and their adventures on the other side (an excerpt)[*]

Jason
Barker

Jason Barker is Professor of Global Communication in the College of Foreign Language & Literature at Kyung Hee University. He is writer-director of the documentary *Marx Reloaded* and author of the novel *Marx Returns*.

Justin
Clemens

Justin Clemens is an associate professor at the University of Melbourne. His recent books include the poetry collection *A Foul Wind* (Hunter 2022) and, with Thomas H. Ford, the monograph *Barron Field in New South Wales* (Melbourne UP 2023).

Sinking not shrinking

Justine & Jacquie arrived at the ferry terminal where the boat was due to depart. Remarkably it didn't require any walking; their feet never even touched the ground. 'Boat', too, was putting it mildly. In fact, the vessel was so huge that when they looked up at the towering masts and the mainsail and two funnels with white puffs of smoke coming out of them, it made them feel quite giddy.

'We're not going to need a bigger boat,' Jacquie said, craning back his neck as far as it would go. 'This one is—ample.'

Crowds were gathered on the quayside to see them off. There were flags, balloons, confetti and multicoloured streamers, a brass band was playing, and someone had made a banner that read: BON VOYAGE HERR DOKTOR

Much as Jacquie enjoyed the recognition, he couldn't help thinking it was all a bit over the top. After all, he was only going to work. 'I can't *wait* to get on board, master,' Justine enthused, straining at the lead. 'Can we play deck games? Can we? Look! They've got golf, and skittles, and bridge, and shuffleboard, and bingo, and—and—*tennis!* They've got tennis, master! I've always wanted to play tennis. Would you teach me? Please teach me to play tennis, master! Please!'

'Wait and see,' replied a nonplussed Jacquie, deck games being the very last thing on his mind. 'Seminars to host, patients to analyse,' he mused, as doctor and hound dodged porters and clambered over mounds of luggage. Jacquie felt underpacked; and, in his Tarzan costume, underdressed. 'I'll be a laughing stock in this,' he moaned. 'It's mortifying, really. I'll have to borrow a suit for dinner—someone will oblige, surely—'

'Good morning, sir,' interrupted the steward at the foot of the gangway.

'Good morning,' Jacquie replied. Despite looking pristine in his white naval uniform, with its shiny gold buttons, there was something unusual about the man. He said 'sir' a lot. There was nothing unusual about that—even if it *was* a tad irritating. Then Jacquie realised what the matter was: the steward wasn't a man at all, at least not a proper one. He was more of a cross between two species: a *rat man*.

'Oh,' said the steward in a high-pitched voice, 'I'm terribly sorry, sir; is this your—dog?'

'My dog?' retorted Jacquie. 'Why? What about her?'

'I'm afraid we don't permit dogs on the upper decks,' said the steward from behind two very sharp and protruding teeth. 'It will have to travel in Hound Quarters.'

[*] 'Justine & Jacquie' is the manuscript of an illustrated novel in twelve chapters. Illustrations by Eugen Slavik.

Jacquie looked aghast, and somewhat lost for words. 'Hound Quarters? *Hound Quarters?*' The doctor took a deep breath and composed himself. 'Listen here, my good rat man,' he said in a lofty voice, 'my dog is Justine, she is very beautiful, and *you* would have heard her speak.'

The steward's watery pink eyes swam in their sockets. 'You mean, it's a—*speaking* dog, sir?'

'Indeed,' nodded the proud owner. 'Say something, Justine. Go on: show the rat man what you can do.'

'Like what?' Justine remarked, casually sniffing the steward's trousers.

'Voilà!' exclaimed Jacquie, looking very pleased with himself. 'What did I tell you?' The steward was barely convinced. He thought about it for a moment with his whiskers bristling. (It is well known that rats think with their whiskers.)

'Like what?' repeated the steward, whose whiskers had stopped bristling: 'Hardly saying much—is it, sir?'

'Quite right,' Jacquie affirmed. 'I said she'd say something, but I didn't say she'd say *much*—did I, now?' The steward was nonplussed. Jacquie, however, sensing a moral victory, escorted Justine up the gangway with his nose in the air.

Once the ship had set sail, Justine wasted no time in playing deck games. Jacquie, complaining of a headache, retired to the sundeck for a lie down. Golf was Justine's favourite, a sport she really excelled in. She was par for the course at skittles, lucky in bingo, and a natural at tennis. Her exploits on the shuffleboard court, meanwhile, were greeted with a mixture of disbelief and delight by the other passengers, and even won her a round of applause. She adored bridge, and one of the players with whom she became very friendly, a jolly uniformed major with a big fat belly and bushy moustache, even suggested they continue playing in his cabin. When Justine said she'd have to ask her master's permission first, the man seemed to lose interest. It didn't matter much, Justine thought; bridge probably wasn't as exciting with only two players.

'I'm so enjoying it here, master,' said Justine, as she and Jacquie reclined on their deck chairs. 'How I love getting out and meeting new people. And the view—well, I never! Why, one can see all the way to—' Justine hesitated, it not being clear *what* exactly she was looking at—apart from the sea. 'That must be why they call it "the sea",' Justine reasoned, 'because all you do is *sea*, without there being anything *to* sea.'

Jacquie looked out from behind his newspaper and summoned a waiter.

'Good afternoon, sir,' said the waiter, who bore an uncanny resemblance to the steward. 'What can I get you from the bar?'

'I'll be having a Scotch on the rocks,' said Jacquie.

'Very good, sir. And for your dog?'

'She'll be having a Vodka Martini,' said Justine. 'Shaken and not stirred.'

'She'll be having a bowl of water,' Jacquie cut in. 'Oh, and waiter,' he continued, 'kindly do something about these annoying creatures,' indicating the seagulls overhead. 'Impound them or tell them to clear off; unless you're going to tell me they're paid passengers—it wouldn't surprise me, frankly—in which case you could at least tell them

to keep the noise down—I'm trying to read my newspaper.' Jacquie rolled up the paper and swung it in the air, albeit more in irritation than anything, the seagulls being far enough away not to take the slightest notice: 'Go on, shoo,' Jacquie said feebly.

The drinks were promptly delivered. Jacquie took a sip of his Scotch and Justine a lap of her water and the pair of them gazed out to sea.

'Look,' said Justine excitedly. 'It's Nigel. Yoo-hoo!' she cried, waving furiously at one of the seagulls.

'Nigel? How do you tell them apart?' wondered Jacquie, for whom any of the 'confounded birds' could have been Nigel. Indeed, there was no point in saying 'he doesn't look like a Nigel', as was sometimes said of small children, if none of them did.

'Ahoy there, shipmates!' Nigel said, landing elegantly and neatly folding up his wings.

'Nigel! Fancy seeing you here,' exclaimed Justine with a growl of delight.

'Arr, shiver me timbers, lass; likewise. I ain't be seein' ye since ye be knee high to a lobster—' said Nigel.

'Technically she'd have still been in the womb,' said Jacquie, somewhat irritated by the idea of his dog's social life.

'Aaaarrrrgggghhhh!' squawked Nigel. 'And who be this landlubber, Justine?'

'Why, it's my master, of course,' declared Justine proudly.

Jacquie, quite unable to understand what Nigel was saying, contrived a little greeting, but declined offering his hand for fear that the giant bird might get the wrong idea and bite it off.

'Nigel,' said Justine, suddenly roused by an idea. 'Why don't you sing us a song? One of your sea shanties—it'll get us in the sea-faring mood. Nigel is ever so widely travelled; he's been all over the world—haven't you, Nigel?'

'Arr, that be true, lass,' said Nigel, cackling like a seadog. 'I'll tell ye a tale of scallywags, scourges, monsters and mayhem of all the seven seas combined.' Then, without further ado, he launched into *The Ballad of Pirate Barry and the Thing*:

There once was a pirate named Barry
Who would cash in all he could carry,
And piled up the bling
With a ring-a-ding-ding—
Which made him as happy as Larry.

With an arr and an arr and a harr-harr-harr!
We're flyin' the skull and crossbones,
And yer know what that means for yer
    hearts and yer spleens,
They'll be morsels for old Davy Jones!

One day as Barry was sailing
On his way to a blood-spattered whaling,
A gargantuan beast
Turned him into a feast—
Oh how fortune is fickle and failing!

As soon as the beast gulped him down,
It plunged back to its murky and brown
Abode in the deep
Where all the drowned sleep—
And Barry felt like a right clown.

As he sat there, morose in the gloom
Of that belly that might be his tomb,
He heard a scritch-scratch,
So, lighting a match,
He peered round the horrible room.

With an arr and an arr and a harr-harr-harr!
We're flyin' the skull and crossbones,
And yer know what that means for yer
    hearts and yer spleens,
They'll be morsels for old Davy Jones!

Well! That beast had been really quite
    beasty
In feasting on all that was feasty—
There were wrecks there aplenty,
Where skeletons gently
Waved ciao to the living and yeasty!

Then Barry's eye fixed on a shape
That was like the preposterous gape
Of primeval disorder,
Like a void without border
Or the sinuous smoke from a vape.

With an arr and an arr and a harr-harr-harr!
We're flyin' the skull and crossbones,
And yer know what that means for yer
    hearts and yer spleens,
They'll be morsels for old Davy Jones!

It was this, it was that—a true Thing!
That was crowned like an infernal King,
Though it hadn't clear parts—
Being all stops and starts—
It was ready to ring-a-ding-ding!

With a voice at once fulsome and flat,
Both a roar and the squeak of a rat,
It said 'Barry, my friend,
This will be your end,
Unless you can act as my hat.

'In order to get out of this place,
I'm going to hop into your face,
And from then on we'll be
In pure synchrony,
The harbinger of a new race!'

With an arr and an arr and a harr-harr-harr!
We're flyin' the skull and crossbones,
And yer know what that means for yer
    hearts and yer spleens,
They'll be morsels for old Davy Jones!

And with that, the Thing did what it said
By burrowing into his head—
Despite Barry's shrieks,
It went straight through his cheeks,
And settled into its new bed.

Once ensconced, the Thing took control
Of poor Barry's piratical soul,
And—assessing its tasks—
Breathed into some flasks,
Infusing old embers of coal.

Along with some gobbets of ooze,
The Barry-Thing tamped in a fuse,
Lit the whole enterprise,
Which it hurled to the skies
(Though a little bit got on its shoes).

With an arr and an arr and a harr-harr-harr!
We're flyin' the skull and crossbones,
And yer know what that means for yer
    hearts and yer spleens,
They'll be morsels for old Davy Jones!

When the flasks hit the quivering wall
They mushroomed into a flame-ball,
And the foul stomach trench
Burst ablaze with the stench,
And blew Barry-Thing down the hall.

His departure was truly atrocious,
For Barry-Thing's path was precocious!
And imagine the shock

Of the migrating flock,
To witness a flight so velocious!

But the Thing had thus started a chain
Of events forged in blood and in pain—
For, hot after Barry,
The wrecks didn't tarry
But followed him like a dread rain.

With an arr and an arr and a harr-harr-harr!
We're flyin' the skull and crossbones,
And yer know what that means for yer
    hearts and yer spleens,
They'll be morsels for old Davy Jones!

And thus Barry-Thing found a fine fleet
Of well-rotted husks and old meat,
Which now plagues the seas
Like a swarm of foul bees,
And sucks the world dry as a teat.

With an arr and an arr and a harr-harr-harr!
The Barry-Thing's 'ere for yer gold—
And he'll feast like a beast from yer soul to
    yer feet,
'Fore he locks all the rest in his hold!

'I be seein' ye, Justine,' cackled Nigel, '—and your good master,' and saluted the pair of them with his wings. 'And watch out for the Thing. It'll run a rig on ye, mind—'

'Oh, Nigel,' Justine whimpered. 'Won't you stay for tea? There's bound to be fish on the menu.'

'Can't, lass,' said Nigel, with his eyes fixed firmly on the skies like a fighter pilot. 'Batten down the hatches: there be a storm a-brewin',' and, launching himself skywards, the seagull was promptly whisked away by the breeze.

Justine & Jacquie watched as Nigel took off from the deck and receded into the distance until he was no more than a tiny speck on the horizon.

'What fun that was,' Justine sighed at last.

'Yes, it *was* entertaining,' conceded Jacquie, taking a swig of his Scotch. 'However, that bird's obsessions show all the signs of psychosis.'

'Are you quite well?' said Justine, who could always tell instinctively when her master was out of sorts.

'Not *quite*,' said Jacquie, with the panicked look of a man who'd mistakenly ingested poison. 'Look—we're shrinking!' And so it appeared; for where previously the ice in Jacquie's glass had been the correct size, now it towered over them like the west flank of the Eiger. At this rate, reasoned the doctor, they were destined to drown in his glass of Scotch, concluding that the only possible solution would be to drink their way to safety.

'I hope you're thirsty, Justine,' said Jacquie, as they scrambled to keep from sliding off the giant ice cube. It then occurred to him that if they didn't *stop* shrinking then at this rate they'd need an army of alcoholics to help drain the glass.

'We're not *shrinking*,' said Justine, grasping the true nature of their predicament. 'But we'll soon be *sinking*.' And so it appeared: the ship had struck an iceberg and was rapidly taking in water. 'Save yourself, master!' spluttered Justine, whose doggy paddle needed some practice. 'Don't worry about me. You're young. Whereas I'm—' she paused mid-paddle to do the calculations '—at least 69 in dog years. I've had a good life; not remotely a dog's life. It's been beyond my pleasure knowing you, master. Think only of the good times we had—'

'Quick, Justine!' said Jacquie, who had commandeered a lifeboat and was already rowing. 'Stop your babbling and get in.' Thrusting an oar into her front paws—and with a 'heave ho!'—Justine & Jacquie managed to row just far enough away to see their passage to the other side disappear beneath the waves, leaving nothing behind but a foamy spot where the mighty ship had so recently been.

'Well, that's blown it,' lamented Jacquie. 'How am I going to get to work on time now?'

As if *that* wasn't bad enough, presently some very dark and menacing clouds appeared from over the horizon, and in no time a storm was raging, tossing and turning their lifeboat like a wooden toy trapped inside a washing machine. It was while on the crest of a mountainous wave that Jacquie observed, somewhat like a man whose life was flashing before him, that if civilisation had any merit, then it must be in knowing that one day, sooner or later, everyone will need a new washing machine.

An anorexic tea party

Once the storm had passed and the seas were calm, Justine & Jacquie drifted for a while, eventually reaching the shallow waters of a tropical island. Reflecting on their ordeal under a palm tree, Justine confessed that she was happy to be alive. Jacquie, however, had other ideas.

'That was all your fault,' he complained. 'You and your Nigel. If it hadn't been for him and his sea shanty none of this would have happened.'

'Nigel?' protested Justine. 'That's so unfair.'

'Look at this suit,' Jacquie persisted, removing heaps of sand from his jacket pockets. 'It's ruined! And those leather shoes the captain lent me are now languishing somewhere at the bottom of the ocean. Whatever you do, I don't want you talking to any more animals. Crabs, for instance. If one of those turns up offering to tell you his life story,' Jacquie cautioned, pointing at an empty shell, 'then kindly make your excuses and walk away. Rats, seagulls—all these animals are cursed.'

'Nigel was only trying to be friendly,' said Justine meekly. 'You can hardly blame him for the iceberg.'

'Plants!' exclaimed Jacquie, as he pulled an endless length of seaweed from his trousers. 'Don't forget those interfering souls. They may look innocent, but oh, no! Anyway, I think I've made myself clear. Now, if I'm *not* mistaken, we should be heading'—Jacquie put his finger in the air and randomly pointed at a gap in some palm trees—'*that* way.'

Beyond the shore the island was covered in dense jungle. There not being a human in sight, and given the prohibition on talking to animals and plants, Justine & Jacquie set off into the unknown, without so much as a pen knife or compass between them, on an epic voyage of discovery.

'Are we lost yet, master?' said Justine, 42 seconds later.

'Nonsense,' said Jacquie, 'we're on the right track. Remember, Justine: this is what I do for a living.'

'What? Jungle exploring?' said Justine, for whom the nearest thing to a jungle she had ever seen was the Tuileries Garden in Paris.

'No! Not jungle exploring,' scoffed Jacquie: 'Sign language.'

'Signs? But there aren't any.'

'Why, of course there are,' said Jacquie, 'you just have to know where to look. It takes training—along with a certain *je ne sais quoi*—which not everyone is blessed with. But signs are everywhere—'

'Er, master,' said Justine in a worried tone, 'I think you're stuck in some quicksand.'

'A-ha!' Jacquie exclaimed, 'so that's what it is. For a moment there I thought I was shrinking again.'

After successfully negotiating some further obstacles, Justine & Jacquie arrived at the entrance to a village, where the natives had erected a sign next to a pile of skulls. The sign read: NO GODS ALLOWED

'What does it mean, master?' asked Justine.

'Indeed,' said Jacquie, scratching his stubble. He thought about it for a little while, before concluding, 'Let's just hope for your sake, Justine, that the jungle people aren't dyslexic.' Jacquie patted his dog on the head and they proceeded into the village, where three men were seated at a dining table.

'More diners, Cook,' one of them declared. 'Light the stove! Welcome, comrades, you're right on time.' The man seized Jacquie's hand and began shaking it vigorously.

'On time for what?' said Jacquie, looking up at the man, who was very tall and skinny, and dressed in a black suit and top hat.

'For dinner, tea, lunch: all three,' answered the man, which generated a merry chorus: 'Dinner! Tea! Lunch! All three!' chimed the others in unison.

'I see,' said Jacquie, regarding the scene narrowly out of the corner of his eye.

'I dare say you're hungry,' said the host, ushering his guests over to the table.

'I'll say,' said Justine. 'I could eat a horse.'

'Here,' replied he, 'take a seat, take two—'

'Take three!' interjected the man with the beard, who stood out as the odd one of the bunch.

'They don't need *three* seats, Chairman,' said the third man, who must have been the cook, owing to the blood-stained apron he was wearing. 'Two people only require two seats:

$1 + 1 = 2$.'

'Ha! That's fine coming from you,' scoffed the first man, 'seeing as you can't even count properly.'

'Er, if you don't mind,' interrupted Jacquie, 'this is all very interesting, but my dog and I have been wandering through this book for three and a half chapters already—might we get the introductions over with so we can move the story along?'

'Certainly,' said the first man, with an embarrassed cough. '*I*,' he announced, removing his top hat and bowing low to the ground, 'am the Count; whereas *this*,' he said, straining to stand up again, 'is Cook.'

'And *that*,' said Cook, pointing at the odd-looking man done up like a scarecrow, 'is the Chairman.'

'I suppose you're both wondering,' said he, 'why they call me Chairman.'

'I wasn't,' Jacquie confessed.

'Is it because you're sitting in a chair?' said Justine.

'To be frank with you,' said the Chairman, who made a funny squawking noise as he spoke, 'I do not know *why* I am called Chairman. But!' he added at once, 'at least I know why.'

'You know or you don't know?' said Jacquie.

'I don't know,' the Chairman replied.

'I see,' said Jacquie, doubting that he really did.

'And,' added the Chairman, nodding sagely, 'I know.'

'Tea time!' interrupted the Count, banging a ceremonial gong. 'How do you take your tea?' he asked, passing cups and saucers to his guests. When it came to Justine he hesitated, unsure whether a saucer would suffice; before deciding—since Justine was seated at the table like the rest of them—that a cup was in order too.

'Without milk,' requested Jacquie.

'I'm afraid we can't offer you tea without milk,' said Cook regretfully. 'We only have tea without tea.'

'Tea without—*tea*,' Jacquie repeated, putting it down to the sand in his ears. Surely what Cook had really said was: 'We only have tea without biscuits,' or 'tea without sandwiches.'

'The tea without tea is *very* good,' confirmed the Chairman, holding up his empty cup. 'I highly recommend it.'

'In which case, perhaps we could skip tea and go straight to the main course,' said Jacquie, who was quite ready to devour whatever was on the menu.

'I'll have you know, comrades,' the Count resumed, after a long silence, 'that we all pay very close attention to what we consume here—'

'Very!' cried the Chairman. 'I agree with him: I'm on a see-food diet, myself.'

'I don't worry about my weight,' Jacquie said, visibly salivating. (As for Justine, she was always salivating; by now, though, she was just as hungry as her master.)

'Why? Does your weight worry about you?' put in the Chairman.

'In which case,' replied the Count, 'you won't mind eating nothing.'

'I beg your pardon?' Jacquie exclaimed.

'Well,' the Count went on, 'since you don't worry about your weight, you needn't worry about eating anything.'

'Or not eating it!' added the Chairman, banging his fist on the table and upsetting Jacquie's cup.

'Which is just as well,' admitted Cook, 'because there isn't anything *to* eat.'

'Nothing?' said Jacquie with his mouth gaping open, and just desperate for something to put in it.

'Nothing,' confirmed Cook.

Jacquie felt like he needed a drink: a Scotch on the rocks—barring the threat of icebergs—or a glass of fresh pineapple juice, which should at least have been possible in a jungle.

'You see,' explained the Count, as if he were reading Jacquie's mind, 'our little jungle retreat provides us with everything we need. We want for nothing. Why, how many people can say that? It's a form of ideal communism we've invented here,' he declared, waving away a cloud of mosquitoes into Jacquie's wide open mouth. They didn't taste *that* bad, but could have done with some mayonnaise.

Jacquie attempted to digest the Count's speech (along with the mosquitoes). 'I have an important question to ask you,' he said after some careful reflection.

'By all means, comrade,' said the Count gleefully. 'Ask away.'

'Is there anywhere around here where I can get me a glass of fresh pineapple juice?'

'And a hamburger,' added Justine, who was fast running out of saliva.

'Hmm,' mused the Count. 'Still hungry, eh?'

'Well,' said Jacquie, gulping down his perspiration, 'a glass of water wouldn't go amiss. To avoid dehydration—it being a jungle. I could even share a bowl with my dog—if your rations were in short supply, that is.'

'Rations?' sneered the Count. 'Why, what a thoroughly primitive idea.'

'Should I read them the tale of *The Doctor and the Patient*?' asked Cook.

'I think you better had,' the Count agreed, trying to contain his disgust, 'before our guests threaten to *eat us alive*. Seldom have I encountered such *voracious* appetites.'

Cook scurried off into a nearby hut before returning with a large book. On the cover was inscribed 'Official Journal' and, underneath in brackets, '& Other Morals'. Having blown off the dust from the cover (which made Justine sneeze) Cook began to read, and at the first mention of food Jacquie fantasised drinking a pineapple juice *with* pineapple juice, and eating a hamburger *with* (oddly enough) the burger—

A venerable quack—a surgeon at that!—
Encountered a bird eating fish.
'Good day,' said the doc, around one o'clock
As the gannet was gobbling his dish.

'How much you consume! It's your taste, I assume
To devour such a fearsome buffet!'
Replied did he, Gannet: 'Oh seldom I plan it,
I eat what I like, when I may.'

'Quite so,' said the doc, 'but consider the shock
If your gut you would ever betray;
Your heart it would stop and your lungs they would flop
And your family would wail in dismay.

'Why, I in my eating, my hunger is fleeting
And rarely leads me astray.
I'm merely entreating—not remotely brow-beating—
That you change your routine right away.'

'What's up with me, doc?' said the bird to the croc.
'I'm afraid you've got food on the brain.
But visit me soon: tomorrow, at noon,
And your health I will help you regain.'

'It's like this, you see,' the next day at three
The doctor revealed to his charge:
'The amount you imbibe, if strictly applied
Need not be incredibly large.'

'So how much is that?' said the bird to the quack,
Who worried he wouldn't eat well.
'It's nothing but wee, on which not a flea
Would ever seriously dwell.'

'So, let's get this straight,' said the bird, 'as it's late:
You want me to give up my food?
For "nothing" might seem a trifle obscene
And impossible if it were chewed.'

'Why, don't be absurd,' said the croc to the bird,
'Nothing is all that I eat.
Just give it a try, you're a reasonable guy,
But avoid the temptation to cheat.'

The very next day, forswearing foul play
Did Gannet commence with his fast.
Then, making his bed, was struck by the dread
That he'd soon be confined to the past.

'This naught I ingest is proving a test,'
Said the bird to the venerable quack.
'Forgive me if rude, or frightfully crude
But nutrition is what I most lack.'

'Well, might I contend, my venerable friend
That nothing is no lack at all?
Why, think of Pascal and Leibniz et al.
Each one to the void was in thrall!

'Imagine a dish, of infinite fish'—
'My God, just how much is that?'—
'And then add but one, you'll see that the sum
Will fail to increase by a sprat.'

'So, what you are saying,' asserted the bird,
'If I am to understand right:
The weight I am sparing not eating a herring
If not naught is enormously slight.'

'Think not of the weight of the food on your plate
But instead the extent of what's not.
Now if you don't mind, I'm getting behind
And advancing my work not a jot.'

Yet try as he might in his dietary plight
The bird soon fell fatally ill.
To the patient's surprise, the doctor arrived
And, presenting his client the bill:

'I shan't be pursuing a cent that's accruing,'
Conceded the quack to the bird.
'I'm here to attest, to own up at best
To any vexation incurred.'

'That's life, I suppose,' in a voice lachrymose
Was the gannet's penultimate plea.
'Watch over my wife, save our children from strife
And visit the family for tea.'

'Rest easy, good man,' the doctor began,
Then, recalling his philosophy:
'But during our meeting, no-one will be eating
Or not them at least, only me.'

'Well,' declared Cook, slamming shut the book at last, 'that proves the point, I think.'

'It was certainly saying something,' said Jacquie, who in truth had found the poem a tad silly and dozed off in the middle.

'Quite correct,' intoned the Count, rising slowly to his feet. 'Selfless to the last, our venerable doctor: suppressing his appetites and attending his patient to the end. A proud servant of the people, if ever there were.'

'That doctor was a crook,' Jacquie surmised.

'No,' countered the Chairman, 'that doctor was a croc.'

'A *croctor*,' asserted Jacquie. 'If ever I carried on my practice like that I'd be struck off.'

'I thought you already had been,' said Justine.

'You're quite an expert, I see,' said the Count with an agitated cough. 'To whom do we have the pleasure, Dr—'

'He's no expert,' interrupted Justine, barking her displeasure, 'he's my master.'

'Calm down, Justine, calm down,' said Jacquie, patting his dog on the head. 'We shan't be hanging around here much longer.'

'Oh? Does our hospitality fail to live up to your expectations, doctor?' enquired Cook, somewhat in earnest, as if he were running a five-star hotel (and sounding like someone who believed it, too).

'On a scale of 1 to 10 I'd give it −1,' Jacquie remarked.

'That's lacking, all right,' said Cook, nodding favourably, as if −1 were a respectable score.

'Well,' observed the Count, 'I wouldn't take *that* for a compliment. And in any case,' he went on, taking a sip from his cup of tea-without-tea, 'you're confusing lack with zero. There may be no tea in this cup, but it certainly doesn't *lack* any. If only you'd learn how to subtract.'

A furious debate began, involving numbers and counting and zeros and lacks that was all incredibly complicated. Jacquie, meanwhile, didn't understand a word, but during the debate did notice some highly desirable tribal artefacts, including an ornately carved statuette that would have gone splendidly on his mantelpiece. 'But how could I ever carry it?' he thought, and, seeing it was far too heavy to lug around, decided that this might be a good time to leave.

'Come along, Justine,' whispered Jacquie, and with the debate between Cook and the Count hotting up, the master and his dog quietly tiptoed out of the village. On their way out, Justine grabbed a bone from the pile of relics at the entrance, which caused the entire edifice to collapse. Suddenly aware of what was going on behind their backs, the tribalists ceased arguing.

'Hey!' cried the Count, 'come back! We never said you could have leftovers!'

A note on the text

Jacques Lacan (1901–1981) was a French psychiatrist and psychoanalyst and one of the most notable thinkers of the 20th century. The signature innovation of psychoanalysis was the theory of the unconscious, which showed, according to Freud himself, that humans were not even masters of their own minds. Lacan brought something new to the witch's brew. His notoriously difficult writings are so steeped in esoteric art, literature, philosophy and algebra that one could be forgiven for wondering just how much of it really serves the task of resolving mental illness, which is, after all, the main aim of psychoanalysis. Isn't it?

Today the expectation persists that a psychoanalyst is a sort of quasi-medical professional who specialises in making people 'better'. It is even the guiding ethical imperative of neoliberal democracy, inasmuch as expressions of unhappiness or disgust with the state of the world are seized on as evidence that the individual, not democracy, needs help. Lacan's ethic of psychoanalysis sets out from here: what moral purpose is there to 'being happy' in a world which is sick to the core?

In the 1960s Lacan's many innovations, both in and outside psychoanalysis, were seized on by students and radical intellectuals. In May 1968, when France was paralysed by a general strike, Lacan broadly endorsed their agenda; however, by December of the following year his sympathies were flagging. An 'impromptu' speech he gave at Vincennes University, during which Lacan's dog Justine walked on stage, concluded with the students and Lacan hurling insults at each other.

What to make of this oddly charismatic figure? 'I'm a clown,' Lacan said, in a judgement since echoed by very many commentators. As for us, we wonder whether Lacan's legacy may best be treated in the form of fanfiction, an expressly fantastic rewriting of his life and times in a para-generic frame.

• • •

Sources
Alain Badiou, *Lacan: Anti-Philosophy 3*, trans. K. Reinhard & S. Spitzer (Columbia UP 2018).
Justin Clemens, *Psychoanalysis is an Antiphilosophy* (Edinburgh UP 2013).
Russell Grigg, *Lacan, Language and Philosophy* (SUNY 2008).
Jacques Lacan, *Écrits*, trans. B. Fink with H. Fink and R. Grigg (Norton 2006).
——. *The Seminar of Jacques Lacan Book XVII: The Other Side of Psychoanalysis*, trans. R. Grigg (Norton 2007).
——. *Television: A Challenge to the Psychoanalytic Establishment*, trans. D. Hollier et al. (Norton 1990).
Elisabeth Roudinesco, *Jacques Lacan* (Columbia UP 1997).

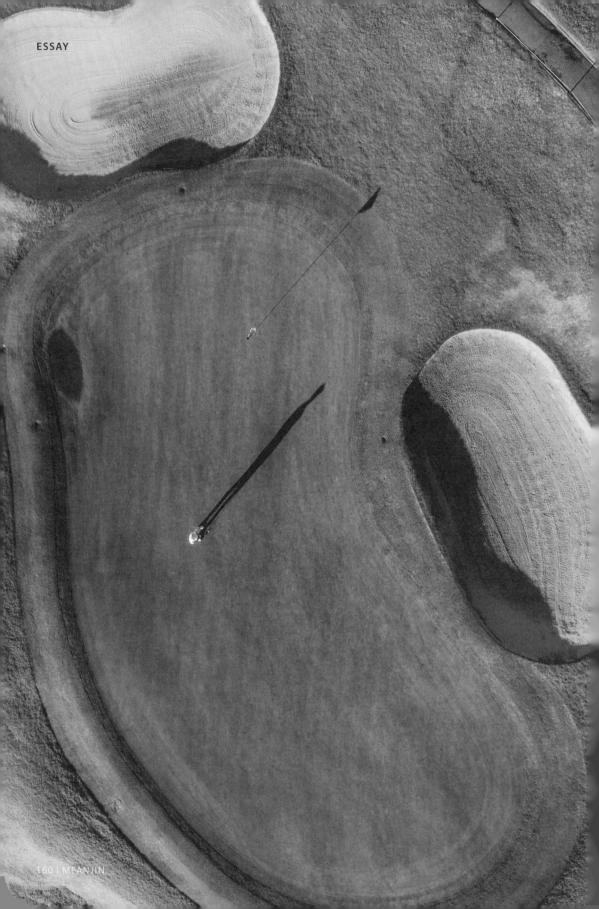

Money Shot: Golf and Public Land

In 2017 a photograph goes viral: three white men in cargo shorts and polos like they just came from a Trump rally, playing a round of golf as a wildfire rages behind them.

Briohny Doyle

Briohny Doyle's latest novel, *Why We Are Here*, is fuelled by golf outrage. Her previous books are *Echolalia*, *Adult Fantasy* and *The Island Will Sink*. She lectures at the University of Sydney.

'In the pantheon of visual metaphors for America today, this is the money shot,' journalist and *Wire* showrunner David Simon tweets. It scores 193,994 likes. I save the image to my desktop. When I look at it back then, my gaze is drawn to two focal points, the fire and the men, each dangerously oblivious of the other. Five years later when I look at the image I hardly see the men. What stands out is the deep green pigment of the grass. The poplars and firs at the edge of a well-tended fairway are the 'wild' in golf terms but are nonetheless tame in contrast to the blazing wilderness beyond. A golf course is a depopulated, managed simulation of nature on which people stage a game you can win.

A golf course reveals itself partially as a liminal space between the urban and the natural, the public and the private. It takes shape as tees and holes, a precise landscape laid over something more unruly. If you're not playing, you might glimpse it through a fence, or via a photograph captured with a drone or a wide-angle lens. You can view it as a healthy hobby, an egregiously unfair allocation of land, or both. You may not have any view of it at all.

Like a ghost sneak-attacked with a white sheet, golf shows it's true form to me in 2020, after which all future hauntings are rendered garishly visible. It starts during the pandemic, in Melbourne, where golf and tennis are the last sports to be banned under the stage-three COVID-19 restrictions. For the first few weeks of what would become one of the longest lockdowns in the world, I walk daily with a friend around Carlton's Royal Park golf course. Daily, we wonder: should we take up golf? I'd never thought about it before, just as I'd never thought of trespassing into one of those cafés where old men gamble at plastic tables. But suddenly it seems golf is the last bastion of leisure and I crave leisure badly.

Later, when the game is inevitably restricted, we stop walking around the edges and step out onto the sweeping fairways. We cut new routes across an old neighbourhood, sit at the edge of dug-outs conjuring beach, our feet swinging over the sand. Lions roar in the nearby zoo. A little later still, someone cuts a hole through the wire fence of the

Players on a green golf course by Jacob Lund. Licensed via Adobe Stock Images.

Northcote Golf Club in Melbourne's inner north. It looks every bit like the David Shrigley work *Sunday Adventure Club. Here 4am*. Every time the council fixes the hole someone cuts a new one. Eventually, the council opens the land for public use until the game can return. When the weather improves and picnics are permitted, the green is littered with groups of people enjoying new social freedoms in hitherto unexplored parklands. How amazing is this? Who knew? says everyone. Locals lobby for the land to be converted into shared use. Their case is strong but golf courses are uniquely hard to share. The sport requires large tracts of immaculately maintained land as well as immense concentration. And golf balls are dangerous projectiles. In June 2022, the proposal is a 3 pm curfew on golf, followed by shared use of the site. By July, the decision is overturned; councillors vote to give the land back to golfers.

Writing for ABC online, sports journalist Richard Hinds declares the community dissonance over golf courses a 'culture war' in which 'non-golfing residents of a Greens-leaning suburb can use the stereotypical image of privileged golfers to mischievously cast the game as an elitist, land-grabbing sport when those using the local course are actually golf's equivalent of working-class battlers'.

A similar battle plays out in 2019 at an eighteen-hole course in Marrickville, Sydney, another rapidly growing inner-city neighbourhood where public and green space are at a premium. This time a proposal to halve the course and convert the remainder to public use is defeated after lobbying. Soon-to-be prime minister Anthony Albanese declares that the proposal to reduce the course 'risks the sustainability of the Marrickville Golf Club and the spirit of the Inner West', which means, I suppose, that a historically working-class neighbourhood should offer gentrifiers the same fringe benefits that wealthy people from long-established desirable neighbourhoods have. They've fought hard to be here after all.

●●●

The comedian George Carlin does a great bit on golf. It's 1992. Carlin is dressed in black, sports a slicked-back pony tail. He strides commandingly across the urban-themed stage for his special *Jammin' in New York*. 'I've got just the place for low-cost housing,' he tells the studio audience. 'I have solved this problem, I know where we can build housing for the homeless: GOLF COURSES!!!'

The crowd cheers, whistles. 'Perfect! Golf courses!' Carlin takes a sip of water. 'Just what we need: plenty of good land in nice neighbourhoods, land that is currently being wasted on a meaningless, mindless activity, engaged in primarily by white, well-to-do, male businessmen who use the game to get together to make deals to carve this country up a little finer among themselves.'

The crowd erupts. Carlin doesn't wait. This is almost-comedy because he also has some hard truths to deliver. 'There are over 17,000 golf courses in America. They average over 150 acres apiece, that's 3 million plus acres, 4820 square miles ... you could build two Rhode Islands and a Delaware for the homeless.' It doesn't get a big laugh, but it hits.

Since I started to notice golf there's been a tiny George Carlin in me, outraged and full of facts. He paces a stage in my mind making declarative statements: Australia has 1616 golf courses, earning us the number-five world ranking and the number-one ranking for number of golf courses per capita. Depending on which golf-sponsored report you read, participation in golf ranges from 1.7% to 4.9% of the population. An eighteen-hole golf course uses approximately 124 megalitres of water per year. My inner Carlin throws his arm in the air to deliver the punchline: all this on the driest continent on Earth after Antarctica! Cue canned laughter, insults, vitriolic public debate, stereotypes, 'culture wars', pure mischief.

• • •

The names of golf courses evoke lush primacy: The Coast, Paradise Palms, The Vines, Meadow Springs, The Lakes, Riverside Oaks, The Links on Hope Island. Money shot. Money shot. Money shot.

There's a theory in economics called the tragedy of the commons. It's grim, much criticised, and the argument golf lobbyists use to justify continued protection of their clubs. The idea is that common property will never be respected like individual property because people only care about what they can own. Further, because our self-interest is paramount in all things, no-one will ever agree on what common good is anyway. The idea dates back to ancient Greece but was popularised in a 1968 essay by Garret Hardin, who writes; 'We want the maximum good per person; but what is good? To one person it is wilderness, to another it is ski-lodges for thousands. To one it is estuaries to nourish ducks for hunters to shoot; to another it is factory land.' To somewhere between 1.7% and 4.9% of the population, we can assume, it is golf courses.

A golf lobbyist's typical addendum to this is that golf is about preservation because if any swath of land wasn't a golf course, it would be apartments already. And now, if any golf course is converted into another kind of public space, like a park, it will be expensive to maintain and inevitably ruined by an influx of people.

A case in point: there is a swath of green in inner-city Sydney that stretches from Randwick to Darlinghurst. This is Sydney Common, a tract of land proclaimed by governor Macquarie in 1811 for Sydney's inhabitants to graze animals. Now it hosts the Sydney Cricket Ground, Centennial Park and Moore Park Golf Course. In 2019, more than 200 years after the land was 'proclaimed', Lord Mayor of the City of Sydney Clover Moore proposed two strategies for reducing 45-hectare Moore Park Golf Course from eighteen to nine holes with the extra land to be returned to public space for the rapidly growing inner-Sydney population. The first stage of community consultation—a random telephone survey of residents within five kilometres of the club—showed 77% support for the proposal. By the next stage, golf clubs across Sydney sounded the alarm. New respondents whose home addresses were outside the council area registered disapproval. The results skewed 50–50. Then deputy premier John Barilaro wrote to Cr Moore and the council in 'the strongest possible terms' to 'keep your hands off' the Moore Park Golf Club.

Perhaps it's mischief with stereotypes to underscore the almost-comedy of a politician facing corruption charges protecting golf. Moore Park Golf Course remains open for minority use. 'Golf has a lobby. Where is the everybody else lobby?' Former Deputy Lord Mayor of the City of Sydney Jess Scully asks when I talk to her. 'In theory that should be our elected officials but when you have Cabinet ministers making submissions in support of golf, that falls apart.'

We are drinking coffee on Sydney's Glebe Point Road in 2022. Around us, a mix of closed and newly opened cafés, the mark of the post-pandemic city. I say post-pandemic not to indicate that the public health crisis is over, but that we are post-response. Golf is back on. But so are school and work and for the most part we are relieved. As we return to everyday life though, it's hard not to wonder if we are missing the opportunity critically to evaluate what we should be returning to.

Golf took form suddenly for Scully, too. She describes flying into Sydney. 'You see all this beautiful greenspace and then you realise it's all golf courses and once that fact gets into your head it's like a bug. You see something totally different.'

The road we are on connects the main arterial road west to the harbour where fishing vessels used to dock but now super yachts owned by the hyper wealthy are moored. It's easy, I realise, to see a city in short hand: land, water, shops, homes. When the aperture narrows, you see a network of claims on how we should live. I too have looked down on this city from the sky and noticed the golf courses. I tell Scully how golf has become, for me, a passive symbol of our unwavering belief in an unsustainable order of things. Passive because golf isn't violent and the land it's played on still exists.

'Golf is the most unfair use of land and the call to rethink these spaces is a fundamental conversation about the allocation of public land.' Scully is unequivocal. This conversation is as persistent as colonisation. Thirty of the 81 golf courses in Sydney are situated on Crown land, a term that dates back to 1788 when governor Phillip claimed possession and vested all land in the name of the Crown.

Today, according to the NSW government website, Crown land is managed in the public interest and includes reserves (and the subcategory 'dedications' that covers golf courses), cemeteries and crematoria, waterways and beaches, national parks and state forests, some roads and specific arts-organisation properties. A further seven Sydney golf clubs are public in that they're situated on council-owned land and therefore open to anyone. Golf clubs, like many sports clubs, also receive tax benefits and subsidies. Their lease agreements are long term, below market value and contingent on upkeep of the land parcel. A golf club on state or local government–owned land is less likely to be negatively impacted by declining participation in the sport, but, unlike privately owned clubs, they cannot sell the land for profit.

'Golf is an ostentatious demonstration of power and control. The landed [gentry] used to build the most absurd displays of power and we have internalised the idea that this is a public good in our cities,' Scully says. 'We subsidise the gating of the commons with every golf course.' Scully worked on the Moore park proposal with Cr Moore, and thinks that, although the project didn't go ahead, the consultation process excited what she sees as a thoroughly 'depleted civic imagination'. That is, it got people thinking about what's possible instead of just accepting what is and what has been.

The term 'depleted civic imagination' sticks in my head like a pop song hook. I'm humming it all the way down Glebe Point Road past boarded-up restaurants, new convenience stores and cosmeticians. It's with me as I cross the dense traffic of Paramatta Road and hit the designated recreation space of Victoria Park, where people are exercising their dogs, socialising or resting; inhabiting a pause in the purpose and momentum of the city.

At some level, our individual and collective lives are enabled through civic imagination. Because we can't be what we can't or won't imagine. We can't create or nurture what we can't or won't conceive of.

• • •

I moved from Melbourne to Sydney during the COVID-19 crisis and rented an apartment on a slice of coastal terrain surrounded by golf courses. From my home, you can walk across four suburbs entirely on golf courses. On your walk you will see lorikeets and cockatoos—black and sulphur-crested—screeching in the trees that dot the edges of the fairway. Striated and white-faced herons, blue cranes and ibis wet their wings in irrigation run-off or bathe in dug-outs after rain. Out to sea you can watch migrating whales, cavorting dolphins and seals. Between the first and the second course there's a small beach, 'Little Bay', that's closed after heavy rain due to asbestos contamination. The Coast Gold Club occupies the same Crown land parcel as Little Bay. In the 1960s a former hospital site was converted into the course using labour from nearby Long Bay Prison. In the busy summer months, the club hires security guards to stand at the edge of the course and stop beach-goers cutting across the fairway. On the other side of the course, property giant Meriton is proposing a high-rise residential development. If the proposal goes through, this golf course will be the main green space for a new suburb with an extra 2000 residents.

Not long after my coffee with Scully, I wait in the lobby of the famous NSW Golf Club. It's two courses down from Little Bay on 59 coastal hectares of Crown land in La Perouse, or Gooriwal, home to the Muru-ora-dial people thousands of years before even the first Scotsman hit a rock over a sand dune with a stick. The lobby has the ambience of an out-of-date luxury hotel: patterned carpet; shabby end tables with lamps, fresh flowers, trophies; prints of colonial gentlemen on the wall; a speaker on the wall playing classic hits. I snicker when Mike and The Mechanics' 'The Living Years' comes on: 'It's too late / when we die / to admit we don't see eye to eye.' The receptionist notices, asks again if I want a glass of water and I politely decline, trying to put her at ease with some golf small talk.

'Oh, I don't play,' she says. 'I haven't got enough time. We have a staff day once a year but otherwise … Do you?' She is utterly unsurprised to find I do not.

My interview is with the club's executive manager, Rob Selley, who worked in a pro-shop while completing his commerce degree in South Africa. He laughs thinly when I suggest he's a lifer. Selley managed the Royal Auckland golf club through an amalgamation with the neighbouring Grange club in 2017. Two 18-hole privately owned clubs became one 27-hole layout with 20 acres sold off for development.

In the bistro, where picture windows take in sweeping views of Botany Bay, Selley lists the environmental and public good the NSW Golf Club does, including community and women's days, and a 30-megalitre dam on site meaning it's rare that they need to access town water supply for irrigation purposes. The NSW Golf Course also works closely with National Parks on native vegetation in the wilds, and on controlled-burning trials. Because they are on Crown land and have an obligation to allow public access, they maintain a walking track that hosts 1500 walkers a year at 'considerable inconvenience' to the game.

I want to talk to Selley partly because I wanted to see inside a club that advertises itself as one of the world's great golfing experiences and regularly makes world top-50 course lists, and partly because it's impossible to find detail on any Crown land lease.

While the 2009 *Government Information (Public Access) Act* establishes a process for the public to access government information, each internal agency decides what's released. To find out lease terms, you need to submit a form that can be rejected, request a review and then an external review. The flashpoint for price transparency is at the point of lease renewal or tender. The information isn't listed publicly, and the only media reporting I can find is a 20-year-old article in *The Sydney Morning Herald* claiming the rent on the entire site of the NSW Golf Club is $40,000 a year while membership costs $10,000, and has a fifteen-year waiting list.

This ignites my inner Carlin. He paces, You're telling me that four club members rent 59 hectares of coastal land in one of the most expensive cities in the world and that's not elite?

Selley corrects the record. Rent, he says, is 'more than four times' $40,000. The waiting list for membership is 'four to five years' and costs somewhere in the 'upper five thousands'. While the club has been at the site since 1926, their current lease runs from 2020 to 2070.

Carlin deadeyes. Thirty-two club members then. It's a mid-sized back-yard party.

Selley is pragmatic about the future of golf. It's a great sport but like all sports it's also big business. Whether any club should continue to exist in its current form needs to be assessed on a case-by-case basis. Some privately owned clubs are a green lung in an otherwise commercial or residentially zoned area and as such need to be protected. Some regional clubs are vital community cultural centres. The NSW Golf Club should exist because paying non-members can play and it's comparable to the best private courses in the world. People come from all over the world to play golf here. He gestures to a table full of grey-haired Americans enjoying lunch and a few frothies after a round.

'These are high net worth tourists who stay in five-star hotels, eat in all the best restaurants, do the bridge climb. And they come here primarily to play this course. This is the jewel in the crown for Sydney.' When I ask him if he has any final remarks, Selley says,

'Well, there will always be people who say golf is a bunch of entitled people using too much land, but I think that, if you start scrutinising all the uses of open spaces ... well, golf is healthy, kids do it. There's a place for golf.'

I suspect that how you feel about the phrase 'jewel in the crown' will be a reasonable predictor of how you feel about the place for golf. In a recent issue of *The Saturday Paper*, Claire G. Coleman argued that in overturning the doctrine of terra nullius, the *Mabo* decision also excluded 'the existence of Crown land on this continent ... The only reason I can think of why Crown land is not being returned to traditional owners is a refusal to give us back what's ours,' Coleman writes. 'Want to prove reconciliation is possible? Return what you have stolen but not used.'

Whether or not golf constitutes *use* probably depends on who you are, your age, income and gender. While it's true that anyone can play golf, only 20% of Australian golf club members are women, with an average age of 64, nine years older than the remaining 80%. There are no reliable statistics on golf club membership and race in Australia.

At a recent forum on First Nations speculative fiction at the University of Sydney, Ellen van Neervan commented on the process of writing their novella 'Water' from the collection *Heat and Light*. It started with walking on country, they said, and then when they sat down to write, country was there waiting for them.

I think about this as I walk the golf courses surrounding my new home. I'm a settler-coloniser walking settler-coloniser country in its most remorseless form. When I sit down to write, it's always there.

●●●

As Selley remarked, not all golf courses have the government support and profitability to survive. Private courses are more vulnerable to declining interest in the sport, the recent challenges of the pandemic, and lucrative offers from developers. Sometimes, critical factors align and something unexpected can happen. Internationally, in Cheshire in Britain and Marin County in the United States, courses have been rewilded to preserve meadow flora species and revive endangered salmon, respectively. In Australia, the first stage of transformation of Melbourne's Elsternwick Golf Club into a nature park reserve and wetlands preservation area has begun. Brisbane's 64-hectare Victoria Park Golf Course is also being reallocated, with more than 10,000 trees, including 80 native species planted since the last round of golf in June 2021. Other plans for the site include a giant treehouse with city views, elevated walkways and Indigenous history areas.

At the edge of the world heritage–listed greater Blue Mountains area in New South Wales, on Gundungurra and Darug land, sits the former Katoomba golf course. The club, which went into liquidation in 2013, occupies land extending out from a gully, with an ancient peat swamp at its lowest ebb. Water flows from this site into the Katoomba reservoir and the water supply of greater Sydney. Now, the stripped pro-shop hosts the office of the Blue Mountains Planetary Health Initiative, a council initiative 'with a strong vision to grow planetary health for the whole city, for all life, and for future generations'. When I talk to Lis Bastian, senior program lead for the initiative, she states their goal is nothing less than to catalyse transition 'from the Anthropocene and into the Symbioscene'. It's not language I've heard council representatives use before. 'Humans are a part of nature and all species have rights. This is a great site to demonstrate that,' Bastion tells me.

A confluence of factors made this possible. The land is council owned. The Blue Mountains City Council is so committed to sustainability that in 2021 it became the first local government body to adopt the 'rights of nature' as a foundational principle. Greens Councillor Brent Hoare declared 'a paradigm shift, where nature is recognised as having its own legal right to exist, regenerate and evolve'. Through this remit, the council has been able to allocate funds to buy the former clubhouse. Finally, recent bushfires mean no-one is lobbying to develop the site for residential housing, or a hospital, both of which are needed by the local human community.

The site will host a convergence of university researchers, creative people, traditional owners and the broader community, I'm told. But Bastion is careful to avoid any murmur of culture war. 'It's systemic thinking that needs to change rather than individuals. We need to rethink and redesign our systems to be more supportive of life. We need to be gentle on ourselves for the mistakes we've made as a species,' she says. 'Golf courses have ignored country for a small group of people to have enjoyment. On the other hand, perhaps this was a good thing. Here, water can still be absorbed into the soil, compared to if it was covered with built structures. And some of those people may have played golf because they loved nature.'

Bastion goes on to describe the weedy brambles at the base of the gully. A group of land care volunteers broke through this dense net of blackberries and lantana to discover pristine bushland behind it. 'The weeds protected the bush,' Bastion says, smiling.

Before the interview, I walk the former fairway looking to plunder colour for my story but melancholy creeps in around me with the dense fog. The grass is still carefully clipped even if it no longer constitutes a bright, outrage-inducing green. Pines and ash trees. Thistle, clover, brambles, the sound of nearby construction. It's hard to imagine this liminal space will ever again resemble the nearby heritage-listed Blue Mountains National Park with its vast, misty peaks, deep gullies and native rainforest. Here then, is my depleted civic imagination. Out for a walk on country that's not mine. I squint and strain my vision. At best I see play equipment, picnic tables, a more sustainable sports field and everything we can never get back.

After talking to Bastion, I don't let my gaze linger on any of that. The space is vast, an open invitation to know less about how things are. If you walk on this country you are looking at a different way to see.

• • •

The Waves

The sea whispered to me
a sad angular cry. Uncomfortable
from the fish, rocks, and plastic
inside of it.
And the placid bodies frozen—
        bastardised from buoyancy.

After a while I step closer.
White tunnels wash over
my feet,
and the world quickly becomes silent.
A deep null in my eardrum, but for now
you can see straight through the sheen of blue
to the generous earth
and the smell of chamomile
reprises a joy that feels newborn.

        Your hands

        a gentle bulldozer,
holding me above water, whilst pushing
inside of me
to the white roses I was gifted;
floating just below
the surface.

Louis
Campbell

Louis Campbell is a
Kaurna Yerta–based
poet and musician.
He is recognised for
his contributions to
the underground
music scene. His
introspective
writing style draws
from nature and is
influenced by late-
modernist writers.

My Year as a Salaried Artist

Jennifer Mills

Jennifer Mills is an author, editor and critic based on Kaurna Yerta (Adelaide). Her latest novel is *The Airways*.

Late in 2021, I attended a conference in Tarntanya (Adelaide) organised by a collective of thinkers called Reset Arts and Culture. I listened particularly closely to a panel about labour and the arts that was chaired by Vitalstatistix director Emma Webb. I'd been writing about these issues, and against the backdrop of the ongoing pandemic, discussions had taken on a new urgency.

As Alison Pennington and Ben Eltham wrote in their 2021 report *Creativity in Crisis*:

> With an eroding and unstable funding base, the arts and cultural sector has been reduced to endless, resource-intensive, short-term grant cycles and philanthropic dependency. Meanwhile, the diminishing pool of available public arts funds has increasingly been directed away from areas of greatest need, such as grassroots arts organisations and independent artists ... Permanent 'good' jobs in the arts have become even more scarce, and precarious work in its myriad forms has exploded (including casual work, gigs, contracting, and freelancing). The consequence of this policy failure is a once-vibrant ecosystem of cultural production in Australia, fed from the grassroots up, has been partly dismantled.[1]

1
Alison Pennington and Ben Eltham, *Creativity in Crisis: Rebooting Australia's Arts and Entertainment Sector after COVID*, Centre for Future Work at the Australia Institute, July 2021.

I stopped to speak with Webb about the panel afterwards. A few weeks later, she called me with an unusual offer. In response to the urgent needs of the sector, the state government had set up a special fund for the direct employment of artists. Would I be interested in a salaried role as artist in residence at Vitalstatistix in 2022? I did not hesitate.

Making its home in the old Waterside Workers Hall, firmly part of the Yerta Bulti (Port Adelaide) community, 'Vitals' is a beloved radical institution that was founded by feminists in 1984, partly in response to the marginalisation of women artists. It now operates as a theatre, a community hub, a place for experimentation and work in development, and a site for progressive public dialogue.

I'd been to Vitalstatistix several times as an audience member. I'd also been there as an artist, collaborating with Alex Kelly in the shopfront in 2018 on her project 'The Things We Did Next' as part of the organisation's annual hothouse, Adhocracy. I admire the way that Vitals encourages experimentation, not just in theatre, dance and other forms of art, but also in methodology: for many artists, it provides space to expand and adapt our ways of working.

Although Vitals has employed artists in residence before, this proposal was different. I don't make theatre, and I wouldn't be producing performance art. Instead, I would be working with the organisation over ten months, with a focus on ideas, documentation and reflection. As part of Vitals' long-range inquiry 'Bodies of Work', I would be able to continue my writing on labour issues and look closely at the working conditions of artists. In the grant application, Webb wrote:

> This proposal ... responds to pressing arts sector issues of precarity and sole trading, the case for salaried artists and resurgence of 'company' models, and the need to see more artists directly employed by, and therefore embedded within the everyday life of, arts organisations. Rather than splitting a grant like this amongst project-based artists fees, we are proposing to work deeply with one employed artist, and in a way that could inform our programming and engagement of artists beyond 2022.

If I could make myself a case study in the direct employment of artists, I reasoned, I could use the experience to advocate for and organise with others. At the very least, I told myself, I'll get an essay out of it.

'I have a sort of communist aversion to labour,' writes Elena Gomez in her contribution to the *Sydney Review of Books*' anthology on writing life, *Open Secrets*.[2] Gomez describes poetry as 'my animal rest'. I can relate; writing is an escape from alienated drudgery. It's a gift, a pleasure and a privilege to do this work; it's also my profession, and I have to eat.

I've been a full-time writer for fifteen years, supporting my creative practice with freelancing. I'm used to the hustle of short-term gigs and multiple projects. I'm an established, mid-career novelist, with five books out and a respectable collection of award shortlistings. It looks and sometimes feels like success, but fiction generates less than one-third of my income.

I usually make $30,000 to $40,000 a year, working 40-hour weeks. I achieved the dubious accomplishment of becoming a full-time writer by living in my car for more than a year when I started. I do not recommend this career pathway.

It does help to live cheaply. The latest national survey found that the average writer makes $18,200 from their work.[3] The Melbourne Institute calculates the Henderson poverty line at around $32,000/year.[4] The minimum wage now sits at $42,255.20, if one is employed full-time, but of course most $21.38/hour jobs are insecure and temporary. Australia has one of the highest levels of insecure work in the OECD. Most of the new jobs created since the pandemic have been insecure. According to the ACTU, there were more than a million independent contractors in Australia in 2020, 2.3 million casuals and a further 400,000 on fixed-term contracts.[5] That makes more than one-quarter of the workforce insecure, by a narrow definition.

In the arts and culture, it's almost half. According to *Creativity in Crisis*, 'in February 2021, around 45% of all employees in arts and recreation services were in casual roles

2
Elena Gomez, 'Secret Poems' in Catriona Menzies-Pike (ed.), *Open Secrets: Essays on the Writing Life*, Sydney Review of Books, 2022.

3
Paul Crosby, David Throsby and Jan Zwar, *National Survey of Australian Book Authors*, Macquarie University, 2022.

4
Poverty Lines: Australia, Melbourne Institute, 2022.

5
Australian Council of Trade Unions, *Insecure Work in Australia*, submission to the Senate Select Committee on Job Security, 2021.

(defined as employment without access to basic paid leave entitlements, like holiday and sick leave, and superannuation)'. Artists and writers are categorised as sole traders, and as small businesses we absorb many of the costs of our labour (studio space, materials, administration, communications). We have no sick leave or protection if injured. We are under-unionised and lack the kind of organising power that might change these conditions for the better.

•••

In his 2011 book *The Precariat*, economist Guy Standing observes a fragmentation of the traditional workforce and the growing prevalence of precarious, gig-based employment. By Standing's definition, the precariat is characterised by multiple forms of insecurity, including a lack of income protection (such as an award wage), a lack of career progression, no protection against illness, injury or abuse, and an absence of organising power.[6]

6
Guy Standing, *The Precariat: The New Dangerous Class,* Bloomsbury, 2011.

Artists and other creatives align with this model of the precariat. In particular, we share the supplicant status that Standing argues is the precariat's defining feature, a relationship of dependence on others for work. Because of that dependence, foiled progression can become a source of shame. Talented artists are driven away when young by the prospect of lifelong insecurity, or when older, by the experience of it. The hustle of chasing work, applying for grants, marketing yourself and surviving on your wits can be gruelling.

There are ways in which we do not fit Standing's definition. Artists and writers have more control over our labour than most precarious workers; within financial constraints, we can be selective about what we do. We often have a strong sense of identity as artists, even if our art is not our main source of income. There are numerous advantages to self-employment over waged work that make it desirable, such as flexibility and autonomy.

But with low public funding, heavy competition for few gigs, devaluation of creative work as either 'elitist' or 'bludging' (but never both at once), mirages of commercial success that encourage exploitative practices, short-term contracts or handshake agreements, and so on, insecurity is baked in to the way most artists are working. Gig work has an impact on our incomes, but also on the kind of work we make: it structures what we can afford to say, who we can afford to piss off, and whether we will sustain our practice into maturity. Many do not expect financial stability from their art; some achieve it with second and third jobs, inherited wealth, a partner's stable income, or temporarily, by entering the lottery of grants and prizes. For those without such supports, flexibility and autonomy are hard-won.

•••

It is a grotesque understatement to say that the pandemic's effects were unevenly distributed. People in secure jobs and owner-occupied housing tended to save money. For others, rents shot up and incomes went backwards. Many freelancers were unable to access JobKeeper payments. Without leave, we couldn't afford time off if we became ill or had to quarantine or care for someone. When the Morrison government offered people the option to draw on their superannuation to get through it, freelancers could only laugh.

The tsunami of cancellations and border closures that swept across arts and culture in 2020–22 had an uncountable effect on our livelihoods. Everyone has horror stories about work from this period: cancelled exhibitions, stranded performers, last-minute digital pivots. When we could work, gigs put us at risk. Despite this, artists showed enormous solidarity to others, offering free entertainment to those in lockdown, raising awareness and contributing to mutual aid.

I was able to keep working, but I took significant hits. I'd scheduled the release of my novel *The Airways* for August 2021, a month after my planned return to Australia. Locked out of the country by border closures and flight cancellations, I launched my novel on YouTube from a kitchen table in Italy, while bookshops in Australia remained closed. I was lucky: I already had readers. It was worse for those in the early stages of their careers.

ilostmygig.com collected data on lost income, surveying 3000 performers, musicians and crew—a small subset of a much bigger workforce. In the 2021–22 financial year, respondents reported $94 million in lost income from 32,000 cancelled gigs; 99% of respondents had no income protection or event cancellation insurance. The survey didn't cover visual arts, literature, craft or other fields.[7] It is impossible to know how many artists and writers have left their practice as a result of these experiences. Anecdotally, people are going back to their day jobs in droves.

Labor has recognised the crisis and begun to address it with a new national cultural policy, aptly named Revive. The policy acknowledges that artists are workers, and should have a right to some security, protection from harassment, and fair pay. New measures such as the establishment of the Centre for Arts and Entertainment Workplaces (since renamed the Creative Workplaces Council) promise to protect our rights. Labor is quieter on superannuation for contractors, access to Australia's notoriously low unemployment benefits, and secure employment for artists. Some have argued that arts organisations have a responsibility to address these challenges directly.

This was the message from Lauren Carroll Harris in her essay 'The Case for Salaried Artists', published in *Kill Your Darlings* in 2021: 'The medium to large organisations and major arts institutions, museums and galleries—many of which benefit from multi-year funding, from both state and federal sources—have to take the lead in restoring some stability to artists' work by modelling the alternative,' she wrote.[8] In practice, it's the smaller institutions that are listening.

• • •

The residency is a shock to my system. Having a regular paycheck is exhilarating. I am instantly afraid I will get used to it. I realise that I have been experiencing the momentum

7
I Lost My Gig, <ilostmygig.com>.

8
Lauren Carroll Harris, 'The Case for Salaried Artists', *Kill Your Darlings*, August 2021.

of insecure work in my body: a metabolic, chronic and possibly addictive form of stress. Can I afford to let that go?

I'm employed for two days a week for ten months. During a historic housing crisis, it's a relief to know that I will be okay for the year. After tax, the residency pays $833 per fortnight. I could live on that, but I'd be paying 58% of my income on rent. I don't stop feeling stressed, and I don't stop freelancing.

It's not just the money that provides relief. It's also the structure, the sense of support into the midterm future. After the disruptions of the past three years, I am able to plan. I have leave entitlements and superannuation. Ordinarily, I have to argue a case for super with each 'employer' I write for. Last year, I received about 30% of the super I was entitled to—an increase on previous years.

A salary changes my relationship to time. Employed for fifteen hours a week, I like the idea of working set hours, instead of being paid per piece. In most of my work, income has little relationship with time. A good book advance, for example, might add up to $3 an hour.

The residency should give structure to my working week, but it soon becomes clear that the role is not going to work that way. I still have to juggle other deadlines, travel and commitments. There are weeks when Vitals will take up all my time, including some weekends and evenings. There are quiet weeks when I can't do much. Having a sense of the hours helps gauge the commitment, but I retain much of the autonomy and flexibility that I like about freelancing.

Performance work treats time very differently. I am used to a slow, iterative practice, with long delays before publication. To an outsider, performance seems to come together in an ephemeral burst. I rarely show my work in progress, and I admire the way these artists invite observation so early, are able to take sustenance and learn from invisible forces and subtle cues. I wonder how a salaried-artist model might support or hinder that temporality and collaboration.

• • •

'If a basic income were achieved tomorrow, it would almost certainly be set below poverty levels and simply act as a handout to companies,' wrote Nick Srnicek and Alex Williams in their 2015 book *Inventing the Future: Postcapitalism and a World without Work*.[9] A Basic Income (BI) is often characterised simply as a tool to alleviate poverty, but it can have more radical outcomes.

One of the arguments for a BI is that it would pay people to do the unpaid work they are already doing: care work, community work, land management, mutual aid, cultural labour and so on. Instead of putting downward pressure on wages, a BI should also redress the power imbalance of employment, freeing up time to organise so we can advocate for ourselves as workers. The unconditionality and society-wide nature of a Universal Basic Income (UBI) are essential to realising its full potential; small trials can't fully explore these large-scale effects.

9
Nick Srnicek and Alex Williams, *Inventing the Future: Postcapitalism and a World without Work*, Verso, 2015.

Artists are a good testing ground for BI. Support between gigs can provide a scaffold, separating creative practice from the hustle. Artists tend to be open to experimentation and are well placed to share observations and reflect on successes and failures. Programs such as Ireland's Basic Income for the Arts pilot scheme reflect a growing interest in this model, particularly in the so-called 'post-pandemic' context. Some of the many regional-scale BI experiments in the United States, such as those in San Francisco, California and Saint Paul, Minnesota, are artist-targeted. Canada's Basic Income Coalition has strong leadership from artists and arts organisations. Though popular with creatives in Australia, UBI remains far from mainstream discourse.

'Many submissions to the National Cultural Policy consultation process raised remuneration, including a basic income for artists,' Revive acknowledges. But that's as much as it is willing to say on the subject. If and when artists push harder for it, I suspect an Ireland-style BI trial in Australia is more likely to come from state or local government.

Among other things, such a trial would address the exclusion of artists from unemployment benefits. Current regimes of mutual obligation don't recognise creative work, making artists look for work outside their profession while ignoring the work they are already doing. Aotearoa had an arts dole in the 1980s, under prime minister Helen Clark. Labor has flirted with the idea in the past, but the new cultural policy only promises to 'develop information' about it.

While there is a lack of consensus on BI, a salaried residency model can illustrate its benefits. A residency is not a Basic Income, but neither is it a traditional employer–employee relationship. As artist in residence, I am undertaking a contract to work and to complete a series of tasks, but I retain a high degree of autonomy. Like a BI, the residency supports the unpaid or underpaid organising work I already do: attending meetings, writing articles, conducting advocacy. Unlike a grant or fellowship, I find I am spending less time on my creative practice.

Although a lack of clarity around the role and expectations is challenging at first, the indeterminacy of the model proves to be one of its greatest assets. In time, I see it as neither a job nor a BI, but a collaboration, with common goals and overlapping interests. Not being paid per project or fee-for-service means that I can adapt and explore. Within a simple salaried structure, there is a lot of flexibility and possibility; like a daily routine, security enhances creativity.

• • •

Vitals legitimises and lends wisdom to my organising work. The year 2022 is a decisive one for freelance organising in MEAA's Media section, which has lately shifted to a much better understanding of the needs and challenges of freelance workers. In February 2022, the Freelance Charter is launched at the union's biggest ever online meeting. More than 500 freelance members endorse the charter, which sets out basic pay and conditions and provides a mechanism for freelancers to bargain collectively with our employers. We begin the daunting task of trying to bring individual publications on board.

In March, the South Australian state election delivers Labor a solid majority. In May, Labor also takes power federally, with a record number of seats won by the Greens. The new Arts Minister, Tony Burke, is also the Minister for Employment and Workplace Relations. After a decade of brutal cuts to arts funding, we have an opportunity for lasting change.

Also in March, I write about the Greens' Liveable Income Guarantee and what it could mean for artists in a piece for *Overland* titled 'A Liveable Income Guarantee should support artists—and artists should support a UBI'. In May, I publish another piece on *Meanjin*'s blog, 'It's time ... to demand fair pay in the arts', calling for structural changes to arts funding, including making funding conditional on fair pay.

These two pieces have a combined length of 3000 words. At union rates, I would be paid $3000, but no-one is paid union rates in the arts. Instead, this work earns me less than $300. The residency income gives me time to research and write about how funding models are failing. In Australian literature, being paid twice is almost as good as being paid properly.

Soon after the election, Burke opens the consultation process for the new cultural policy. I write my own submission and share it widely, then contribute as an author to Reset's group submission. I attend Burke's speaking tour and read up on what other organisations and peak bodies are asking for.

At state level I speak about the conditions of my work at a 'Meet the Minister' event organised by the Arts Industry Council of South Australia. I say the bit about success and the Henderson poverty line. Several people, including salaried arts workers, thank me afterwards for my frankness, with varying degrees of surprise. I wonder about this for days afterwards. Don't salaried arts workers already know how broke most artists are? We make plenty of art about it. But the experiences of working artists are rarely prominent in policy discussions. A regular income means I have time to contribute.

In August, I co-organise an event called Artists Organise! along with Sam Whiting, lecturer in creative industries at UniSA. The event brings unions and artists together to talk about the issues we face and how we can work together. The event connects people working on these issues at the grassroots, with representatives from literature, visual arts, music, games, theatre and retail. It takes time for us to organise the venue, the Welcome, invitations, travel, accommodation, facilitators, poster art, live-streaming, transcription and publicity, and to pay everyone properly. Unlike writing, I recognise all this as labour I would not do for free.

As artist in residence, I also contribute directly to the work at Vitals in a variety of visible and less visible ways. I conduct and publish interviews with artists, contribute to strategic planning, participate in the curation of 2022's Adhocracy program, hang around and listen or watch while artists test their ideas, offer my perspective when invited. Part of the reason we don't organise better in the arts is because every project is different. The conditions of our work vary a great deal between and even within art forms. But speaking with artists about the demands of what they're making, I'm struck by commonalities in how we navigate the tensions between paid work and art work, collaboration and friendship, structured labour and play.

I take my role seriously, but there is room for less formal and more playful responses to the work at Vitalstatistix. I'm dazzled by The Rabble's production *YES*, but I don't have critical distance; I compose a creative response, a collage poem that draws on the work's themes of violence, consent, power and complicity. Later in the year I write a grant application for a project I call 'Sick Leave'. I propose to use a single $50,000 Australia Council project grant to pay two days' sick leave to 90 artists, drawing attention to precarity and insecurity by writing and speaking publicly about this. Unsurprisingly, it doesn't get funded, so the publication of the unsuccessful application becomes the work:

> *Sick Leave* is a performance, intervention, and inquiry into the nature of art as labour and the relationship between creativity, economics and rest. This project asks: how do we care for and support working artists during a time of funding scarcity and the structural devaluation of art as labour?

In September, Adhocracy returns, with twelve projects in residence at Waterside and Harts Mill over four very busy days. I attend a showing of every work in progress and manage to interview almost all the artists about their work during the weekend or in the days following. There's rarely a chance for this scale of reflection, and I'm heartened by the honesty of the artists and their appetite for change. 'Art in the works' is published in *Artlink* in January 2023. The essay concludes: 'Artists, beyond exhausted, are reaching for transformation.'

Crisis demands change. Looking back, I can see this same reaching in myself. I've been looking for a more sustainable way of working, a practice that balances plenty with animal rest.

The year 2022 was one of change for Vitalstatistix, too. After the pandemic's many additional pressures, the organisation has been reflecting on its ways of working, coping with burnout and staffing changes. The residency's process of active, participatory reflection is of benefit throughout the year, both formally and informally.

The expansion of my capacity to organise and advocate has extended beyond the employment contract. I am already finding ways to continue that work: becoming a director of the Australian Society of Authors, joining the Reset Arts and Culture collective, standing in solidarity with unionised booksellers, and working on campaigns to end fossil-fuel sponsorship in the arts. Most of this work is unpaid.

While the residency took time away from my fiction, it also fortified my sense of its purpose. With a friend, I recently joked: 'Can't decide if these things take away from my creative practice or are becoming my creative practice.' Really, I am happiest in the place where this distinction is unclear. In my week, activism and writing are experienced as competing demands, but over a lifetime, they are simply two ways of making change.

The residency is a public act, and I remain responsible for sharing the experience. In writing this, I hope that other organisations are encouraged to test and implement forms of direct employment for artists. With exceptions such as Alana Hunt and

Fiona Kelly McGregor's residencies at Carriageworks in 2021, the employment model is rarely funded. More organisations, not only in the arts, should be willing to put an artist on the payroll and see what happens.

There are risks inherent to the model, given its dependence on collaboration, but those are offset by the nature of an employment contract. It may be slightly costlier than working on a project basis, but the Vitals team saw no additional administrative burden, and flexibility meant that I was able to carry some of the communications load during the year. The length of the relationship facilitated richness and depth. The grant required us to identify clear outcomes, which we provided and have fulfilled, but the real benefit of this model is its adaptability.

Precarity is harming culture at the roots. To build solidarity in the arts, we need to admit the inequities between freelance artists and salaried arts workers; but we should also attend to common ground. Artists and arts workers share a culture of overwork and a reliance on goodwill. Witnessing each other's labour as colleagues is essential to improving our lot.

I've returned to full-time freelancing in 2023, but I see my working life in a different way. I don't want to spend the rest of my career hustling for badly paid gigs, on a treadmill of prolificacy and promises. My writing practice has never been very attached to money-making, but maybe it doesn't need to be about individual success or failure either. Belonging to an organisation for a time has helped me to make space in a community, and to understand that secure work is also a collective practice.

•••

In April 2023, the Department of Employment and Workplace Relations updated its advice regarding mutual obligation requirements for freelancers, including writers, artists and musicians. Activities such as pitching stories, applying for grants, attending auditions and contacting publishers or performance venues can be counted towards the new points target. Unpaid writing, art-making or music still does not count as 'work'.

Snow Gums

Snow gums at dusk after the first
Or second snowfall of the season, summer
Shrinking to the yellow liver on the big middle
Tree's middle. Purple and green, lavender mist
On the outer. We bought it on our honeymoon,
The second cheapest picture in the gallery.
The proprietor was a lewd who'd done a portrait
Of Charles Waterhouse in his chambers
With two crouching bikini models.
You were shocked. You love winter.
I pretended to be impressed but gentlemen prefer
Landscapes. It (the snow gums) hangs in the bedroom.
How he gets his trees behind from misty trunks
To off-tint smudges a hundred yards behind.
It's the light, as they say, he gets so right.
The view and the distance, the grass poking through,
What will clearly melt before the big freeze.
The snow caught in the crook of a limb,
The quiet of someone walking just beyond the frame.

Lucas
Smith

Lucas Smith is from
Gippsland and
California. His work has
appeared in *Southerly*,
*Australian Poetry
Journal*, *The Rialto* and
many other journals.

Untold Histories: The Last Days of Major Sir Thomas Mitchell

Belinda
Paxton

Belinda Paxton is
currently enrolled in
a Master of Creative
Writing. She has
published work in
the *Grieve Anthology*,
*The Mascara Literary
Review* and *Meniscus*.
Her work 'Clinging
to Space Hardware'
was runner up in the
2019 Deborah Cass
Writing Prize.

Mitchell: 35.21°S, 149.49°E. Light industrial suburb in the Australian Capital Territory. Named after Major Sir Thomas Mitchell, surveyor-general, explorer, legislator, mass murderer. See also: Major Mitchell Cockatoo, Mitchell Hopping Mouse, Mitchell Grass. Mitchell (locality in Queensland), Mitchell (Victorian local government area), the Mitchell Highway, the Mitchell River.

3 October 1855: Each day he waits for me, the groundsman. That's why we watch each other. Me here, propped up on my pillows like a fish lying on the bank, mouth opening and closing slowly. He on his chair under the window with the light spilling over his hair and his arms, which are crossed over his chest, and over his lap and his glinting boots, which are planted like flags on the floor of my bedroom.

I pull at my shirt when the breathing is hard and strew the sheets about. The groundsman has been brought inside to replace the house-girls who are frightened by my floundering and my bared chest. The girls call him by his surname, Daron, which I first misheard with a start as 'Charon', the ferryman. He is strong enough to hold me down and to lift me up. He is not afraid. I see him smiling sometimes, over there by the window. Waiting to take me.

Yet when he leaves me, I am all at sea. For then the woman comes to me. The woman who, through all these miserable years, through my colleagues' rumours and hateful whispering about her, through their smug malice, I had somehow forgotten.

She appears in the lull between breaths. I have never seen her face. Always, I am above and behind her, looking down on her naked back. I don't understand her posture, hunched over with her shoulders pushed far forwards like wings. So disturbing. She shudders to some strange regular beat. The brown skin gleams. She is wet. And all around the landscape moves and is alive with the tea-trees rattling, the breeze raking through the dry grass. Above us both, the woman and me, the deep arch of the sky rises and is silent. I am filled with terror. My throat constricts, my heart hammers. It is the moment before. I would cry out but my breath is too scarce. God help me, I need my groundsman.

4 October: The groundsman is all at ease with my body. As my weight falls away, he shifts me easily. Lifting me off the commode he says, 'Your body forgets its high station, Sir.' Smirking. Once I would have beaten him soundly. Or had him beaten. Now I understand that his derision comes with the sweet chafe of his fingertips, his pinching grip, the cool cloth he slides into my creases. I am as tender as a fish's belly. The infection forms a sour crust in the corners of my mouth, which he swabs with the cloth. I suck at the damp fabric as he moves it over my lips. 'You'd like water?' he enquires innocently, eyebrows raised. He squeezes the cloth and one or two soiled drops fall into my parched throat. The shadow of a smile passes across his features.

Still my yearning for him increases with each minute narrowing of my airways. In the stillest part of the night when fear is my only companion, I whisper to myself, 'I must not panic, I must not panic. In the morning, the groundsman will come and wipe me clean.' He is free with my possessions also. Replacing the basin on my nightstand, he notices my bible and picks it up. He glances over at me, grinning. 'I can't read,' he says and replaces it but not before feeling carefully between his thumb and forefinger the silk ribbon that I use to mark its pages.

If my family were here—but they have abandoned me to him. I hear them moving around downstairs but I cannot call out and they don't come of their own accord. Not even my wife, though she must have loved me once. I recall a moment before the woman, when my wife and I had just married. Both of us were on the white sheets in England, lit up by the soft light. Her naked arm was flung across my chest, dimpled and white, and her laughter fluttered in the curve of my neck. Looking across us both, I saw that the morning light had fallen on her body and that her skin was beautiful.

After the woman, storms formed inside me and there is this moment: my wife is standing flush against the wall in the dining room and her face is turned away from mine and her expression of startlement is so profound I see only the whites of her eyes. My hand is pressed down hard on her throat. Crockery clatters to the floor. Behind us, our children are standing up from the table and shrieking. But for Dicky who, though he is no higher than my knee, has squeezed between me and my wife and is hammering with his small fists against my thighs. His tiny body is stiffened against my shins by the force of his screaming and when I look down upon his upturned howling face, I note with dim surprise that all three of us—me, my wife and

Dicky—are standing in a puddle. It seeps from beneath my wife's skirts and spreads slowly across the floorboards. My lovely lady has pissed herself.

Last night I saw the woman again and I saw that her strange shuddering is made by her own gait. She is running and water is scattering all around her and she is lifting her knees up very high, so very high it seems they might touch her ears. Is that possible? Only a demon could run like that.

Grunting, the groundsman leans across and hauls me further up on the pillows. With the movement, he shifts the air and then I breathe it in along with the warmth from his body and minute fragments of his sweat and breath. He smells like a hare or some other form of game. I turn my head into the crook of his arm. The coarse fabric of his shirt rasps my nose and lips. I open my mouth to inhale more of him.

5 October: He stands at my nightstand and takes up the ribbon from my bible. I watch him with my chest heaving like an ocean. He smiles at me. Keeping his eyes on mine, he unbuttons his shirt and tucks the ribbon inside. It's a hanging offence. 'Fair,' he says, referring to a fair recompense for his work though it's possible he means 'fare'. He is right to feel free. Only my eyes follow him, flat as a fish's. I am drowning in slow increments. Last night, when he was gone, the woman came in her entirety. Now I remember. We came upon them at the river; they had been tailing us. They wanted us gone. I thought I'd show them what's what. I thought I'd show them I wasn't frightened.

The woman started running first. Coming upon her on my horse, high above her, I noticed her hunched posture and saw the reason. Flesh and shoulder bones used as protection, body curled around something precious. She gripped to her breast a small child. Her legs were horrific machines, knees lifted high above the water so that she could step down into it. Her mouth, seen in profile, was a rectangle, lips curled back from her gums and teeth. It was in the shape of a scream but she was entirely silent, every fibre in her being focused on only one thing—more air. I knew in a moment what was in her mind—the fastest way through the river, that she might get her child to the other side before she is shot. I only ever saw her side-on. It was all I could bear. And she remained unseen to me after I pulled the trigger.

How it was told: afterwards, we journeyed out from the river until we could no longer hear the keening. We lit a fire, for it was getting dark. We stood around the fire together. Convict crew and gentlemen stood together like brothers. We agreed, 'They are savages. Little more than animals.' We all agreed and we said it was a necessary thing. I walked among them and we told each other how it had happened. We told each other the same story. We fixed it in our heads the same way. I walked among them and we talked. We talked and talked and agreed, and told the story until I was sick to my stomach.

Then this from my dunderheaded surveyor's assistant: 'Anyway. They're too dead to tell their own stories.' He said it and then it could not be unsaid. The next day we beat him until he could barely stand.

The groundsman leans across me and I clutch at his shirt, bunching the linen in my hands as once I clung to my mother's apron. Each breath dies in me and waits. I am again in my mother's kitchen with dripping spattering on the stove and the smell of paraffin and burnt fat in the air. His hands are dry at the nape of my neck as he lifts me off the pillows. Sitting up like this, I can see my mother at the stove. Her back is to me. Her shoulders shake as she stirs the pan and she hums a tune I knew as a child: 'Sing a song of sixpence, a pocket full of rye / Four and twenty naughty boys baked in a pie.'

He takes the pillows away so that I am flat on the mattress. With a palm against my forehead, he says, 'You're burning.'

The light in my mother's kitchen is from an oil lamp that hangs from the rafters. Shadows swing like oars on the ceiling. He slides his palm over my face until it is clamped over my mouth, and with the fingers of his other hand he pinches my nostrils. I long for my mother to turn from the stove and see me. He says, 'It's too late.' Each breathless heave is a stroke that carries me further and further across the water. I flail on the mattress. I need more time. Tell him. My mother might turn and peer through the thick darkness. She might see me, her own child, weighed down by my unseen crimes. I might yet be forgiven. I might yet die free of shame. Oh God. It is some sort of legacy.

•••

outtakes nine to thirty-eight

Cynthia
Troup

Cynthia Troup (she/
her) lives on Dja Dja
Wurrung Country.
Her creative work
is often concerned
with the inherent
musicality of language,
and the allusive
richness of fragments.
<cynthiatroup.com>

Through the chase-and-grab of British Bulldog at lunchtime__unchosen for the centre *it* gang__mauled by shame I keep running in the small body given to me so__scared of the half-hearted tackle that says we know you don't count for the boys' winning side__you're never *it* just plain OUT__In a family of girls I still hope I'm like my father__

I run how I can at nine__by now the faithful given form's begun to be parcelled OUT__all my stubborn sisters and me trying to be and become__what we're not__In headband and short shorts the new PE teacher tests one day how we run__the biomechanics__Each Grade Four in turn sprints toward Mister Crean__I chase me on rough asphalt__in the short body given to me she crashes past his elbow biro clipboard__it's clear you can't run he announces to the class__whole__class__breath won't__be caught sweat creeps OUT__clings to her face everywhere I see laughter__hear no difference between able and allowed you__can't run__but after school there are tennis lessons with the slender Brownells__

Shoes with grief in them__Go on maybe every test is a trap__line up__again too close to the net__What's the end of competition?__

Brownish spots bloom on my schooldress__Me and the given rounding form fall OUT__dog eat dog running on willpower I stalk a mirror of her__no clear thought or feeling about the final shape of success though about__how to belong these holey bones to it__

Slick months of calorie counts and scale readings were wildly OUT__the surface body I judge find wanting__dear wanting is pent for strict bedrest in Ward 21__a room opposite Reception__alone and she's *not* to be conversed with__My father writes__right: either you make every effort to eat more or you threaten the chances of being OUT__by Christmas we want you home with us__

One nightshift nurse does speak with me__When she strips the bed I stand__hopping leg to leg in the ground of her goodwill__jog of voice sway of feeling cue here I exist!__She figures me a fan of the dating quiz show *Perfect Match* hey__you get the compere's codeword for sex is romance? Oh__

And none of me gets I could press for news of Martina__her latest grand slam__Miss Navratilova who knows she knows the game inside OUT__A letter the same week adds but maybe you've OUTgrown the holiday pantomimes__At fourteen and scant on all sides I__don't yet understand that yes if true *if*__true is dead-simply a secret of love__

Instead of the worst something saner with grace__furred strong and lithe__gains the centre *it* place in me__Gradually__OUTpacing shame__

Snug café clatter sounds harsh and high-pitched__like a dog (not a child) in despair I think__and scan for my mother__Having guessed the blood obvious hasn't been__this lunchtime I for us needs must declare Alice and me we're lovers since last August Ma__

Her jaw tilts belly clenches I'm sensing higher up in mine and__sip water__game set and match a grown daughter's OUT and OUT__lost favour she never knew she had__Our table empty but for pepper and salt__two pairs of hands wait apart__

It's a Friday midyear after orchid season and Alice's calm when I asked to kiss her eyes__sure bless nowise out of the blue__Ma doesn't accept they you can be real__mutters God I have to tell your father and__what happens now? Who we are is happening always beginning comes the reply__maybe at thirty-eight I'm across the difference between able and allowed__

D'you remember smash happy Ma__how nothing in the body's a hard straight line?__Loneliness in marriage is where the next breath takes her__dashed free of the net we just listen raw__

Tears later with ourself I run__night run quiet and dream the Brownells my sisters__all edgy unique too early flattened OUT__the strain of learnt hope__Depths ever faithful the given body lets us give to become being whole at life and lucky__ swing arms open in their own grammar __ greet the playground full willing __ rise turn bristle as if the light __ possibility __

distinct enough

Foot Notes

Melanie
Pryor

Melanie Pryor lives
on Kaurna Yerta. Her
non-fiction has been
published in *The New
York Times*, *Meanjin*,
Southerly, *Overland*
and more. She has a
PhD in creative writing.

breunloch	dangerous sinking bog that may be bright green and grassy **Gaelic**	
brochan	miry soft ground (literally 'porridge') **Gaelic**	
carr	boggy or ferny copse **northern English**	
clachan sinteag	stepping stones across boggy areas of moor **Gaelic**	
currach	bog, marsh **Irish**	
curhagh-craaee	quagmire **Manx**	

—Robert Macfarlane, *Landmarks*

A few days before I flew from Australia to travel alone through Scotland for three months, my eye caught on a book behind the counter of a book shop: *Landmarks* by the British nature writer Robert Macfarlane. The blue-and-white cover looked like a wood cut. I asked the assistant for the book, and opened it to a glossary of words under the title 'Lights, Hazes, Mists and Fogs'. I mouthed the words listed there: *brim'skud*, from Shetland, was the smoke-like haze that rises from breaking waves. *Maril'd*, also from Shetland, described the sparkling luminous substance seen in the sea on autumn nights, and on fish in the dark. The contents page of the book was divided into regions such as 'Flatlands', 'Waterlands' and 'Coastlands', and each section was followed by a glossary of place-terms for weather, landscape and nature gathered from Norn and Old English, Anglo-Romani and Cornish, Welsh, Irish, Gaelic and the Orcadian, Shetlandic and Doric dialects of Scots.

Flicking through the introduction, I paused when Macfarlane wrote of the chapters, that 'all are fascinated by the same questions concerning the mutual relations of place, language and spirit—how we landmark, and how we are landmarked'.

I clasped *Landmarks* to me. This was a dictionary of vanishing words from the landscapes to which I was about to depart. I bought the book and took it with me to Scotland. I read it on long train rides. I read it over hot chips in bars as rain lashed at the window. I read it on ferries, squinting at the bright sunlit page. *Landmarks* set new words under my tongue that I tested out over the next few weeks sitting in silent, drizzling forests watching red deer, or staring up at unfamiliar star formations at night. I drew on these words as I scribbled descriptions of places in my journal, trying to capture the way colour and light shifted in the landscape. I took Macfarlane's lists of words to heart, determined to incorporate what I could of them into the language I used. I shared what I thought of as his urgency, his grief at their diminishing in our lexicon to speak about landscape. Was it presumptuous that I called it grief, the thing that drove him to write his book? I was gripped by my own urgency towards the wild, towards the solitudinous, to what is found in the lesser-known places, and I thought I understood some of his urgency. When place-words die, a specific way of seeing vanishes from the world.

If the word *blinter* is forgotten, will we still notice the icy glitter of distant stars and the particular experience of beauty and trepidation that accompanies this sight?

On the western coast of Scotland, the Rannoch Moor is a 130 square-kilometre bog, a wilderness of moorland and lochans through which Macfarlane walked when he was writing *The Wild Places*, a paean to what he thought of as the last remaining wild places in Britain. That I could follow Macfarlane across Scotland thrilled me profoundly. I was mapping tracks in the wake of his writing, following in his footsteps—perhaps literally, though I would never know if I did—but making my own at the same time. I had been reading avidly as I travelled, devouring books about people spending time in wild places in nature: Macfarlane's oeuvre about walking the old places in Britain, *Wanderlust* by American writer Rebecca Solnit and *The Living Mountain* by nineteenth-century Scottish poet and writer Nan Shepherd. I was enthralled by these writers. I leant irresistibly into the pages, trying to see the landscapes through their eyes, to feel what they felt in the places they wrote about, and to understand what it meant to each writer to be there. They came to feel like companions with whom I shared my last waking thoughts each day. Their words gave shape to another kind of map that led me forward geographically: a kind of terrain of the psyche in which I was also discovering myself.

As I headed southeast to the moor, I saw through a kind of double vision. I was seeking out that which someone whose writing had permeated me to the core had seen, as well as looking at the landscape for myself. Alongside my own impressions, I was seeking the small, ordinary signs that someone else had noted, that, in their noticing, had become extraordinary to me because they were extraordinary to someone I admired.

The ecocritic Ian Marshall calls this kind of immersion 'a kind of research, involving a different kind of "foot notes" than most literary scholars are used to'. This sense of putting into practice an interconnectedness, or reciprocity, between written word, lived experience and geographic place compelled me. While I was not interested in checking the accuracy of how Macfarlane described Rannoch Moor, I wanted to get as close as I could to the places from which he wrote: the geographical place through which he travelled, and also the psychological place that comes about when geography seeps into the thought-scapes of the walker. To achieve this particular closeness to Macfarlane's thought-scape, I could do little more than read his words.

But as far as tracing his footsteps went, and immersing myself in Macfarlane's moor, I could do this—to a degree. I traversed the moor in a car, rather than walking through it, and experienced visually in a few hours what took Macfarlane a few days to walk. It was a strange, ephemeral experience to know that he had been there. To know that this flat and, at times, bleak expanse might have dismayed him at first as it did me. From the moving car, the colours of the moor blurred into a dark, coppery brown; I could not see the boggy expanses of water that Macfarlane would have crossed, nor make out the individual clusters of heather and their small bells that would change colour with the seasons.

Whose trail was I following across the moor? Whose footsteps had I followed already, without even realising? It could have been a contradiction, the feeling that I was discovering for myself ways of being and walking and seeing through the words of others. But it was one of the most intimate things I have ever known, the phenomenon of recognising, in someone else's words, like a sudden, electrifying flare, the same urgent tug of wild places, and the need to understand why in them I felt most fully realised.

Across a landmass that was not my home, but which felt like the word *belong* wherever I touched it, I traced the footsteps of people who thought like I did; who I suspected dedicated, in their own, private ways, much of their lives to pursuing, seeking to understand, the lure of the wild. In finding them, this community of people I had never met and likely never would, I was discovering my place in it. Macfarlane, whose passions and longing came back, always, to the old places, the old ways; Solnit, articulating the interwoven nature of discovery of self while walking; and Shepherd, whose craving for mountains and remarkable, exquisite insight on being in a body in place was only recognised half a century after the publication of her work. How many other women, in the 1900s and earlier, had their gazes fixed on mountains but never had the means to follow this wild call? It left me with a lingering melancholy but also a small, fierce kernel of gratitude and kinship to think on it. These women I would never know, but who had existed, and who had maybe, without knowing my name, dreamed of women like me who could do what they could not.

It was overwhelming, the thrill of being able to track these writers, these companions in thought, whose thinking affected my own so profoundly, across the landscapes in which the genesis of their ideas—those first visceral, joy-filled, provoking sparks of experience—had come into being.

Places are always storied. Going into them is an action simultaneously embodied and imagined and remembered. The landscapes into which I went were more than just the geography of the plateau, the valley, the ridge. As I wove slowly through the moor, my window down, breathing the cool, boggy air, the world seemed to shift, revealing at once the place I saw and the place I imagined Macfarlane saw. This moor that swept out around me—I could barely see it for how it had been storied before me.

•••

Australia beyond the Crown

Liberation, Emancipation and Unity

Craig Foster

Craig Foster is Co-Chair, Australian Republic Movement.

Australia is growing into its contemporary skin and in that unfolding, unifying reality, there is no further place for the Crown. It's an age of awakening, conversations previously unspoken, taboos broken. It's a cultural and psychological liberation and we're coming to understand that it is not to be feared—rather, it is both empowering and deeply inspiring.

As tortured as the process is—amid arguments over the practical manifestation of solidarity with First Nations Peoples and the usual political posturing that Indigenous Australia has become attuned to over a more than two-century-long fight for justice— there is a therapeutic sense of release and relief. The historical vacuum of national silence is being filled with knowledge, truth, love and respect for our First Peoples as the oldest living culture on earth.

This liberating process of truth-telling that First Peoples are teaching us will help us move past a number of blockages in the national psyche that all rest on our fear of looking back: the misplaced notion that it will diminish us as a people to acknowledge that this land was stolen when the very opposite is the case.

The truth can be our superpower

We are only stifled, suffocated, if we continue to refuse to make right what we know is wrong. This process of healing will ultimately make us whole as a people, bringing more than 65,000 years of history together with the beautiful face of contemporary Australia in all our colours, cultures and vast capabilities. First Peoples knew this long, long ago and we are coming to the same realisation slowly, painstakingly. As a country, that truth is our real strength—our superpower—if we grasp it.

Our future relationships between all of us, among every culture, will start from a position of justice: all of us knowing that we live in a country courageous enough and capable of building a new national identity formed from an absolute commitment to truth, justice and democracy.

Visibility and conversations are one thing, justice is another. Symbolic actions that have increased the visibility of First Nations rights such as Welcomes and Acknowledgements of Country, Indigenous rounds in sport, and the proliferation of Indigenous art in corporations and public spaces, can only be authentic when part of a broader journey of equity. This is why Australia is charting a collective course through the Uluṟu Statement, starting with the Voice to Parliament.

We are so very tired of the culture of denial, the endless history wars, the needless fight for control of our children's education

We want it. We crave it. Both for First Peoples who are our colleagues, our friends, our partners, our community members but also, selfishly, for those of us who are not Indigenous, for ourselves.

We are so very tired of the culture of denial, the endless history wars, the needless fight for control of our children's education that seeks to hide the truths of history, and we are deeply thankful that they're now learning that of which we were kept unaware. We are tired too of seeing a proud people decay in front of our eyes, a people who despite every atrocity endured are still the most open, gracious and giving, still prepared to offer their hand in partnership, to ask us to walk with them rather than demand. It's a profound demonstration of the beauty of a culture that has survived tens of thousands of years despite every attempt to erase it from these lands they nurtured for millennia, and which needs their spiritual guidance to heal.

It has become clear to us that we are really fighting with ourselves, with our own misgivings about the beginnings of our nation, and that First Peoples are simply the vessel through which these national anxieties are played out. Until we speak the truth, we cannot move on from the past and hold our Indigenous peoples in a place of eminence, as the overwhelming majority of us would so love to do, because it reminds us of the fundamental contradictions in our national mythology.

We want to begin the journey because we know it's the only way forward, it's right, it accords with our modern values, and because the more our minds are opened through new knowledge, the greater our commitment to make amends. The gifts that First Peoples are giving us are those of listening, holding complex realities simultaneously, and keeping dialogue open on subjects that go to our very core as Australians by helping us to confront unanswered questions.

How can we talk of egalitarianism when our own compatriots are too often reduced to subhuman conditions and excruciating incarceration rates? How do we explain the Indigenous children filling our juvenile centres and later jails—and is the issue really about Indigenous kids, or also about us? How do we reconcile the concept of fairness, the old 'fair go' with the unfairness at the heart of the national story? How do we accommodate intellectually our pride in multiculturalism with the racism our non-white communities face every day, and our unwillingness to talk about it?

Our changing conception of multiculturalism is part of the same journey because as we learn to listen, we develop an ability to hear every community, and there is a whole conversation ready to happen that will help us shape how we think about ourselves. True multiculturalism means both access and representation. Where barriers to participation and power exist, they are antithetical to the demography of modern Australia and our belief in genuine inclusion.

The current Australian Parliament—the most diverse in our history—shows that we are, at last, manifestly growing into our modern skin, in large part because our diverse communities are becoming more vocal, organised and visible. This is the real Australia coming to life, breaking old barriers and emerging into a new future.

This is the country that is so inspiring to be a member of—not one that continues to deny, that refuses to account for injustice, or that fights endlessly over simple truths that we have known for a very long time. It's a beautiful vision of a nation at ease with itself and its past, completely open in our institutions to Australians of any background and ancestry, founded on secular and democratic principles, which provides a framework for us all to interact respectfully even amid significant differences of thought and belief.

We can maintain immense hope because change does happen: it is important to remember that what I am now writing was once heresy. Many of those who spoke these simple realities in past decades going back to first contact in 1788 were silenced, demonised and often incarcerated, so we cannot underestimate the importance of the steps being undertaken.

A shadow is starting to lift that has suffocated the nation, and it is emancipating: a release from the chains that have bound us all to several hundred years of pretence and the silencing of voices of truth. I strongly suspect that when we reconcile with our true past and bring the fullness of our modern demography to light, our relationship with each other and the world will fundamentally change. We will better understand our tendency to demonise newcomers, telling them to 'go back where they came from', or our obsession with border security, torturing of refugees and terror at 'the floodgates being opened' to be swamped by the 'other'.

When we accept the reality that this land was stolen, and work with First Peoples to make amends, we will surely be less fearful of this continent being stolen from us. Walking in truth means that we can also confront historic, systemic, cultural and institutional racism. We cannot truly shed ourselves of the legacies of the White Australia policy and the racism that non-white migrants face every day until we accept that racism underpinned our foundation.

The insistence on turning the International Day for the Elimination of Racial Discrimination into 'Harmony Day', and thereby rendering invisible the racism faced by too many Australians is one such example. On this day in 2023, we saw progress with truths emerging in the public discussion; increasingly, we are peeling back these layers of denial and confronting issues long dormant, buried deep inside, making them all the more limiting and damaging. They include the eighteenth- and nineteenth-century view of First Peoples as subhuman; our first legislation as a nation, the *Immigration*

Restriction Act 1901, to restrict non-white and non-British migrants; the racially motivated constitutional powers that persist today. All of this can only be overcome by the process of coming together through truth and lowering barriers for any and every Australian, by seeing the face of Australia in every institution.

The coronation of someone else's king

With the utmost sensitivity, love and respect, this is a year when First Peoples must rightly take the microphone. This is a year that will further crystallise the journey we are on, and bring into sharp focus the historical ties that are predicated on the very denial we now unseat. The coronation of King Charles III, King of Australia, took place on 6 May. In this context, we can more easily see that the Crown not only has no relevance to contemporary Australia but also that any further formal relationship is irreconcilable with our evolving conception of Australia since 1788.

Australia's reaction to the news that the Reserve Bank would celebrate First Nations history and culture on the $5 note, instead of the British king, who would ordinarily have been expected to replace the former queen of Australia and 14 other realms, was instructive. We just nodded in agreement. It was a natural step, with no need for histrionics, nothing to debate.

We should go further and have an Australian on all our currency, remove portraits of the British king at official functions, and change the pledge or oath of allegiance still used in numerous fora to allegiance to Australia alone, not to the Crown. We have slowly come to realise that our true 'kings' and 'queens' are our Indigenous Elders, carrying eons of wisdom and cultural lore. The distance between Australia and a foreign, unelected, unaccountable, privileged monarch has never been greater.

The cord of attachment has snapped. It is time for our institutions to reflect that reality. There are many views on the historical inheritance of the British tradition: finally, we are able to acknowledge the positive with the negative. It is not necessary to ridicule the British monarch or monarchy, nor make any Australian who holds the king in affection feel in any way uncomfortable, because in moving into the new reality of contemporary Australia, we can all hold very different views of the past.

Some will consider the British tradition, Queen Elizabeth and our democratic institutions with reverence; others will be more focused on the Frontier Wars, dispossession of Australia's First Peoples without recognition or recompense; and every shade between. What is indisputable, though, is that the legacies of the Crown preclude any further association—because of the connotations it carries, the pain it presided over, the lies it profited from.

Republicanism is about creating the best version of contemporary Australia built on an acknowledgement of the complexities, injustices and triumphs of our past, about bringing the different historical threads, ancient cultural survival, British traditions and the migrant contribution together. Many of us fundamentally disapprove of the concept of hereditary title, and believe it should hold no further formal place in Australian society. I personally had cause to see inside the true nature of royalty in my advocacy for Hakeem al-Araibi in 2019, when princes and kings from Thailand and Bahrain traded the life of a young man, contemptuous of international law. Had I not already been a republican, I certainly would have become one then.

Australians should consider, too, the damaging effect on the human rights of people around the world and particularly in the Gulf region where royal families preside over societies such as Hakeem's former country of Bahrain, and oppress their citizens—amid the legitimacy provided to these regimes by all other royal institutions around the world. Bahraini, UAE or Saudi Arabian royals can point to Australia as an exemplar of support for the concept of a birthright and divine right to rule that so often has violent, fatal consequences—something that we should rectify as soon as the opportunity arises.

> The distance between Australia and a foreign, unelected, unaccountable, privileged monarch has never been greater. The cord of attachment has snapped.

We can now more appropriately contextualise the Crown through long-awaited conversations that have been normalised, such as Invasion Day—and know that there is no longer a place on this journey for a Crown responsible for the systematic, racialised destruction of a beautiful people.

A large portion of Australia is still unaware that a foreign monarch is our head of state, the highest office in the land. Our international representative. The elder who should embody the best of our qualities, and uphold the greatest of our aspirations. The only value of 6 May is that our lingering ties will become clear to us all, and kickstart further conversations about a fully independent, self-led Australia where our sovereignty no longer rests abroad but in us, the people.

An Australian republic: not *if* but *when*

Taking this step, as the Albanese government has foreshadowed for the next parliamentary term, is another important part of our continuing decolonisation culturally, intellectually and formally.

This process is occurring across other former colonies, with India demanding a formal apology and return of stolen treasures, Barbados becoming a republic in 2021 and Jamaica committed to doing likewise, both calling for apology and reparation for the enslavement and oppression of their people.

Other Caribbean nations anticipate becoming republics in the next few years, leaving just a handful of the 56 Commonwealth nations as realms of the British monarchy. The reach of Charles' family and institution has been decaying for many decades. The question for Australia is not of *if* but *when* we will take this final, natural step.

It is deeply ironic that despite having been considered a 'dying race' at Federation where our first attorney-general and second prime minister, Alfred Deakin, felt able to forecast that within 100 years there would be no Black Australians, our First Peoples are growing in cultural power and authority. They are renewing culture and language, deepening the cultural understanding of all Australians, and emerging as one of the most recognised cultures globally at the very time the Crown is losing its meaning, trust, relevance and place in the modern world. That is at least some justice.

Change is building—even in Britain itself. Some British commentators are now calling for the monarchy to release the 14 realms outside Britain, to apologise and make reparations. As Australians watched the King of Australia crowned for the first time in 70 years, it was fundamentally different this time. Odd, in truth.

Australia still saw itself as part of the British Empire in 1953. Today our concept of ourselves is shifting in a way that places the royal succession as something diametrically opposed to our sense of meritocracy, equality and social mobility. It strikes us as an abuse of the public purse when so many people are suffering economically, including when any royals visit these shores at our expense. I would imagine their reception today would be similar to that in the Caribbean last year, with the visit of royal family members disrupted by calls for justice and separation.

The vast majority of Australians want this formal separation. The need has never been clearer for Australia to move from colonisation and Federation to the third era of Australian life: reconciliation, independence and true multiculturalism. Australia could be a beacon for the world on how to live together in truth and inclusion, a nation of many cultures, all peoples—and more than 65,000 years in the making.

In the coming months and year—and hopefully, following a successful referendum on the Voice, which is a once-in-many-generations opportunity for growth—we will begin conversations about what an Australian head of state looks like, building a new consensus on constitutional change that makes us uniquely, proudly and independently Australian.

The two proposed referenda are separate but deeply interlinked: a republic must carry forward every one of our tens of thousands of years of history, and reconciliation is a fundamental part of any Australian future founded on truth. It is the only future worth fighting for. It is time for the historical ties to the British empire to be brought to an end, the monarchy placed in its appropriate historical context, and the Australia of today able to fully bloom on the domestic and international stage.

The process of decolonisation is unfinished business. We are culturally and psychologically ready as a nation to walk together with First Peoples in all our contemporary, multicultural beauty. This can only truly be done by us alone—without the Crown.

•••

nine points in time

a dark slug traverses a ripening papaya
in the fruit bowl; the barest film of rain

three chicken bones sucked clean
in a pyramid on the abandoned plate

time measured in whale fall: the feast
of a carcass on the deep ocean floor

an angophora wears the bark ribbons
of a neighbouring mountain ash as its own

doomed ice off glaciers beginning to melt,
the edges dissolving: hold that thought

a row of bushes crouched low and still
in the shadow of a leaning fence

the chipped bowl of a morning arrives
through the long narrow windows first

squeeze the half-grown oranges bunched
on the elderly tree, warm now in the sun

lying on the footpath, a white bird's wing
a small angel felled with feathers intact

Jane
Gibian

Jane Gibian's latest
collection of poetry is
Beneath the Tree Line
(Giramondo, 2021).
She works as a librarian
and also writes about
libraries, history and
the environment. She
lives on Bediagal land
near the Cooks River.

Is the literary industry even worth saving?

Matilda
Dixon-Smith

Matilda Dixon-Smith is a writer, editor and bookseller living on unceded Gadigal land.

This year I reach an important milestone: ten years working in the literary industry. In 2013 I entered my first 'real' lit job, as an editorial assistant at a small magazine publisher in North Melbourne. I had worked as an intern at two other publishing companies during my master's, but this was the first time I would actually be *paid* for what I had studied for five years to do—really, as a voracious reader and writer, for my whole life.

As I think back to my first day in my first lit job, I can remember the sickening mingled exhilaration and horror of finally being able to work in a field where I truly felt I belonged. Yes, I was scared, but I was also entitled. I was *meant to be there*, working with words. This was my *calling*.

What a difference ten years makes. The literary industry in so-called Australia is a strange, small and spirited space. Unlike in larger markets, as in the United States and Europe, in our colony the industry is tight-knit, communal and quite prolific for such a small sector. It's also ruthless, both in how it welcomes newcomers to its circle and in how it rewards and provides for its community.

In ten years working as an editor, journalist, academic, author and bookseller, I have rarely earned over the median Australian income. On average, I've spent less than a year in most of my positions in the literary industry. I've done so many different things in the lit sector—I've worked in almost every kind of job it's possible to do—but, as I look back on my ten years as a member of the community, I feel I've accomplished virtually nothing. My super is lacking but so is my enthusiasm for the work I do now.

Work in the literary industry is hard, unending and viciously underpaid. Editors are expected to work overtime for little (or no) pay; arts workers drop out of the industry in droves due to low pay and outlandish demands on their time and person; academics are being casualised into oblivion; bookstores plot against their workers to cut costs and increase the workload; and writing is not a vocation but rather a hobby that only sometimes yields reward in the form of payment and recognition.

It's seriously tough out there. The workplaces are unyielding and perilous, and the work never stops, but still our pockets are basically empty. Despite all this, complaints are not well tolerated. In the literary industry, you work not because you have to but because you *want* to. The passion—not the pay, not the recognition, not the *respect*—is the reward.

On 30 January 2023, the federal government published its new National Cultural Policy—Revive: a place for every story, a story for every place. Interestingly, the announcement also marks an anniversary: Revive is the first National Cultural Policy to be established in ten years (the last was Julia Gillard's Creative Australia). Part of this announcement, which marked the government's renewed interest in and support for the arts sector, was a new national funding body for the literary industry, Writers Australia. Many in the lit world were cautiously optimistic about this announcement—especially those who had made submissions to help shape the National Cultural Policy. Perhaps Australia's lit industry was about to see an unprecedented and dearly desired injection of stimulus. Perhaps the broader population really did value our work with words.

One day in February, I left work early to sit down and watch a webinar produced by the Australia Council for the Arts, designed to give the community information on Writers Australia and to collect feedback on the announcement. I felt trepidatious about this webinar. What would Writers Australia look like? How would its establishment impact my beloved lit community, my colleagues and my friends? What did renewed interest from the powers that be mean for the industry?

Unfortunately, none of my questions were answered. The webinar did not go into great detail about what Writers Australia would look like, how it would function or whom it was designed to support. What little we were told sounded similar to the funding apparatus already at work at Australia Council (and in every state government and many local governments): a pocket of wealth from one group, divvied up among those who are skilled at writing grant applications. Nothing felt different or monumental or exciting about Writers Australia, the way it was presented to us. It was all too vague, too grossly familiar to constitute real change for our industry.

Writers Australia will start its work—whatever that will be—in 2025. I suppose then we will really see how the federal government supports and fosters the so-called Australian literary industry. But what's really interesting to consider between now and then is not what this support looks like in the industry; rather, it's worth asking whether we deserve the support at all. We're struggling financially in the sector, that's clear. But what about all the other problems: the terrible bosses; the oppressive workplaces; the exclusion and the nepotism; the race and gender and class inequity; the misconduct, harassment and trauma? I mean, is it even worth saving the lit industry?

'I don't love the lit sector, I love the people who manage to write outside of and despite it,' says Panda Wong, poet, editor and communications officer at the Melbourne City of Literature Office. Wong has been working in the literary industry for about five years and, while she writes and edits, she explains that her work in the university sector is 'definitely my "money" job'. Wong, who is a recent shortlistee for the Judith Wright

Poetry Prize, tells me the sector can be 'such a toxic little sore sometimes'. 'I feel like it is (for the most part) a super white, elitist, boring, classist and risk-averse place,' says Wong, 'and while Australia manages to publish some really amazing work every year, there are still certain kinds of stories that get prioritised or published.'

This is a view that's shared by many in the industry—and on its fringes. Will Cox, a writer and bookseller from Melbourne, has just self-published a novel, *Hyacinth*. Cox describes the book as 'the sitcom *Keeping Up Appearances* rewritten as a gothic fable'. Cox is interested in hauntology, which he tells me is where you refer to the past in the spirit or atmosphere of the art you are creating, 'giving a mythological quality to the slightly uncomfortable recent past'.

The book is certainly for a niche market, but it's a wonderful creation: beautifully presented in millennial pink and full of spiky, transporting writing. I ask Cox why he chose self-publishing for *Hyacinth*, and he tells me, 'Partially, this is the pathway for it. But I did think initially, I'll approach some publishers. And then I looked around at the Australian landscape. And there aren't any for this.' Cox spoke to one small Australian publisher about *Hyacinth* before deciding to self-publish. 'They were very kind about it,' says Cox. 'They said, "We really like this, this is great. But it's too weird, we can't sell this. It doesn't fit on our list."' So Cox decided to self-publish *Hyacinth*, which began as a weekly online newsletter. He hired a friend to edit the book, and he designed and typeset it himself. 'I'm a proper book nerd,' he says, 'and I loved having control over everything.'

Ceinwen Langley, a self-published author and screenwriter, had a similar experience to Cox when deciding how to publish her work:

> I write various shades of fantasy, none of which is set in the contemporary world or has any ostensible connection to Australia, and when I looked into local publishers I could submit my debut novel to, I found that very few were accepting submissions for fantasy books. When I looked at the Australian publishing landscape at large, the only genre books being published (and there weren't many of those) were science fiction and dystopian fiction. The rest was, as it still broadly is, Australian contemporary or historical fiction. It made me realise there probably wasn't much demand for what I'd written at an acquisition level, and so rather than navigate the confusing process of querying to the more genre-friendly American or UK publishing industry, I decided to flex my project manager skills and pursue independent publishing.

Cox points to the size of the local lit sector as a huge motivating factor for him to self-publish. 'It's just such a small scene and a small community. It feels more like a scene than an industry.' Cox avoided the grant pathway for funding *Hyacinth* for much the same reason. 'I looked into it and it was pretty thin on the ground,' he says. 'And I didn't want to wait and do it on someone else's timeline.'

Access—especially to funding—in the industry is something that concerns many in the community. 'Literature makes space for deep, weird thinking, for human feeling,' says Jinghua Qian[1], a full-time freelancer who describes emself as 'at the intersection of arts,

1
Jinghua's pronouns are
ey / em/ eir.

media and publishing'. 'It's rich in everything but money.' Qian has been working 'at the fringes' of the publishing sector for nearly 20 years. When I asked em what made em angry and frustrated about the industry, ey were not short in supplying answers:

> Unliveable wages, opaque industry norms, no clear entry or career progression. I say wages but I've never been a salaried employee, so what I really mean is fees—the fees are absolutely disconnected from economic reality. All this means that working in the literary sector is a privilege few can afford, and in turn that means a narrow literature.

Wong agrees. 'I don't think it's enough for rich white people to be cognisant of these inequalities on a surface level,' she explains:

> I think there should be an attitude of mutual distribution—sharing resources, knowledge and funds—instead of this weird gatekeeper energy that proliferates the whole sector. The most generous people I know are not the ones with the most to share, that's for sure.

Charlotte[2], who has worked as a freelance critic, bookseller and fiction writer, agrees that pay is a huge issue for the sector, especially in terms of who gets to be a part of it. 'What makes me angry is the absolutely dogshit pay received by so many workers in the literary industry,' she tells me:

2
Not her real name.

> Publishing assistants are living off $45,000 a year. Booksellers are earning minimum wage. Authors are earning basically nothing (with very few exceptions). This means that often the people who work in the literary industry come from privilege—otherwise they wouldn't be able to afford to do it. This means that, in turn, we see a lot of work being published that reflects a certain kind of 'Australian' experience—often this experience is straight, white, and middle class.

Charlotte tells me she no longer works as a bookseller because the bookshop she worked in 'was no longer a place of calm or positivity for me. Management continuously underpaid staff and workplace bullying from management to floor workers was rife.' Her experience is replicated all across the sector. Clare Millar, a bookseller and the books editor at *The Big Issue*, tells me, 'I feel safe at work, despite being an active organiser. I do feel safe, but I have seen my peers [...] targeted and can see that my safety is a result of various privileges (white, cis, permanent position rather than casual).'

In 2021, amid COVID lockdowns, Sydney bookstore Better Read Than Dead[3] reached a 'historic' agreement for, among other things, better job security and increased workplace health and safety measures with management after a year of organising efforts and an escalating series of industrial actions. The deal was hard-won: the unionised staff's industrial actions saw management implement a 'lockout' against organising staff, send cease-and-desist letters to staff they claimed had made 'defamatory' statements on Facebook, and the 'unlawful' retrenchment of key organising staff members. Despite management's claims that the industrial campaign was 'aggressive' and that

3
The author is the kids manager and buyer at Better Read Than Dead bookshop, and a proud member of RAFFWU.

demands were 'simply not affordable to our business', they signed an agreement with workers that gave staff a base rate of $25 per hour, 26 weeks of paid parental leave, and domestic violence leave. The staff organised under the Retail and Fast Food Workers Union (RAFFWU). Union secretary Josh Cullinan called the accord 'a landmark agreement'.

The following year, negotiations escalated between workers (backed by the RAFFWU) and management at the iconic Readings retailer. Readings, which corners the independent market in Melbourne bookselling with a number of stores across the city, was embroiled in a highly publicised battle for better conditions that was endorsed by many in the industry, including Miles Franklin–winning author Jennifer Down. Despite the best efforts of organising staff, a 'non-union' revised enterprise bargaining agreement (EBA) was accepted by a narrow vote (61 to 58).

Bookselling is not the only place where union organisers are advocating for change. In 2019, Penguin Random House's union-negotiated EBA was accepted by the Fair Work Commission. The EBA, which enshrined pay increases for editorial and publicity staff among other gains, was voted 'overwhelmingly' by staff in those sectors, and was the first union-negotiated agreement in so-called Australian publishing history.

These victories often come at a cost: they're won at the expense of—or despite—workers' safety and contentment in the workplace. And safety is a concern outside union battles for better conditions. Millar explains she 'generally' feels safe in the community, 'but always have people I would avoid based on harassment and assault issues'.

In the early days of COVID, in mid 2020, news came that beloved literary magazine *The Lifted Brow* would close temporarily. The *Brow* had traditionally been a home for more experimental and esoteric artistic expression than the other lit mags, and it appeared to be a supportive ally to people of colour in the overwhelmingly white lit sector, having previously made space for a collective of First Nations writers and editors to publish an exclusively First Nations–run issue of the *Brow*, called *The Blak Brow*. The publication's board announced the closure in a release that pointed to the difficulties arising from COVID as its reason for closure.

In reality, behind the scenes the *Brow* was crumbling. Reports of an internal investigation into alleged sexual misconduct began to circulate in the community and, as the reports circulated, so too did a series of connected allegations about sexual harassment and ethical (race-related) misconduct concerning the upper management of the *Brow*. The internal investigation, which was ruled inconclusive by members of the board because the complainant was unwilling to make a 'formal statement' (which would give their alleged abuser a right of reply), disappeared—and so did the *Brow*. The community called on the board to resign, and a new board was appointed. Since their appointment, the *Brow* has not reopened for submissions, nor has it published another issue, either online or in print.

In her investigative article about the allegations and *TLB*'s collapse, Caroline Overington wrote, 'Rumours that some senior staff were having inappropriate relations with those who were more junior, or else taking advantage of young people just starting out on their careers in the arts. These and other gossip—all of it to date unverified—have now taken down the entire board.' Once the allegations were made public, Overington reported that

> staff within hours began quitting their posts, and the Brow's beautiful website soon started coming apart, as people began demanding their names be taken off the masthead. Some left because they felt the investigation had been flawed, and others thought the conclusion was wrong—there had been a toxic workplace culture, and some people had been exploited and hurt, and some of the rumours may indeed have been true.

It's scenarios like the one at the *Brow*—a collective of supposedly like-minded individuals, working together to create art, destroyed by alleged misconduct—that give many pause in an industry that's so small, so cliquey and so unregulated. 'There's lots of other incidents of racial and misogynist violence that get swept under the rug,' says Wong. 'While I feel safe and supported in my job at the Melbourne City of Literature Office, I know this is a privilege. I don't think any workers should be pushed out of this sector due to feeling unsafe.' The community's whisper network often works in overdrive, disseminating reports of bad actors in the industry who should be avoided.

Marginalised lit workers experience the worst kinds of exclusion and discrimination you can imagine. Alison Evans is an author, children's bookseller and the winner of a Victorian Premier's Literary Award for their novel *Ida*. '[Minority writers are] constantly distracted by mistreatment or circular, bad-faith arguments,' says Evans. 'So much energy is stolen by these things that we could be using for our art instead.'

Wong tells me she's 'always re-evaluating' whether she wants to stay in the literary industry. 'As a writer, of course I want to leave this racist and elitist space sometimes. It doesn't pay well, it's traditionally inhospitable to people like me and it can really chew you up and spit you out with its precarious conditions.' Wong speaks in concert with many marginalised lit workers who feel that the industry does not create space for them. I ask Qian if ey feel safe in the industry, and ey reply, 'No, but to be fair, I would say that some of the precarity I experience is inevitable in this industry, and some I have chosen in order to protect my independence.'

Roz Bellamy is the editor-in-chief at *Archer Magazine*, which is now owned by Drummond Street Services, an organisation that offers a service to 'help people facing personal challenges and societal barriers connected to living situations, health, identity, relationships and community'. Bellamy tells me, 'I feel safer than I have in any position, ever. I also feel paranoid saying that, because it could all disappear tomorrow. But I feel safe in terms of ... there's a lot of supervision, support when things come up, say, around the mental health of our writers or our team. There are processes in place to support us.'

'It was a safe workplace before we were part of Drummond Street,' Bellamy explains. 'My boss, the founder, is an amazing person to work for and has always had the backs of everyone in her team. But I think, even with an incredible individual doing that, you still need supports in place, which we now really have. And I haven't found that elsewhere in the industry.'

Charlotte says, 'We need more books reflecting the diversity of our population—and a huge part of how we might achieve this is by making sure literary industry workers are paid enough to make working in the industry viable for people who aren't already rich.' Isobel[4], an editor for one of largest commercial publishers in the colony, says:

4
Not her real name.

> I think the willingness to consult sensitivity and cultural readers is a great sign of change, and also the willingness to publish writers from marginalised groups. I think publishers are seeing that these books do sell and taking more chances. But it also has to be said that the majority of staff are white, and I'm sure that it's true that we are publishing the kind of queer and POC writers that white [straight, cis] readers find palatable.

5
Not her real name.

Emily[5], a trade-published author and literary magazine editor, points to inequitable distribution of funding as a huge contributing factor to the lack of safety and diversity in the literary sector. 'There's a lot of value in supporting new writers and lifting up the industry as one, and they're being missed,' Emily explains. 'It's good to see more opportunities for marginalised writers, but they're generally not being awarded the big financial support that can do a better job of equalising what's able to be published.'

Isobel is also concerned about how pay and working conditions in publishing affect who joins the industry. 'The low pay, especially in editorial, is frankly embarrassing. I have colleagues with master's degrees who are earning around 50k and can't even afford to buy lunch or coffee because rent is so high and they literally have no money until pay day,' she says. 'We're expected to do multiple jobs in addition to actual editing—author care, project management, bookkeeping, finding and hiring freelancers—and when you factor in all the unpaid overtime it's really not much better than minimum wage.'

But many of the lit workers I talk to are ambivalent about funding increases from the government solving the problems of discrimination, exclusion, poor conditions and misconduct in the industry. 'I don't know how it will change the sector, but I hope it will create more opportunities for writers who would otherwise not be able to produce work,' says Emily. 'I worry it will direct funds to even more of the same people who already have every possible opportunity afforded to them. Does a multiple Miles Franklin winner need funding over an emerging writer who can't afford to share their work without it? I don't reckon.'

Leanne Yong, whose YA novel *Two Can Play That Game* was published in February, but who tells me writing fiction is 'not my main job', agrees that funding can't solve everything. 'Just throwing money at the problem won't help, structural changes are needed too,' says Yong:

> This means not throwing more money at the same old established publications, but creating programs and pathways for more experimental stuff and works by marginalised creators. More publications for genre fic by marginalised creators, as it's more commercial and accessible to the general public than 'highbrow' lit that seems to get the bulk of the awards, visibility, funding.

Yong, like others in the sector, worries that funding increases will be directed to the wrong (or old-established) areas 'with, shall we say, narrower scopes of view'. She also wonders if more funding 'will go to organisations that purport to champion diversity but the people deciding who receives the funding as it trickles down do not share said marginalisations and therefore prioritise works written for the gaze of those on the outside'.

Bellamy says, 'There's very few resources and a lot of people wanting them, so there's a lot of competition between us in the industry.' Wong agrees that competition is fierce, but she tells me, 'I get frustrated with the way that the lack of funding creates this scarcity complex within the literary sector. I think that obtaining grants and funding, for example, can be a system that really favours people who "can play the game". I don't like that we have to compete for scraps, and that applying for grants can be such an obtuse process. There need to be more transparent, straightforward processes that don't make us jump through flaming hoops.'

Evans says these poor conditions are the worst for writers. 'From where I am, it feels like authors are treated as the lowest rung on the ladder, so to speak,' they tell me. 'Why is it that authors provide the work for the whole publishing house, but are paid the least? Authors' positions feel so precarious because there will always be someone who can replace us. It's like casual work—you can be dropped at any time. Except the pay is worse.'

Marlee Jane Ward, an author who has published books for children and adults, is also disheartened by the low pay for authors in so-called Australia. 'When I broke down the fucking money I was earning—about eight bucks an hour for like two years of work.' Even when advances (the commission fee paid to writers by publishers to secure a work) increase, the issues with how books are published and promoted are kneecapping promising writers. 'I don't even know how you solve the problem. Like you say, is it worth saving? Like, can you solve this problem?' Ward asks. 'I've heard of a few people who have gotten big advances and they rarely ever earn out.' (A writer 'earns out' when their book makes more than its advance in sales and they begin to earn royalties. Many writers never see any money for their work beyond a publisher's advance.)

Charlotte agrees that the lit industry's advances system is a huge problem for writers' ability to earn a living wage. 'We need to change the "advance" model for authors. It is wild that authors only start earning money from their books once they sell a certain number of copies. This does not happen in other industries and it's a totally moribund practice.'

Cox, who paid out of his own pocket for *Hyacinth* to be published and will receive all the profits from its sales, agrees that author pay is problematic. 'I think writers are probably paid the least out of anybody involved in the book. It seems absurd to me, but I'm just resigned to there not being any money.'

Langley says she is not motivated to move from self-publishing to a traditional publishing model because conditions across the sector are unsatisfactory. 'The biggest draw to try to move into the traditional publishing space is, for me, the editorial teams, the marketing, and letting someone else check my sales numbers,' she says.

But I am hearing from author friends that that level of support—particularly in marketing—is really dropping away. More and more, publishers seem to want submissions to be edited and almost ready to publish on acquisition and the back-and-forth author–editor relationship is diminishing. And if your book isn't chosen as a big lead title, a huge amount of marketing these days falls to the author themselves.

Both Cox and Langley can see the perks of avoiding the inherent problems in traditional publishing, though Langley tells me self-publishing is 'a gruelling process'. For Langley, a key draw is the independence she retains. 'There are real perks to owning your books and the associated IP outright, and not being locked into a contract,' she tells me. 'I've known too many authors with wonderful books that received little to no marketing, only to see them fall out of print.'

Cox compares the literary sector to the fine arts and music communities, where 'self-publishing' your work is commonplace. 'A lot of my friends are visual artists, or musicians, and my partner's a painter. And in those circles, doing it all yourself is cool and kind of punk. But in writing, in the literature world, it's like vanity publishing, and it's kind of embarrassing. Which I don't really agree with. So I just try and convince people.'

Despite myriad issues, literary workers feel a great affinity with those who are doing good work in the sector. 'I'm excited by the number of independent collectives and groups that are doing things for themselves,' Wong says:

Libraries like Melbourne Art Library, Murmur Library and Incendium Radical Library continue libraries' long tradition of being a space for accessible knowledge and exchange. Amplify Bookstore is a really amazing champion of books by BIPOC (Black, Indigenous and people of colour). There's *Crawlspace* and *Runway Journal*, [which] both publish really innovative and exciting digital work and have that really great open-source attitude towards creating. Another World Library uses spec-fic as a way to imagine new and better futures through workshops. I could go on and this is just a small section. I'm excited to see lots of small collectives and groups coexisting and connecting and sharing with each other.

Qian says, 'Growing class consciousness excites me. I think there's real potential in a precariat of media and culture workers challenging the current frameworks of production.' Bellamy reflects, 'I just keep thinking about places like *Liminal*, and what they're doing. I absolutely love the voices that they're platforming. Of course, I'm going to mention *Archer*. Our founder Amy Middleton has always been about platforming unheard voices.'

And some lit workers see potential—however dim the glimmer—in the promise of more investment from the government. Evans says, 'My hope is that it will make the writing side of things more sustainable. I'm more than ten years into my career and it feels much less sustainable than it ever has. I want to see the government really invest in us, and in particular children's and teen fiction. So much of the popular kidlit is imported from overseas, or [includes] celebrity books. I want to see writers given a basic income so that we don't have to move so precariously through our lives. If we're trying to live from grant to grant, from unstable work to more unstable work, how are we supposed to create?'

Millar says, 'I'm really excited about the possibility of literature being a larger part of national conversation/consciousness. And, hopefully, making writing a more feasible way to live. I don't imagine the funding will mean anyone new can live entirely off their writing, but it's a start.'

And even though the sector is rife with issues, from pay to conditions, from inequity to a lack of safety, most of the workers I speak to don't want to leave. 'If I leave the sector, I can't try to make it better,' Charlotte tells me. 'I write about women and queer people, and I review books by women and queer authors. This matters. The fact that I earn about $200 per 4000-word essay is not ideal, but I feel strongly that it is important work, and I work other jobs to supplement this.'

Emily tells me what she appreciates most about the industry is the reason she'd never leave, though she also appreciates that 'I'm a writer, there's no other industry.' Still, she says, 'I love finding new voices and having the opportunity to share my own voice. I love the community of people within it, and being able to collaborate, support, challenge ideas.' Evans says their experience with readers is 'perhaps the only thing' that keeps them in the game:

> I talk to young trans kids who need my work. Almost every event I do, someone will come up and tell me how my work has helped them through a tough time, or reflected something of their own experience that wasn't being reflected elsewhere. To write for these kids is a huge privilege and honour, and for me is the most important job in the world.

But Evans also loves the process and experience of being a member of the lit community. 'I love writing and the act of creating. I love workshopping ideas and stories with others to help them. If I were to stop writing professionally, I would still do these things.'

Yes, the industry has problems, and chief among them is how we're all bound to it by our passion to create. But the industry, the sector, is also a community—one that fights hard (on a worker level, at least) to protect its members. The increase in collective action across the sector; the power of the whisper network (even if that does not always lead to measurable consequences for bad actors); the demands for *more*—all these things excite me, even as I feel the fatigue of ten years of Sisyphean work settling on my bones.

Perhaps a real, measured funding increase across the industry will be implemented in new and exciting ways by Writers Australia; perhaps we will one day be able to create and share art for a living wage. But more meaningful change will not just come from funding but also from motivated action, if it comes at all. For now, although I'm trepidatious and sceptical about the future of the industry I love so dearly—despite its many flaws—I'm not quite willing to throw out the screaming baby with the bathwater.

•••

Not talking about typography in 2022

'*The first rule of fight club is you do not talk about fight club.*' Within a few months that single sentence of dialogue from David Fincher's 1999 film *Fight Club* was catapulted (via Brad Pitt) into both popular culture and ubiquitous quotation. I have often thought that talking about typography is just like that. The easiest way to discuss typographic matters 'outside the club' is not to talk about it at all. Instead, we use that most useful of literary devices that can describe anything except itself—the metaphor. See, I just did it in that opening paragraph. So, following that happy spirit of metaphor, my summary of typography in 2022 will be discussed *through* life in 2022—looking at some of the bigger social and cultural undercurrents that ran through the past twelve months and how those popular interests and concerns have been reflected in letterforms. Let's start right at the very beginning—New Year's Day 2022. For typographers this was a happy occasion. We're always glad to see the end of a year that has a '1' in it, because of the incessant kerning to correct its overly wide spatial position in any date. So that was an easy win on the first day.

Reconnection

During the recent pandemic years a lot of people developed an individual engagement with typography, either by choice or by circumstance. What had previously been discussed in office conversations, chats in the elevators or in the street over a take-away coffee, suddenly had to be replaced speedily by its digital (and therefore typographic) equivalent. Fearing ambiguity in their communications, we saw the uptake of emojis and expressive punctuation as a way of clarifying emotional states.

By 2022 we were hesitantly emerging from several years of social isolation. As we emerged blinking into the (natural) light, there was an understandable need for social connection, on both a personal and a societal level. This widespread deep yearning for human intimacy was reflected in the popularity of script typefaces and lettering.[1] As an

Stephen Banham

Stephen Banham is a typographer, graphic designer, writer, lecturer and curator. His primary research interest is typography— particularly the social and cultural readings of letterforms.

1
Here I specifically differentiate typefaces (a mechanical and unified set of reproduceable letterforms) from lettering (hand-generated letterforms).

Opposite:
The display typeface composed of both ultra black and script weights, *Nostra* designed by Lucas Descroix.

Epicene *Epicene*

Epicene *Epicene*

AaBbCcDdEeFfGg*HhIiJjKkLlMm*
NnOoPpQqRrSsTt*UuVvWwXxYyZz*

emulation of handwriting, scripts are purposefully intimate in nature, promising direct thoughts straight from the human heart. As type scholars have noted:

> The current embrace of scripts, especially those sporting a riot of swashed and flourished letters ... is a continuation of the decades-old rebellion against the less-is-more philosophy of Modernism ... Scripts are malleable. Most importantly, they are personal. They encompass a variety of styles, and they suggest a plethora of emotions. Scripts are human. As the digital world takes over more and more of our lives, they provide a link to the physical and tangible world we are leaving behind.[2]

2
Paul Shaw and Abby Goldstein, 'The Line of Beauty', *Eye*, no. 83, vol. 21 (2012), pp. 54.

Several years ago the popularity of script typefaces transcended just their online purchase to the uptake of lettering courses in how to hand-render scripts (the face-to-face element being of particular appeal in 2022). We know deep down that the scripts we see are most likely simply typefaces, but (like our experience of film and theatre) we suspend our disbelief in the hope that Britney Spears really did handwrite that album cover just for us and only for us.

Either or

In the past year it has become more common to see scripts melding with other typeface styles such as sans serif to create fusions that defy traditional typographic classification. This indicates two interesting forces at play: first, a stylistic revival of the early 1990s 'Franken-fonts' (typefaces deconstructed and reassembled digitally using during the first wave of font-editing software); and second, the questioning of even

Above:
The typeface 'without gender', *Epicene*, designed by Kris Sowersby.

having a classification system in the first place. These developments coincided with the abandoning of the well-established Vox typeface taxonomy,[3] developed in 1954 by Maximillian Vox. Its rejection rightfully acknowledged that its classifications no longer reflected the nuanced, multicultural, multilingual digital environment of contemporary type design. In a bigger sense, 2022 saw a more intensified questioning of cultural binaries. As design writer Ellen Lupton describes:

> Binary categories are under attack. Advocates for racial justice have challenged racial binaries, which marginalize people of colour whilst enshrining White supremacy. LGBTQIA+ activists are dismantling the male/female polarity, which enforces gender norms and compulsory heterosexuality. Environmentalist are unravelling oppositions such as nature/culture and human animals ...

Given this context, it has not been surprising to see the emergence of typefaces that appear deliberately to avoid the typographic binaries of sans/serif and roman/italic, for example. Fairness and diversity in representation are all desirable and essential elements of a functioning democracy, but to equate typefaces as a microcosm of community is to overly anthromorphise the letterform. Although the non-binary argument is well intentioned as a broader cultural virtue, it is misplaced when applied to typographic design—one of the few endeavours requiring clearly differentiated compositional hierarchies. To make all typographic elements on a page equal in emphasis would be to strip the page of readability, purpose, clarity and indeed beauty. The design of letterforms likewise requires stylistic unity, powerful contrast and convincing differentiation simply to function.

3
This de-adoption was announced by the International Type Organisation, ATypi, in 2021.

Above:
The contemporary fusion of geometry and the organic, *Funkyfont*, designed by Silvertag.

6 Styles AND
Matching Italics

F

Forrest

a typeface with a familiar feel

Thursd ay

Forrest Bold

Cooper Black.
Cooper Black Italic.

Indeed, the gender of typefaces developed as a topic of vigorous discussion throughout 2022, resulting in the publication of several books on the topic as well as interest from the mainstream media. Although typefaces are technically incapable of having a gender,

> describing things as 'masculine' or 'feminine' in design and typography is historically and culturally loaded. Language is powerful, typography makes language concrete. Language has a shared meaning and heritage. When they write 'delicate and light' is feminine, 'strong and bold' is masculine, they're really saying 'women are weak, men are strong'. It's that simple. This language is corrupt and bankrupt in today's society'.[4]

4
Kris Sowersby, *Epicene* webpage: <klim.co.nz/blog/epicene-design-information/>.

It should be pointed out that this debate is not proposing that typefaces have genders but rather that our descriptions of them are gendered. Again, this debate is reliant on the anthropomorphising, as Marie Boulanger, author of *XX, XY: Sex, Letters and Stereotypes*, admits, 'We treat and describe letters like human beings.'

One of the most eloquent and thoughtful contributions to this debate has not been a book, article or essay but rather a new type family, *Epicene*, by Kris Sowersby, which, as the title and definition suggest, has 'characteristics of both sexes or no characteristics of either sex; of indeterminate sex'. As Sowersby attests, *Epicene* is 'an experiment in modernising Baroque letterforms without muzzling their ornamental idiosyncrasy nor falling into the trap of gender codifications. It's a firm statement that fonts have no gender.'

This greater societal debate around diversity is reflected in the field of typography

Top:
The self-described 'typeface with a familiar feel', *Forrest*, designed by Fenotype.

Bottom:
The iconic advertising typeface, *Cooper Black*, designed by Oz Cooper in 1921, affectionately echoed a century later in *Cooper Black*.

"Tom, why didn't you wake me SOONER? Oh, Tom, don't! It makes my *flesh* crawl to hear you. Tom, what is the matter?"

The Adventures of Tom Sawyer, Mark Twain

Gooper Black.
Gooper Black Italic.

through the rising popularity of 'variable' fonts—a reasonably new type format that offers a system of interpolating different weights, slant or any parameter, all in the one font file. This removes the need to load multiple individual font files—a key consideration for web typography. As it relates to the wider societal debates around diversity, variable fonts represent a real paradigm shift—removing the explicit distinctions between different weights and styles, which have existed since the early days of typesetting.[5]

Just for now

A curious cultural parallel during 2022 was the ongoing appeal and convenience of the transient: think pop-up shops, food vans and subscription streaming services. Notwithstanding the revival of vinyl records, the privileging of *access* over *ownership* has led to a popularity in typefaces that reflect that sense of the temporary, the movable and the agile (yes, I squirm just using that last term). Typographically, nothing answers that cultural desire more than stencil typefaces. During those twelve months many existing typeface families were further expanded to encompass stencillised versions, seen as big sellers in the type market.

Curiously, stencil typefaces simultaneously nod to two specific undercurrents of 2022: the militaristic tone of stencils refers to world conflicts (primarily Ukraine), while the stencil's familiar use as the voice of protest in populist and rebellious movements echoes the corresponding political tensions and instability.[6]

As a more positive counter to this cultural reflection, French designer Philippe Apeloig observed the 'see-through' power of the stencil: 'When the letters are stencil, they seem to be cut out of the paper. They give a kind of visual illusion, something like transparency,

5
See <https://fonts.google.com/knowledge/introducing_type/introducing_variable_fonts>.

6
In occupied France, the stencilled letter 'V' for Victoire became a powerful symbol of resistance, while much of the poster typography of the Occupy movement (2012) was stencilled.

as if it will be possible to see through the letter shapes.' I would like to think that the stencil positively represents one of the major political and social shifts of recent times: the public demand for accountability through transparency and clarity.

Just for then

The choices we make everyday from a font menu can also reflect patterns of societal disruption and anxiety. The answer lies in the perfectly natural human response to fear, which is to cling to the known, the safe. According to the *2022 Type Trends Report* published by the international font vendor Monotype, 'the appeal of nostalgia offers a sense of familiarity and comfort during "crappy and stressful" times'.[7]

Within the world of typography, nostalgia is an ever-present element because each typeface, by its very nature, is a variation on a predecessor, making the evolution of type design a noisy echo-chamber of endless revival and remixing. Nevertheless, 2022 presented some distinct forms.

The return of the 'slur serif' is a revival of heavy, soft and rounded forms, reminiscent of 1960s styling (itself a revival of the 1910s)—producing updates of *Cheltenham* (1906), *Souvenir* (1914), and the famous *Cooper Black* (1921), making this a revival of a revival. One of these recent releases is *Forrest* (2022). Its marketing spiel draws heavily upon its nostalgic appeal: 'A lot of times, an old trick is better than a bagful of new ones—all you might actually need would be a good, reliable font family with soul, providing that comforting, familiar feel. This is where *Forrest* comes in: a type family born out of a lifelong passion for digging into old archives of fonts, in search for that good ol' type— simple, honest, made with love.'[8]

To add further complexity to this situation, another trend described as 'Neue Nouveau'[9] refers to an updated Art Nouveau, described by Monotype as 'type with organic lines and dramatic curves that speak to nature and biodiversity, and at the other end, there are legibility-challenging, psychedelic, flowy forms speaking to the push-pull of pandemic time'. These forms are then combined and mixed together to become a wave known as 'Mix-Up'. Monotype contextualises this style by noting, 'Individuals, groups, and the culture at large are embracing diversity—fluidity—ambiguity—inclusion. 'Mix-Up' is typographic diversity ... the idea is sublime: embracing differences.' What these micro-trends all have in common is a desire to express a diverse and ambiguous typographic form.

Yet a nostalgic counterforce to this diversity is the yearning of 'modern' graphic design to return to the safety of its womb—namely, the postwar neutrality of the European sans serif. This has been seen primarily in the corporate branding sector, seemingly deaf to the undercurrents of recent change. As the design critic Alice Rawsthorn observed: 'A defining theme of European modernism was the application of new technologies and rationalist design principles to produce huge quantities of identical objects ... This approach to design favoured standardization over diversity'.[10] Throughout 2022 we saw the continued popularity of the quintessential 'standardised' symbol of the sans, *Helvetica* (1957), along with its armies of clones. A similar pattern of

7
Monotype Type Trends 2022 Report, p. 4.

8
See <https:// www.myfonts. com/collections/ forrest-font-fenotype>.

9
The 'Neue' reference is a nod to Neue Haas Grotesk, the original name of Helvetica.

10
Alice Rawsthorn, *Design as an Attitude*, JRP Ringier, 2018, p. 81.

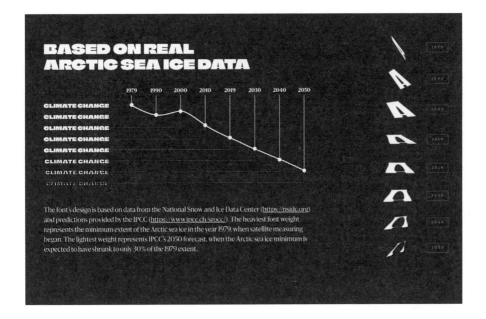

BASED ON REAL ARCTIC SEA ICE DATA

1979 1990 2000 2010 2019 2030 2040 2050

CLIMATE CHANGE
CLIMATE CHANGE
CLIMATE CHANGE
CLIMATE CHANGE
CLIMATE CHANGE
CLIMATE CHANGE
CLIMATE CHANGE
CLIMATE CHANGE

The font's design is based on data from the National Snow and Ice Data Center (https://nsidc.org) and predictions provided by the IPCC (https://www.ipcc.ch/srocc/). The heaviest font weight represents the minimum extent of the Arctic sea ice in the year 1979, when satellite measuring began. The lightest weight represents IPCC's 2050 forecast, when the Arctic sea ice minimum is expected to have shrunk to only 30% of the 1979 extent.

behaviour was seen in the closing years of the past century when we were all anxiously staring into an unknown millennium.

Even in 2022, sans typefaces continue culturally to reflect our collective sense of 'the modern'. Yet the symbolism of 'the modern' is not derived from the typeface design itself (since the sans has existed in some form for 3000 years), but from its cultural associations, how it is perceived, the ways in which it is used and where it is used. A quick glance at recent rebranding in the fashion and app development industries, for example, indicates the increasingly generic complexion of sans-based identities. A look across the top 20 bestseller list of 2022 on MyFonts (the largest of the international font vendors) shows that 17 of the top 20 are sans. Unsurprisingly *Helvetica* remains a very firm (and dare I say, safe) number one.

From here

Now that we have typographically mapped the contours of the previous year, let's move away from the safe comfort of hindsight and instead look at what remains of 2023. To make these predictions less precarious and avoid stylistic or aesthetic fixations, I will anchor these to larger cultural speculations. A political realignment to the left will see a further cultural momentum for greater diversity and representation, eventually eroding the persistent homogeneity in corporate brands and the unhelpful nexus between 'modern' (current) and 'modernity' (European sans). A strengthened sense and appreciation of local communities will encourage correspondingly localised typographic languages, and the long overdue customising of the tools of design to break the stranglehold of Adobe and Apple. Given that these are all positive speculations they could be viewed as much as hope as predictions.

Above:
Produced for the Nordic newspaper *Helsingin Sanomat*, the typeface structure is based on climate change data.

11
See <https://
www.itsnicethat.
com/features/
forward-thinking-how-
typography-can-make-
a-more-inclusive-
future-graphic-design-
040123?utm>.

12
A reference to both
Baz Luhrmann's
film *The Great
Gatsby* (2013)
and Jenny Holzer's
1989 installation
at the Solomon
R. Guggenheim
Museum, *Truisms,
Inflammatory
Essays, The Living
Series, Under a Rock,
Laments.*

13
Tyler Durden.

Bringing many of these strands together is an increasing 'inclusive thinking' among font developers. As the Tokyo-based designer Ray Masaki notes:

> Fonts are part of a cultural ecosystem that has ways of closing the doors for minority cultures. I did a quick search for *Grotesk* (sans) on a well-known font marketplace, which resulted in 5744 matches. After filtering the results for Vietnamese support, the results dropped to 241, roughly 4% of the original matches ... when you consider that a Vietnamese typographer only has access to 4% of the same tools, it places into perspective how typographic expression can be stifled by a lack of inclusive thinking.[11]

These reflections are based on a deep belief that typography plays a cultural role within our lived experiences. They reinforce that, instead of operating in some isolated void, letterforms are intrinsically connected to our cultural life—they are made *by* us and they *represent* us. Yet two forces continue to hinder this connection in the public mind: letterforms are so ubiquitous in our everyday environment as to render them seemingly invisible; typography's deep origins within the printing trade continue to depict them as an arcane, technical endeavour.

Yet there may be a strategy to counter these elements. The most powerful way to ensure letterforms are viewed as a creative expression parallel to other forms such as visual art, film, literature or performance is to refer to those very connections when we discuss typography. If cultural references and metaphors work, we need to use them. For example, to describe a piece of typography as '*Great Gatsby* meets Jenny Holzer' generates an immediate melding of 1920s decorative titling scrolling along a long LED strip[12], complementing its more technical description as an animated 'all caps modern grotesque with inline'. This opens up the possibilities of a more connective discourse, inviting a diversity of voices and references into the discussion of typography. It not only makes it more accessible to those not 'within' the field, but also reinforces the parallel, concurrent nature of ideas and creativity.

So perhaps Brad Pitt's character[13] in *Fight Club* had a point—that the first rule of typography is not to talk (internally) about typography but instead about how typography represents our lives and the times in which we live—our embrace of the transitory, our yearning for intimacy and safety, and our growing dissatisfaction with simple binaries. Looking across the past year in typography, 2022 may have just signalled the beginnings of this radically connected transformation.

• • •

Past

I'm more at ease
with the past
than I've been—

and as I write
it's up ahead
in clear sight—

if still a mystery
as it comes out
of white hills

unbidden
and through
shadowy trees

that shake
in autumn wind
leaves tender

as they fall
under a sky
of milk.

Simeon
Kronenberg

Simeon Kronenberg
has published poetry,
essays, reviews and
interviews in Australian
poetry journals and
anthologies. He has
also published widely
in the contemporary
visual arts. His first
poetry collection,
Distance (Pitt Street
Poetry), was published
in 2018.

Seismic Shifts

Shannon Burns
Childhood

TEXT PUBLISHING

Zowie
Douglas-
Kinghorn

Zowie Douglas-Kinghorn is a young writer living in Tasmania. Her essays and short stories have won the Scribe Nonfiction Prize and the Ultimo Prize. She is the previous editor of *Voiceworks*.

Childhood is a formative experience. And reading can be a transformative experience; between the lines and shelves of books there are spaces to inhabit and new ways to metamorphose. I found myself thinking about the contours of these experiences while reading Shannon Burns' *Childhood*, which felt invigorating and courageous, at times breathtaking in the execution. Burns has the past interacting with the present with graceful uncertainty, tracing rifts and voids in memory. Often in life-writing there is a sense of mining the past, processing and refining its contents into a narrative that seems irrevocable and crystal-clear, leading to conclusions that point to redemption. Instead, many of the events detailed in *Childhood* remain uncertain due to the nature of their origin.

Traumatic memories are often blurry and elusive—the memoir provides room for shapeshifting rather than closure, such that their exploration points to more possibilities. The narrator is never pulled from the crevasse he finds himself in, but its boundaries become tangible. In an interview with *Australian Book Review*, Burns refers to his younger self as 'the boy', almost a foreign body dislocated from his present self by his tumultuous, unforgiving childhood: 'No one is coming in to help him out or to rescue him in that moment, in those moments. I do feel a great distance from him. I think that I really left him behind, just like everyone else.'

The events in *Childhood* are rendered in fragments of experimental essay and memoir, as Burns, an academic and literary critic, documents his upbringing among Adelaide's underclass during the 1980s and 1990s. The book includes parts of previously published essays, but they have been reworked substantially to suit the broader context of the book, so a second reading reveals new facets. Burns retains a childlike perspective in the boy narrator without sacrificing the clarity of adulthood.

This is powerfully executed in depictions of the boy's mercurial parent: 'My mother's derangements coexist with her brand of love and tenderness. I know that she is on my side, even if she is incapable of mothering sanely, and even when her dysfunctions place me in danger.'

The fraught allegiance to a parent who continues to endanger the child is a tension that runs through the book from beginning to end. Towards *Childhood*'s ending, a story is included from a workshop for prospective foster carers: 'A young boy lies in a hospital bed, frightened and in pain. Burns cover forty per cent of his body. Someone doused him with alcohol, then set him on fire. He cries for his mother. His mother set him on fire.' The child cannot escape the entropic vortex, which also happens to be the source of life that sustains him. In foster care, these cadences remain suspended at a distance. Holding on to formative relationships is like holding a whirlpool in your hand, impossible safely to extricate yourself. As the author writes of his parents, '[They] embodied the storm.'

Throughout *Childhood*, details are necessarily blurred by fragmented memories, challenging the narrativisation of events; as well as referring to his past self as 'the boy', Burns often slips between 'he' and 'I', creating a dissociative effect. As the narrator is ferried between foster care and parents who cannot adequately care for him, the seismic shifts of each upheaval give the memoir a filmic quality— moments are encapsulated in movement rather than static description. Lines such as this reverberate: 'I experience it like a click of the fingers, a rapid movement during which the universe resets and the deepest things are recalibrated while the surface remains unchanged.' Moments of sweetness and humour sting and pulse against the sobering backdrop.

The world the author inhabits as a child is one of bewildering rules and pressures, shifting goalposts that simultaneously confuse and constrain him. The idea of adults being reliable or consistent is alien: 'As far as I can tell, adults are compelled to do the most improbable and destructive things imaginable, and it's their children's job to come to terms with this however they can.' The abuse from his primary caregivers is met with ambivalence from others around him, and the outcomes continue to veer between abandonment and violence. 'There were no good options,' Burns writes. Yet, rather than reducing to caricature those who failed to care for him, characters are illustrated with generosity and complexity. They are expressed with a poetic gravitas that seems to expand beyond their context, suggesting that abuse and trauma don't exist in a vacuum, but instead refract through generations. Of his grandmother, Burns notes: 'This is the image I carry with me into the future: a woman overburdened, under-resourced, ground down. Yet she smiles at me.'

Burns' prose style is lucid and forthright, with currents of eddying, lyrical rhythm. As I read I found myself reminded of Patti Smith's *Just Kids*, where the singer writes of her experiences of living on the street, of being hungry before work, of being ostracised due to her partner's sexually transmitted infection, of being mocked and then abandoned by nurses during the birth of the child she wasn't able to care for. In both books there is a sprawling sense of progression, without the narrative constraints of inevitability or linearity. Painful and joyful memories are interwoven so that traumatic experiences are not exceptionalised, nor are they diminished. In her memoir, Smith frequently references literature (poetry by Arthur Rimbaud and Vladimir Mayakovsky, to name two examples) as constant companions. Likewise, in *Childhood*, literature becomes a way of communicating with the world beyond its constraints. For Burns, his literary lodestars include James Joyce's *Ulysses*, Fyodor Dostoyevsky's *The Brothers Karamazov*, Thomas Hardy's *Jude the Obscure* and Greek plays, which 'offer a way of articulating truths he can't dislodge, softening them by making them unexceptional'. But these truths are framed by the act of reading itself, which often takes place in unbearable situations. Rather than being presented as a panacea or portal into class mobility, literature seems to offer a sense of belonging: for example, Burns writes that reading Russian literature feels like 'discovering his true parents or a lost homeland'.

Reading offers a window of reprieve in the last section of the book, 'Freedom', where Burns recounts working as a labourer at a recycling factory, alongside another job washing linen in an industrial laundry. Here, work is intense and degrading: 'Working with waste stains you. His eyes are focused on rubbish for more than forty hours each week. It seeps into his consciousness and colours his dreams.' These environments evoke a sense of taintedness that persists throughout the memoir: of being simultaneously burdened and abandoned by those around him, carrying the weight of hidden shame.

This is a world of outsiders, of those who have been thrown on the scrap heap. 'The welfare class has long been regarded as a kind of human waste,' Burns writes early on, a kind of foreshadowing for the rest of the memoir, noting that the process of reflection is not often afforded to lower-class writers. What is impressive about *Childhood* is its refusal to adhere to tropes and straightforward trajectories, which often undergird memoirs that centre traumatic experiences. The book eschews bootstrapping narratives while acknowledging the sacrifices made in order to survive childhood. Rather than through fighting or bravery, survival is achieved by withdrawal, trickery, the ability to forget, to change and discard old selves.

This process of metamorphosis suggests that childhood is something one transforms with rather than transcends, especially as attempts to improve his circumstances (working, going to school, seeking help from friends) repeatedly lead into traps of exploitation and betrayal. 'The abject misery of childhood is over,' *Childhood* concludes, yet it's not a 'happy ending'—we get the sense that this mark of abjection never truly fades. Here I was reminded of Julia Kristeva, who writes in *Powers of Horror: An Essay on Abjection* (1980):

> I expel myself, I spit myself out, I abject myself within the same motion through which 'I' claim to establish myself. That detail, perhaps an insignificant one, but one that they ferret out, emphasize, evaluate, that trifle turns me inside

out, guts sprawling; it is thus that they see that 'I' am in the process of becoming another at the expense of my own death.

Similarly, Burns writes that he had to shed his younger self in order to escape his circumstances; he describes writing as a process of 'shedding skins every other week'. As a child he practises imaginary self-erasure, fantasising about a world without himself in it. The world outside, in his imagination, is 'a saner, friendlier place than the one he knows', yet it continues to ensnare him as he grows.

Tragically, the boy attempts to take his own life as an adolescent by swallowing a mixture of cleaning agents and painkillers. He purges them, poisons that literally turn him inside out. Afterwards, 'whenever a severe bout of despair takes hold, the boy understands that the ghost of his former self is trying to reinhabit his body, and he expels him. Again and again.' He describes writing as a 'kind of exorcism that continually fails to expel the demon'. Books, meanwhile, become steady companions: 'Literature, only literature, can be trusted.' Reading becomes an act of introjection, absorbing voices and ideas from elsewhere, while the blank page becomes a vessel for containing loss and change. As Burns writes of his mother, 'I had to kill her off, for pragmatic reasons.'

This ongoing cadence of expulsion and flux imbues the book with a post-structuralist bent, which is, at least in the context of Australian literature, reminiscent of the work of Brian Castro,

particularly *Shanghai Dancing*, for its disorienting shifts in identity. In an academic essay, 'Arrested Motion and Future-Mourning: Hybridity and Creativity', Castro writes that 'Introjection is the process of accepting the wound, taking in loss, transforming it and translating it into something new.' These ideas are echoed in Burns' letter to his mother towards the end of *Childhood*, where Burns writes: 'I now know that we must liberate ourselves from our stories—our creators—by relentlessly rewriting and reshaping them. These are not mere repetitions, re-creations, recalibrations, new translations. The walls must crumble and be rebuilt, over and over.'

Throughout *Childhood*, literature becomes a way of navigating constant transformation and an unstable reality. Whether living between boarding houses, sleeping rough or in a car, in housing without electricity, the narrator Burns is always reading. In between shifts at the recycling factory, he describes reading from the light of a nearby train station: 'It feels impossible to save up for anything, so he accepts the situation and adapts to the new rhythm: Work, home, reading, work, home, reading.' This was where I recalled my own experiences reading a dog-eared copy of *Persuasion* at age fifteen, curled underneath a towel at a public park, where sprinklers came on at two each morning. *Childhood* shows how books can transport us to another world, where the future is not foreclosed.

•••

The Longing for Belonging

Elisa Shua Dusapin
The Pachinko Parlour

(trans. Aneesa Abbas Higgins)
SCRIBE

May
Ngo

May Ngo is a Teochew Chinese Cambodian Australian who lives in Prague. She is a former academic in anthropology, and is now a freelance writer and editor as well as founder of the Prague Writers Workshop. See <mayngo.net>.

'I walk over to the picture window, look down at the station; a central spine, four walkways fanning out like limbs. A lizard lying in wait.' One of the most striking things about *The Pachinko Parlour,* besides a style of writing that shines in quiet descriptions like this one, is how untethered and lonely all of its characters feel. Regardless of their centrality to the story, they seem to lead temporary, floating lives.

Claire is a Korean-Swiss woman who goes to visit her grandparents in Japan. She is about to turn 30 and spends the month of August in Tokyo, where they live, and in September plans to take her grandparents back to Korea for the first time since they left the country nearly 50 years ago. Her grandparents are zainichi, Koreans who migrated to Japan to escape the war that was unfolding in Korea in the 1950s. Young adults then, they are now nearly 90 years old and run the eponymous pachinko parlour.

Pachinko is a mechanical game similar to pinball or slot machines, where balls are loaded into machines by players who press a spring-loaded handle; the balls that fall into a catcher drop into a tray in front of the machine. The pachinko balls are then exchanged for items such as a bottle of water, chocolate bars or an electric razor, which are then swapped for money as a way of circumventing gambling laws. Koreans invented pachinko when they first came to Japan, and it is now still only those who are ethnically Korean who are exempted from the heavy tax imposed on these parlours. In a sense, the pachinko parlours are symbolic of the zainichi presence—an indication of an industriousness that comes with migrants setting themselves up in a new country, yet this association also silos them off from wider Japanese society. Today, pachinko parlours are still operated mostly by zainichi and their descendants.

Claire's grandparents' pachinko parlour, called Shiny, sits at the centre of the novel. Their apartment is located opposite it, and her grandfather, despite his age, goes to work there every day of the week. As the days pass, Claire notices the sandwich-board woman paid to advertise Shiny on the street, whose cry she can hear from their apartment: 'Shiny and bright, shiny and bright, shiny, Shiny every night.' She also notices Yuki, a pro player paid by her grandfather to stand outside Shiny each morning, solely to create the illusion of demand. As Claire continues to observe these characters, which include her grandparents, an unsettled atmosphere pervades. These turn up in some of the most unusual images in the novel—for example, when Claire and her grandmother wait for her grandfather to come home for dinner, she notes: 'On the table, our three bowls make the shape of a face. My grandparents', the two eyes; mine, the mouth, rounded as if in astonishment.'

While in Tokyo, Claire answers an ad to provide French tutoring to a student named Mieko. Mieko and her mother, Madame Ogawa, also known as Henriette, temporarily live in a former hotel. Mieko's father, a designer of Japan's shinkansen, has abandoned them. A sense of desolation surrounds Mieko and her mother's world, which is further enhanced by the description of their surrounding environment. Mieko's bedroom, a swimming pool, is described as follows:

'The floor of the pit slopes gently down to a drainage hole. In one corner sits a single bed ... Mieko sleeps here, for the time being.'

It is these descriptions of the external environment that give us a clue to the mental state of the characters. Elisa Shua Dusapin is able, through the excellent translation of Aneesa Abbas Higgins, to convey a sense of what each character may be feeling, not by focusing on their interiority but by reflecting it onto the environment around them. When Claire takes Mieko on a trip to Disneyland, she describes the parade thus:

> Ariel, Cinderella, Minnie Mouse, Mickey Mouse and Donald Duck file past, one by one, waving their arms in the air to the jolly music and lip-syncing the words to 'Happiness is Here' ... On every face the same tightly stretched grin, the same vacant happy look ...

This can be interpreted as a mirror image of the one-woman sandwich-board parade and its claim to shininess and brightness. In contrast to what the theme park is trying to cultivate, grimness instead suffuses the air at Disneyland—a raspberry tart is 'compact and rubbery-looking'.

Amid these disjunctions, the sense of loneliness is perhaps best conveyed through the characters' complications with language and communication; they frequently struggle with the limits of language/s. Claire, who was born and raised in Switzerland, used to be able to speak Korean when she was younger but lost most of it to French as she grew older. She had wanted to study Korean at university, but as it was not offered in Switzerland, took Japanese instead. The many layers of language that Dusapin's characters simultaneously inhabit and are dislocated from reflect the complexity of their biographies and migrations.

Her grandparents moved to Japan from Korea; Claire's mother left Japan to move to Switzerland; and Claire who was born there has come to Japan. While there, she speaks to her grandparents in a combination of simple English, basic Korean, gestures and facial expressions. Despite the fact that they are able to, they do not like speaking Japanese with her. Although the reason for this is never disclosed in the novel, we learn that it was illegal to speak Korean when Korea was under Japanese occupation. Claire's grandparents now live and speak in the occupier's language.

These knots show that national identity is not linear, and speaks to the nation-state as a mythical notion, particularly when so many people's lives incorporate many movements across geopolitical borders.

Yet ideas of national identity do exist, if only to satiate the universal human need for belonging, which often results in demands for demarcation between 'insider' and 'outsider' status. When Henriette asks Claire about her grandparents ('Couldn't they find work where they lived?'), it shows how her ignorance of Japanese history results in her inability to see Claire's grandparents as truly belonging in Japan, or having a reason to be there at all. At another point in the novel, Henriette says to Claire, 'You'll never really be able to speak Japanese, will you?' These remarks demonstrate how the rules for national belonging are extremely narrow when tied to arbitrary criteria such as linguistic ability and ethnicity. Through migration, forced or otherwise, it would be naïve to think that unbroken lines of heritage always exist in a nation.

Paradoxically, Henriette is fascinated with Switzerland and wants to send Mieko to school there. This obsession with Swiss culture becomes clear when we learn that Henriette herself went to university in Switzerland and is enamoured with it. Now a French teacher, her fascination with the country is symbolised by an eighteenth-century children's book she owns, *Heidi* by Johanna Spyri, about an orphan girl who lives with her grandfather in the Swiss Alps.

Later, Claire takes Mieko to Heidi's Village, a theme park just outside Tokyo, which Dusapin uses as a device to cast an inverted gaze on Western culture. At Heidi's Village, European culture is on display and othered, with replicas of a church, town hall and Alsatian-style houses. A log cabin is described as 'a single room with a wooden table on which artificial foods are arranged, with labels written in Japanese: "cheese", "meat", "bread"'.

It is refreshing to see this represented from the other side for once—this othering of Europe must be a mirror for how we in the West often view other cultures. Henriette's fascination with Switzerland demonstrates that although the nation-state demands complete belonging, most of us do not completely belong. Many people often have multiple allegiances, which can be erased or unrecognised in simplistic nationalist discourses. Even adherents can't maintain a strict national identity, for there are always other longings.

Unspoken longing, then, becomes the common thread that runs through the characters in *The Pachinko Parlour*—Claire's grandparents, Mieko, Henriette and Claire. Dusapin's skill is in her ability to vault these faltering longings into the air through the gestures of the characters and in the few words that they do say, so that it suffuses the atmosphere of the novel. It is an excellent reminder that for many of us, our longings remain unarticulated, sometimes even to ourselves. Higgins as translator does a remarkable job translating Dusapin's French into an English that is restrained and economical, yet pregnant with what is left unsaid.

In a scene towards the end of the novel, Mieko tells Claire that she hadn't communicated something clearly after a minor interaction: 'You didn't make yourself clear. [...] Calearo [...] Like your name. Calairo.' These scenes occur frequently throughout the novel—characters experience trouble with communication whether due to linguistic barriers, cultural differences or generational ones. It can be argued that this struggle to communicate crosses national borders and is a common human experience. If communication remains a conflict between humans, it highlights that language itself cannot be the sole basis of belonging.

All the characters in *The Pachinko Parlour*—whether ethnically Japanese, zainichi or biracial—display different ways of belonging and longing that don't rely on language, that often remain unarticulated because difficult to express; formed as they are by migrations, wars, geopolitical conflicts and interpersonal tragedies. Dusapin demonstrates that other ways of belonging can and do exist, where what is unsaid can be just as important and binding.

•••

In the Developing Solution

Janet Malcolm
Still Pictures

TEXT PUBLISHING

Jonno
Revanche

Jonno Revanche is
a writer and critic
originally from
Adelaide, currently
living in Sydney.

From the years 2010 to about 2016 I believed, and was proven right, in one way or another, that I could wield dominion over the petty narrative structure of my life by taking to it with a camera. Born into a generation that didn't yet take the existence of the internet as the status quo, watching it develop in much the same way we were developing. Images created almost solely to publish online were perfectly set to become representations of our lives—frames from what simultaneously *could have* been a life, but maybe wasn't; a sensorial view into a hollowed-out inner space. An imagined visual representation of the world, one which did not always require compatibility with the so-called 'real' world.

If life in the meantime was unremarkable, the biased view of a camera, smartphone or polaroid could become the means to understand extrinsic forms of information, and to translate something. You could omit unnecessary details in order for things to look more remarkable—even *become* that, by proxy. The viewfinder became a means to orient images in a highly selective way, and to transpose them into a garish, but not unbeautiful, sequence, lo-fi and desperately constrained. By being taxonomical about memory, you could be relieved of the expectation to know or say who you *truly were*. It involved a certain level of self-mythology, a little bit of delusion. The mission was to get one's preferred story back.

Like many people of my cohort, I've known the power and pitfalls of being devotionally, and sometimes casually, delusional. One fine evening I lay on my bed as I watched a video of Lil Nas X accepting a trophy at the iheartmusicawards, the rapper admitting that he had seen a TikTok professing the strengths of such a view: if he wasn't delusional about his prospects, he would never have made it to that stage. This Didionesque view on 'telling ourselves stories in order to live' is a sensibility that is, of course, not just a Gen Z principle, but an organising system of an unsatisfied life.

We live in a time when it's become increasingly clear that our economic systems are delusional and so are our leaders, as are their republic of followers. *Delusional*. There has never been a word so apt in describing postmodern neurosis, a necessary and often involuntary response to a future that won't arrive in the expected form. It's bathetic because most people know the feeling. Delusions have kept me occupied when the automation of the affective inner world grinds to a halt, leaving me with nothing to do but confect something in response—as if, to quote Adrienne Rich, the spectacles produced by capitalism 'carry the messages of those social relations and power mechanisms: our conditions are inevitable, that randomness prevails, that the only possible response is passive absorption and identification'. Yet if we were to believe that our values are worth upholding, we may have to delude ourselves into thinking otherwise—like microdosing insanity, if you will. Some, like Lil Nas X, are insistent on this as a methodology; others, such as Janet Malcolm, see it as a release, or something inevitable. 'The mystery of madness hangs over the world like a cry at night,' writes the collagist and journalist. 'The children of psychiatrists are no less crassly derisive about crazy people than the rest of the world.'

If there's someone who can be considered an expert on self-delusion, much less the delusions we tell of ourselves and others, that person would almost certainly be Janet Malcolm. In her long career she was critical of psychoanalysts, and critical enough of journalists to psychoanalyse them. The psychology that undergirds the best photographers received no quarter. Her being a photographer herself, and married to a psychoanalyst, is only tangential. No-one else could get away with the level of cheek she does, her navigational expertise and sometimes charmed distance. That remoteness troubled her.

She indicated as much in a 2010 essay for the *New York Review of Books*:[1] all her life she had tried writing some kind of autobiography, recoiling at her attempts more than once, binning what she had written and returning to the comfort zone of reportage where her involvement could be more concise, elegant, not too revealing. Like seeing yourself in the mirror of a fancy building where the light reveals just enough to appear flattering. Not too close. Not like passing a bathroom mirror and seeing all the undereye purple from having aged ten years in three. 'My efforts to make what I write interesting seem pitiful,' wrote Malcolm in that essay:

> My hands are tied, I feel. I cannot write about myself as I write about the people I have written about as a journalist. To these people I have been a kind of amanuensis: they

1
Janet Malcolm, 'Thoughts on Autobiography from an Abandoned Autobiography', *New York Review of Books*, <https://www.nybooks.com/online/2010/03/25/thoughts-on-autobiography-from-an-abandoned/>.

have dictated their stories to me and I have retold them.

She attempts to rehabilitate these feelings and their representations in *Still Pictures*, a collection of essays published posthumously about two years after her death in 2021. She makes this clear near the beginning of the book: 'Autobiography is a misnamed genre; memory speaks only some of its lines.' To bookend her life, she ventured to justify this claim by doing what she had once tried and failed to do, to finally write a memoirist's memoir. Instead she did what she had always done best.

The daughter of a psychiatrist who doted on her, she returned the favour (detailed in a chapter called—funnily enough—'Daddy') by enhancing, in herself, the features she loved in others. You get the feeling she would be telling on herself by admitting any disappointment in this larger-than-life figure; her mother, while present, lingers in Malcolm's life like a footnote. We find out why later, when she reveals that she is not yet ready to write about her mother. When she eventually does, the mention is fleeting, changing subject to focus on her grandmother. If her mother is present, and technically she is, her presence is not always strongly felt. Was this an influence? This is not the question she can decisively answer. As Malcolm says, 'parents have their own mythologies'. A writer smart enough to know that boundless freedom is not true freedom but a prison of infinite, potentially overwhelming options, Malcolm handles the oceanic possibilities of memory by using a time-honoured tool of discriminatory thinking: constraint.

Her miniatures, not quite essays in the traditional sense, more like an elongated caption or a 'snapshot', are juxtaposed only to select photographs. A Czech term Malcolm uses—*Skromnost*, the title of a chapter about a girl she loved in her adolescence—could substitute for such an ethos. A fulgid term, a little geological, sounding like the word for a crest of a mountain, it translates more literally into 'modesty' but acts as a synonym for resourcefulness. As a descriptor, it manages expectations of her form, which she identifies as 'a culture of conservation ... one of being satisfied with what comes our way'. Malcolm thereby follows the tools of the erotic toolkit without being necessarily sexual or sensual. After all, the erotic is as much about what's withheld as what's teased or revealed. Not quite scarcity or overabundance, but a balance between the two is what any good artist should be inclined to pursue. Using what's close at hand, admitting limits, not overcompensating. Or, in her words: 'Campbell's soup was not associated with Andy Warhol. We ate it.'

Although other critics have described her as almost frozen in time—impossible to imagine as young, yet not beholden to age—it's precisely that cheekiness that comes through in the vision of her younger self, making her countenance as an adult whole. In one essay, 'Slečna', about a teacher at a Czech school Malcolm attended as a child, she looks upon this younger self with a perennial view, of being 'part of the background of ordinary girls, who secretly loved and, unbeknownst to ourselves, were grateful for the safety of not being loved in return'. She shows affection for her inner child and those often ill-made early assumptions and their associated precocity and unknowingness, qualities some would hesitate to evoke even after years of practised self-compassion.

I note this if only to reiterate how useful such a stratagem may be when asking, what is the point of this? becomes too overbearing a task, obscuring the real point, about being the main character in your own life. When you're young, appearing often posed in photographs convinces you of your belonging there—if only because another's cruelty has yet to suggest otherwise. Delusion's foundations are maintained by parents and society; it's taken as fact that children would be unable to operate without any of those foundations, as if adults can readily do so. As Malcolm suggests, children are 'mythological minded creatures' who 'sense the strangeness of it all', and 'as we settle into earthly life, this sense fades'. The triumph of grand storytelling must eventually take its notice.

In *Still Pictures*, each segment of Malcolm's life is measured not by the obvious milestones, but through what seem like mini-reviews of an image, and then of the conditions that made up the respective photographs. A little funny to think about Malcolm looking at these deeply personal images and bitchily evaluating them as if they were professional photos taken by someone trained in portraiture rather than say, a family friend. But they are not just family photos; they do not even feel like vignettes. In a section called 'Camp Happyacres', about a childhood photo she barely remembers, she remarks that some hold 'no artistic merit and summons no memories'. Perhaps aware that picking and choosing the most interesting lines from one's autobiography is, in some way, 'dishonest', she is careful to include the uninteresting and the terrible. At no point, however, does the word 'trauma' appear.

Allegedly, the body keeps the score. This is to say nothing of the mind that lies within it. A process called Eye Movement Desensitisation Reprocessing requires one to enter a pseudo-hypnotic state to let the brain play catch up. Though it's not 'me' doing that work, in a sense, I feel the same exhaustion afterwards. I learn to do the rearranging, to follow self-reportage like a script, eschewing a diagnosis or even prescription. I don't leave feeling 'better' per se, but I do feel more clear-headed, like after I've cleaned my room—able to understand a version of the truth that isn't so loaded with emotion, hurt, disappointment, even shock, surprise, joy, belonging. Malcolm's writing, which is always at odds with the distance between the more apolitical nature of everyday phenomena and the charged bias of memory, is not dissimilar.

In 'Fred and Ella Traub', Malcolm is looking at an image of two family friends, in an effort to understand how even somewhat peripheral characters shape her. She has somewhat of a breakthrough; somewhere along the way her direction shifts. The chapter is no longer about a marriage of sentimental and material feeling. A line becomes the working ethos for the 'failed autobiography': 'I am struck by the character disparity between the dramatic character of the stories we hear and tell about people we know and the prosaic character of the people themselves.'

As I read, each time I suspect I'm getting closer to 'the real Janet', she turns on her heel and devotes a number of pages to what's seemingly unrelated. In one essay on Hugo Haas, whom she describes as 'the most minor of celebrities ... a Czech-Jewish actor who fled Prague in 1939', it appears to exist only to give an insight into her diaromic thinking, painting a 'fuller' picture of the personal, historical, cultural ephemera that surrounded her in some developmental stage yet complicates things further, leaving me to think: perfect! Trust the journalist who had spent her whole life thinking of conceit to reflect it at us. That very same 'us' is suspect, as we should be, imagined as the most unabashed of possible audiences, the most carnivorous of readers, a sensible interpretation likely influenced by her 1990 investigative book *The Journalist and the Murderer*. She thinks she might know better. This is why only the daughter of Czechoslovakian refugees could survive in the highly literal, arid world view of US journalism, being so good at it, so effectively un-American, that she would set the standards of US journalism for years to come. Even her parents could not exist in that all-encompassing supernatural landscape without losing some of

themselves to its logic—her father, she writes, had 'scarcely stepped off the boat before becoming a Dodgers fan'.

Janet Malcolm lived in an era when writers were seen to have the ability to function as journalists, rather than the other way round, as happens often in Australia; it is impossible to imagine her having written a book on 'vulnerability'. She had no wish to literalise her memories or formative experiences. Janet Malcolm would not do as Leigh Sales did, for example, writing a book about her elderly parent dying and selling it as some kind of trauma memoir. What I now think of as impossible to perform under the rigid, News Corp–style apologia that almost entirely constitutes 'Australian journalism' (right-wing or otherwise), the kind that has basically garnered no respect by any free-thinking person outside the continent, I can conceive of as understandable by (some) American standards. Instead, Malcolm found the middle. I have read many of her books, but it isn't until now, with evidence of her past suddenly clear, that I put two and two together. I guess it was my fault for not reading between the lines.

• • •

Only the Cry Remains

Stephanie LaCava
I Fear My Pain Interests You

VERSO

In *The Culture of Pain*, David B. Morris offers a provocation: if every era has its 'characteristic crime', then it has also its 'defining or representative illnesses'. And in the Anthropocene, we know pain better than ever. Thanks to increased understanding of how the nervous system works, it is now apparent that sensitisation is the source of chronic pain—with sensation arising in the brain rather than from ongoing physical stimulus. The solution to this is an approach that incorporates medicine, but also psycho-education and community support. This is to say: yes, pain hurts more when other stuff is painful too.

Alex
Gerrans

Alex Gerrans is from
Meanjin. She has
a Certificate III in
Horticulture.

We are in a pain crisis, at the level of the real and of its representations, with the increasing prevalence of chronic pain (a chicken-and-egg situation where mental health is also concerned). It is often the subject of the digital writer's first essay, the memoirist's first book, the poet's blasted landscape. Pain—physical, emotional, sexual—sells, if at most for a few hundred bucks a quarter. For young women writers, or emerging writers of marginalised identities, it seems there is an audience for nothing but their pain and trauma. In the face of this torrent of pain, of about-pain, through-pain, and pain's-impact-on, Stephanie LaCava asks: what if there were no pain?

In *I Fear My Pain Interests You*, LaCava's second novel, Margot Highsmith has known since childhood that she cannot feel pain. She has instead learned to perform it. Early in the book, she describes staging this mirroring as a kid: 'I kept pretending, taking cues from reactions. I mimicked the onlooker's level of intensity.'

Margot is the 20-something daughter of famous and neglectful musician types. Swaddled in a world of art-making, she naturally assumes the role of actress. But Margot is not a sympathetic figure; she is shielded by fame and wealth. When she needs somewhere to live, she gets her grandmother to mail her the keys and kick out the tenants—the family owns the whole building. She wears a golden choker that once belonged to Alice Coltrane, stolen from her family's possessions. Her grandmother, Josephine, orchestrates Margot's teen acting career down to what she may wear and how she is to conduct herself around a potential employer. Unsurprisingly, Josephine has access to the surveillance cameras where Margot lives.

As a young adult, Margot has a situationship with a man in his fifties she refers to only as 'the Director'. The Director tells her, before he leaves her without warning, that 'he'd deliberately created a life for himself that brought people to him'. Likewise, her father shares with young Margot his philosophy on relationships: 'When someone shows you who they are, you move away. Sever.' Like many parents who are not good caregivers, he has no concept that she is merely a child; when Margot's parents go on tour, she has no choice but to 'pretend the severing was my doing'.

The pain of women and gender non-conforming people is our culture's favourite ulcer, at once disregarded and feasted upon. Margot reflects on the way the Director has manipulated her, but it could just as easily be LaCava's perspective on withholding both easy message and scandalous detail in a novel where the protagonist is less actor than someone who is simply acted upon, a flickering point in a constellation of coercion and control. 'That was the important part about saying nothing,' Margot notes privately at some point in the novel, ostensibly about the Director's conduct, but really about far more than that. 'You could come back and fill in the gaps left unsaid [...] Only emptiness as evidence, a void with every version of the worst.'

In Jamie Loftus's podcast about Vladimir Nabokov's novel *Lolita*, there is an episode about online fan communities. It is one of the best 'histories of online' I've encountered, documenting online spaces such as LiveJournal, Tumblr and YouTube as they were burgeoning in the 2000s. On these platforms, many girls and women used them to express their idolisation and dissections of imagery from the two film adaptations of *Lolita*—the deeply disturbing 1997 version in particular, as embodied expertly by an adult Lana Del Rey at the beginning of her career—but they also reflected adroitly among themselves about the real-life exploitation they had experienced. This is perhaps not what some might imagine for an online community of young women, that they would move beyond aesthetic fandom to providing one another real space to be heard, and to inhabit the complicated vectors of woman-girl-victim-survivor. Margot could well be reflecting the experience of Dolores Haze—dolorous, pain—when she reminisces about the Director: 'This is the dangerous thing about a breakup with someone so much older and so much more accomplished when you are young, desirous of credibility and short on self-love: when he goes, he rips those little medals right off your chest and carries them away with him.'

The novel's epigraph is a quote taken from Reddit: 'Cows are not sentient beings.' This is not, as it first appears, an indication of the novel being 'about the internet'. There are no depictions of technology more advanced than the telephone. Margot sends a few texts, but that's about it. Instead, the epigraph sounds like a justification—if cows *aren't* sentient beings, then this is all the permission we need not to think about how they might suffer. It also gestures to the reality that others with more power than you make, as they obfuscate another's truth behind their own. Margot's grandmother maintains that there are 19 cows in a field nearby, though child Margot only ever counts nine. It is forever known as the field with 19 cows.

Later, Margot has her legacy admission to a fancy North American college informally revoked when someone snooping through her stuff finds drugs in her room. She flees the expulsion, and subsequently her rumination on the Director's abandonment, to a friend's family's property in rural Montana. This friend, Lucy, is another child of famous artists. We learn that there are film reels from the cancelled 1968 Cannes Film Festival in a studio out the back.

In Montana, Margot is very depressed. She gets to be depressed and disorganised in a way that readers with similar experiences will find joy in. But this is not the kind of malaise that involves wine in the bathtub and crying then back to a full-time job. It's months of not showering or eating, going outside in the cold with shirt on and underpants off. Of course, it goes without saying that someone without wealth's safety nets would not have the privilege of falling apart and staying undone so long or in such well-appointed surroundings; in a house stocked with enough supplies for months of solitude in the name of making art, Margot leaves only filth in the conversation pit.

Much of the novel involves Margot glacially exploring the enormous country house. '*What's behind painted door number eight?* Each day, I'd be allowed to crack open a cabinet. A lottery to occupy the what's next.' The house is isolated and slightly dilapidated from disuse, but filled with cultural artefacts. She serves her only guest, an alleged ex-trauma surgeon she meets after a cycling accident, a drink in an irradiated glass from Lucy's mother's collection. He becomes fascinated with her inability to feel physical pain. It turns out it was his area of specialty. He suggests experimenting with emotion and feeling to see if it affects her ability to feel pain. She is noncommittal. He does it anyway, but without telling her.

For those who understand the emotional turmoil that is naturally a spillover effect from abusive family relationships, there is a certain recognition that comes from seeing the hypervigilance it instils replicated in art. LaCava writes it well; the reader almost inhabits it. Child Margot says of her mother that it 'was easier at home when she wasn't around. I wouldn't have to wonder about her state of mind, worry I might say something to upset her, something apparently harmless; she was easily set off.' In her rural exile, Margot notices distantly that she has not heard from her mother in a long time.

Margot dials, and no-one answers. If she feels fear or trepidation about this, we don't hear about it. Anxiety is displaced onto the reader; the suspicion and fear are ours, and we gradually find out we are right. Meanwhile, Margot keeps having sex with the alleged ex-trauma surgeon, who lectures her about the significance of the old film reels from the shed. He enjoys the access fame provides to a world of representation in parallel with his vicarious enjoyment of Margot's inability to feel pain, which makes her his perfect subject.

LaCava's depiction of depression behaviour is particular, ritualistic and perversely delightful, if only because it's so true to life. Margot's 'standard evening meal' is a smashed frozen chocolate bar in a plastic bag, with Benadryl mixed in: 'On very bad days, grind them with the bottom of a can, my makeshift pestle. Then put them in the plastic bag, shaking it up so that the hot pink dust stuck to the white nougat.'

I Fear My Pain Interests You revolves around experience and experimentation. LaCava seems to suggest that these may bring harm, knowledge or both. Margot's family are 'obsessed with control', 'simultaneously harping on about resistance to state or corporate interference' even as they exert control over others. Margot sees her two terrible older lovers observe her, watches them watching themselves use her. They are both drawn to her proximity to her famous family, of course—she is not the point of

any of it. Although she knows well how and why they treat her as they do, she is deeply destabilised by the loss of these people anyway, whether by distance, abandonment or death. She doesn't know how to conduct relationships otherwise. But Margot does not wallow in feeling, she reports actions. Her parents' neglect, and other formative events alluded to be worse, are bloodless. Assaulted during sex but not feeling the pain of it, she notes only that her back is wet.

How we represent and anticipate pain has real effects on the treatment that people who are not considered a 'neutral' subject (i.e. white cisgender male) receive. In *The History of Pain*, Roselyne Rey notes that culture shapes how we anticipate women's experience of pain. Either they 'had a lower pain threshold than he and that, consequently, little notice should be taken of her cries and tears', or women are 'more used to suffering' and 'ultimately more resistant'. The most affecting details in LaCava's novel could be missed by a reader primed to look for physical violence alone, but as we now know, physical pain interstices with the emotional. Numbness is the star of the book, not Margot. Margot feels pain at the end, but it is not an epiphany or breakthrough or healing or development. It's just something that happens. No longer sensorially unusual, Margot withdraws from the reader's view—privacy, at last.

● ● ●

Opaque Gems

Elfie Shiosaki
Homecoming
MAGABALA BOOKS

Ruby Langford Ginibi
Don't Take Your Love to Town
PENGUIN (1988 EDITION)

> *How to punctuate an aesthetics of suffering, its vizibilization regime, with a counternarrative of NDN possibility? Hypothesis: be negative space.*
> —Billy-Ray Belcourt, 'Red Utopia'

Something has been bugging me lately, like a seed stuck in my teeth. In a review of Amy Thunig's *Tell Me Again* for this same publication, I considered the memoir alongside my own doubts about the utility of exposure: what compromises do I make to be seen, and how much control do I really have over whether I am seen or merely watched?

Ellen
O'Brien

Ellen O'Brien is a Guringai (Garigal/ Walkeloa) writer and editor living on Bidjigal land. Ellen's poetry and prose have been published in *Sydney Review of Books, Meanjin, Overland, Cordite* and *Rabbit*.

Like many Aboriginal writers, I'm well aware of the complex nature of publishing autobiographical writing, especially as I navigate the contradictions of describing my existence through a language and a form introduced by a colonising force. After all, our stories first appeared in written English in the diaries and letters of colonisers—told under a gaze that, as Mick Dodson so aptly put it, 'Aboriginality changed from being a daily practice to being a "problem to be solved".'[1]

Of course, there's a power in claiming and distorting the form and imbuing it with our own cultural practices, so that we can tell our stories in the way we want to. But I'm increasingly conscious of the fact that this telling is often mediated through a market of settler readers to whom publishers are catering—or rather

1
Mick Dodson, 'The Wentworth Lecture— The End in the Beginning: Re(de)fining Aboriginality', *Australian Aboriginal Studies*, no. 3, 1994, quoted in Anita Heiss, *Dhuuluu-Yala* [To Talk Straight]: *Publishing Indigenous Literature*, 2003, p. 21.

2
I want to note here that there are many definitional issues that cannot be addressed in this essay. Chiefly, an issue arises with defining the terms 'Black life-writing'. What is a 'Black life'? What is a 'Black voice'? How do we define these terms—and should we? For further discussion of these definitional issues, I point readers to Anita Heiss's *Dhuuluu-Yala* [To Talk Straight]: *Publishing Indigenous Literature*, particularly Part 1, and Osca Monaghan's chapter 'Milirrpum v Nabalco Pty Ltd (1971) 17 FLR 141', in Nicole Watson and Heather Douglas (eds), *Indigenous Legal Judgments: Bringing Indigenous Voices into Judicial Decision Making* [Routledge, 2021].

3
Oliver Reeson, 'A Communal Genre', *Sydney Review of Books*, 14 November 2022,

4
For other recent examples, see Lur Alghurabi, 'Against Memoir', *Sydney Review of Books*, 7 November 2022; Jeanine Leane, 'On the Power to Be Still', *Sydney Review of Books*, 3 August 2020; Amani Haydar, 'Writing from and Through Trauma', *Sydney Review of Books*, 29 August 2022; Imogen Dewey, 'Readers are hungry for stories about trauma. But what happens to the authors?', *Guardian Australia*, 19 November 2022; Karen Wyld, 'White Lenses, Blak Stories', *Meanjin*, 12 October 2021; and Cheryl O'Byrne, 'Aboriginal Women's Life-History Writing, Settler Reading and not Just Black and White', *Australian Literary Studies*, 37 (3) (2022).

5
Jeanine Leane, 'Cultural Rigour: First Nations Critical Culture', *Sydney Review of Books*, 7 February 2023.

6
Anne Brewster, *Reading Aboriginal Women's Life Stories* (2016).

the buyers, whether they read it or not. We are constantly being asked to explain, to help them understand. The irritation at my gums is caused by this kernel: how do these market desires shape my writing, and other writing by Blackfellas, particularly when we write about our lives?[2] How can our life-writing resist the settler desire to control and consume Black lives, while also operating within its remit?

There's a long history of critical interest in texts that deviate from what Oliver Reeson calls 'memoir of answers'[3]—the kind of life-writing that offers up too-simple solutions to the problems faced in one's life or is stapled firmly to a singular identity.[4] Yet when you look at the Black books that sell really well, you'll see that, outside of children's books, many bestsellers on this continent are life-writing by Blackfellas with a public profile—athletes, musicians and, increasingly, influencers. While this trend may reflect a more general inclination towards celebrity memoir, in the context of Black literature it provides an indication of how book sales hinge on having a coherent identity that a (settler) reader is familiar with, influencing the kind of work that publishers seek out. As Jeanine Leane has written, there's a kind of 'celebrity colonialism in publishing and marketing that seeks to sell a particular stereotype or brand of a minority group at a particular time and place at the expense of ignoring the diversity of stories and the life-experiences of the rest of the community'.[5]

When we trace the genesis of visible Black literature on the continent, life-writing was the genre that first sold big, starting with David Unaipon's *My Life*

Story (1954), and later Sally Morgan's *My Place* (1988).[6] From this point the genre proliferated, perhaps catalysed by the publication of the *Bringing Them Home* report in 1997, which included testimonies from many Blackfellas who were forcibly removed from their families as children. Arguably, for some (settler) readers, this was when Black lives became 'a human rights story',[7] something to be understood and learnt from, so that they could absolve themselves of their guilt. But to many Blackfellas it was just the latest iteration of a long-held settler stare. As Richard Bell puts it, Blackfellas are 'the most studied creatures on earth ... They are stuck so far up our arses that they on first name terms with sphincters, colons and any intestinal parasites.'[8]

This gaze has been compounded by an enthusiasm—largely fomented on the internet—for personal essays, which picked up around the mid 2010s when websites began accepting submissions in the 'true story' or 'it happened to me' genre. The writing was popular and hotly confessional, like talking to the worst one-upper you've ever met: Oh, you've seen some fucked-up things? Wait till you hear my story. Yet the choice to write such personal stories may have been dictated by market forces as much as it was an (albeit misplaced) desire for catharsis. As the popularity of these stories increased, publishers and editors seemed to seek out stories that would go viral for their provocative and salacious content rather than their artistic sensibilities. A similar kind of sensationalism was in vogue on video platforms too: 'Storytime' YouTubers racked up millions of views in 2016–17, often using melodramatic and misleading titles to elicit clicks on their videos. Similar storytelling styles have since appeared on TikTok, with trends such as #DramaticStory keeping viewers hooked.

This is the context we write in today, this realm of readers consuming Black life-writing perhaps because they want to *understand the native* and/or be titillated by a good ol' traumatic story. As Black writers, it feels as if we're supposed to be grateful for anyone even looking at our writing, despite the fact that we're being watched all the time. This is tempered by a false belief that by having eyes on our stories, we'll be able to change things. We're playing right into the hands of 'neoliberal politics, which [has] seen the incorporation and absorption of dissenting interests into the orthodoxies of power',[9] as Helen Fordham writes, while abandoning our own. It is in this context that I return to some texts written by Aboriginal women in recent and more distant times. I am curious to see how they evade the eyes of the (settler) audience, or refuse to perform to the assumptions of (settler) readers, and in doing so challenge what Maddee Clark has noted as 'the colonial ontological assertion of progress and nationhood'.[10]

• • •

I don't think it's a coincidence that many Black writers spend time in the silt of poetry. It's one of the few places where we can escape the constant call to explain our existence and dwell in opacity, holding 'that which cannot be reduced' in order to be understood, objectified and contained within the paradigms of Western thought.[11] This is not to say that

I am an advocate for the pure potential of poetry—I do not wish to wade into Western literature's odd demarcation and defence of genres—but that I acknowledge the benefits of a particular kind of poetic approach that appears in some Black life-writing, allowing us to acknowledge gaps and inconsistencies, and not rush to resolve them.

Noongar and Yawuru writer Elfie Shiosaki's *Homecoming* disrupts the 'I' from the get-go. Her poem 'Story Tree' weaves the voices of Shiosaki's great-grandmother, Olive, and Olive's father, Edward, with Shiosaki's own voice. The owner of the 'I' in the poem becomes lost over time such that it ceases to matter. The poem is followed by two pages of Edward's and Olive's handwriting, retraced by Shiosaki, deconstructing the illusion of authorial ownership or control. After all, we are all just tracing over someone else's story as we walk through our lives.

Homecoming does not adhere to linearity in its depiction of time and relations. In the poem 'Reborn', a grandmother becomes a child, and a granddaughter becomes a mother, a carer, a receptacle of safety: 'reborn / as mine / comfort you / always / just as / your own mother wanted to'. Likewise, in 'Legacy', the logics of Western time do not constrain or control comfort: 'that time / he broke me / into uncountable pieces / I dreamed / your strength / to piece myself / back together / bit by bit'.

Elsewhere, Shiosaki quotes her ancestor William Harris, who between 1904 and 1927 wrote words that still reverberate today: 'hundreds out back / die of starvation / without seeing / tasting / the miserable dole / they call Government

7
Kay Schaffer and Sidonie Smith, *Human Rights and Narrated Lives: The Ethics of Recognition*, 2004, pp. 94–5, quoted in O'Byrne, 'Aboriginal Women's Life-History Writing'.

8
Richard Bell, 'Bell's Theorem: Aboriginal Art—It's a White Thing!', November 2002.

9
Helen Fordham, 'The power of the personal: situating Aboriginal memoir in the Indigenous public sphere and as a mode of public intellectual intervention', *Media International Australia*, 168 (1) (2018), pp. 167–8.

10
Maddee Clark, 'Are We Queer? Reflections on "Peopling the Empty Mirror" Twenty Years On', in Dino Hodge (ed.), *Colouring the Rainbow: Blak Queer and Trans Perspectives*, 2015, p. 238.

11
Édouard Glissant, 'For Opacity', in *Poetics of Relation*, 1997, pp. 191–2.

12
Ien Ang, 'Comment on Felski's "The Doxa of Difference": The Uses of Incommensurability', *Signs*, 23 (1) (1997), pp. 57, 60.

13
Ruby Langford Ginibi, 'My Mob, My Self' in Kerry Reed-Gilbert (ed.), *The Strength of Us as Women: Black Women Speak* [Ginninderra Press, 2000], p. 17, quoted in Anita Heiss, *Dhuuluu-Yala* [To Talk Straight], p. 36.

Rations // can you wonder then / why the blacks don't love the whites?' Shiosaki acknowledges this ongoing connection, while also remaining cognisant of the distance between us and our ancestors, particularly if we only know them through words on a page in a colonial publication: 'I go along thinking / this is what you would do / or say / or how you would be / but I never really know / I'm only guessing.'

There's a pain in only being able to guess at our ancestors' subjectivities, when the world we inhabit can feel so far from theirs, and the recordings of their lives—at least in the colonial archive—tend to be patchy. Shiosaki acknowledges, however, that there's a joy to be found in being illegible and therefore free:

> I do not find this story about my great-grandmother enjoying the excitement of her youth in the archive. A story that makes my grandmother's eyes dance when she tells it to me. These are some of the years of my great-grandmother's life when she evaded the surveillance of the government. When she cannot be found in the archive.

• • •

Ruby Langford Ginibi's iconic *Don't Take Your Love to Town* disrupts the 'I' as well, albeit in a different way to Shiosaki, with a style that is beautifully descriptive at times and mercilessly blunt in others. There's a tender, even soothing familiarity in the way Langford Ginibi writes—she inhabits a somewhat blasé, emotionally distant persona while recounting the traumatic events of her life, reminiscent of many older Black women I know. This may be the only way to speak or write about certain 'areas of experience ... that are, in some fundamental way, unspeakable, expressable only circuitously'[12]—experiences such as the deaths of a number of children far too young, another child's escape from the hellish colonial prison system and subsequent persecution in the media, or the generational removal of Blackfellas from Country and kin, which Langford Ginibi expresses:

> I told him that was the home of our Bundjalung tribe, they were the Richmond and Clarence River tribe. The river ran into the ocean at Evan's Head and we were approaching the turn off when we saw a big sign saying BUNDJALUNG NATIONAL PARK and I told him he was now in my territory, and that he was the only one of my children who'd ever been there.

Here, Langford Ginibi is speaking to the reader, but not trying to prove or explain; for the most part, she is merely stating the facts of her existence, even if there was an affective drive behind her work. She has said:

> I thought if I wrote about my experiences as an Aboriginal person, it might give the other side, the 'white side', some idea of how hard it is to survive between the Black and white culture of Australia, and they might become less racist and paternalistic towards our people.[13]

It is understandable in the context of the 1980s, when terra nullius was still believed to be a legal fact, and the greater settler populace had not yet begun to reckon with the legacies of colonial violence on which their lives were built. Of more interest is another stated aim of Langford Ginibi's work, expressed at the end of *Don't Take Your Love to Town*: 'that we are here and will always be here'. She refuses the disappearance of Blackfellas into the annals of history, and reaffirms our sovereignty by simply stating her truth, alongside that of her peers and children:

> Halfway into the shop I saw myself in the long mirror, close up. Here was a pregnant woman with blistered hands like a man's, her face peeling like flaky pastry and black, she started black, but her arms were BLACK and the hair ginger. I stared at myself for a long time and then I bought a sleeveless cotton dress and went outside.

While *Don't Take Your Love to Town* centres Langford Ginibi's experience and is told from her perspective, it's not just *her* story—it's the story of Black women in a particular time and place, and the communities that surrounded them. As she says in the acknowledgements that introduce the book, her work is dedicated to her children and 'also to every black woman who's battled to raise a family and kept her sense of humour'. Much like Shiosaki in *Homecoming*, Langford Ginibi recognises the path she walked is not hers alone: 'We shared our fun, we were all in the same boat. No money no land no jobs no hope.'

By choosing not to diminish her flaws, Langford Ginibi ensures that she does not become a static individual, to be easily understood and consumed by outsiders. In one section, she accompanies her youngest son, Jeff, to a doctor's appointment, where the physician states that Jeff is experiencing stress-related chest pain after losing his job. Langford Ginibi narrates: 'I sat there thinking stress, at nineteen years old, how stupid.' Then, further down the page, she continues: 'I knew work wasn't the real problem. Jeff was three when the older kids died and didn't understand about death.'

This is not the only instance of multiplicity; Langford Ginibi also complicates the public narratives told about her other sons, Nob and David. Throughout the book she provides glimpses into an aspect of Nob that she, as his mother, knows, and which is made invisible by the mechanics of carceral punishment:

> Later Nob went out for my toiletries, Lo-Cal drink and flowers. He hired a TV, put a hundred dollars in my purse and every night he came to visit. His job at the picture framers was going well, he had a car and money in the bank. It really seemed like he'd survived gaol and would be OK. This was the first time Nob had been around to help when I was in trouble and I was glad to have him close ... On the day I was discharged, Nob came to pick me up and took me on a grand tour around the city. He realised I'd be stir-crazy from a month in hospital so we sat near the harbour.

While some may interpret this as Langford Ginibi constructing Nob as 'worthy' within a Western paradigm

14
Michael McGowan,
'Long Bay prisoners
spell out BLM after
guards use tear gas
to break up fight',
Guardian Australia,
8 June 2020.

(car, job, money in the bank), I am more inclined to think that Langford Ginibi was highlighting the values integral to her world view: the acts of care and attention by a child from whom she was so cruelly separated while he was incarcerated. There is a certain joy here that sits alongside the devastating circumstances of their relationship.

A subversion of linear time is also apparent in *Don't Take Your Love to Town*. Langford Ginibi tells her story mostly chronologically, but at times deviates from linearity to provide details that must be immediately recognised. Speaking of her father, Langford Ginibi writes:

> Near the end of his time at this job, he had a coronary, and he died of a heart attack at the age of forty-four. He was a man who worked too hard, had a lot of stress, and who lifted the anvil for white men to win bets.
> But at this time we thought he would live forever.

Elsewhere, Langford Ginibi recounts Nob's experience of police violence in 1973, and protests held in response by those detained in Bathurst Gaol—a scene that is gut-wrenchingly contemporary, reminding me of a Black Lives Matter protest that occurred at Long Bay in 2020.[14] Much like the quotes from Shiosaki's ancestor William Harris, reading Langford Ginibi's account in 2023 disrupts the settler-colonial fantasy of progress for Blackfellas in colonial systems predicated upon our erasure. Without the destruction of the colony and the rightful return of Country to Blackfellas, reverberations will surely continue.

• • •

What is the role of the Black writer in contemporary times? We're no longer in the same place as Langford Ginibi, where there was a hope that if only settlers could hear our stories, then perhaps meaningful change would follow. Terra nullius was eventually proven to be a work of fiction, yet our sovereignty is still challenged in big and small ways. There have been royal commissions upon royal commissions, and yet deaths in custody and police brutality are ongoing issues. Our stories are now out there winning awards. Settlers at the very least 'acknowledge' our presence, sometimes even acknowledge the problems created by *their* presence, even if they don't know what to do with it.

The central issue appears to be one of power. If you have ever been in a position of relative powerlessness, trying to explain to a doctor or a cop or a parking inspector or a judge why you deserve to be seen as human, you understand that the act of explaining yourself as an appeal to power is rarely successful and often draining, if not outright humiliating. For Black writers, then, exposing so much of ourselves in this dynamic—where most publishers and readers are settlers—makes it near impossible for such exposition to be anything but an act of contortion, as we appeal to a greater power to understand us within the neat lines of their world. You see how I am doing this now.

What Shiosaki and Langford Ginibi offer us, as Black writers, are alternative ways to write about our lives and selves outside the grasp of settler understanding, and therefore decentre the power of the settler public. It's an 'if you know, you know' poetics. These authors show us it's possible to write without trying to fit predetermined narratives of Blackness, or relegating ourselves to the role of 'negotiator and interpreter'[15]—the same roles some of our ancestors were forced to play. It's possible to write in a way that explores the gaps, the differences and complexities of our existences in the settler colony, and how our journeys overlap. It's possible to write without striving for legibility in a system that wants to write us out of it, and instead centre our sovereignty and our collective power. In this it might serve us to return to the words of Driftpile Cree poet Billy-Ray Belcourt:

> Identity
> dies hard
> and
> the world is not so simple
> not always realistic.
> Worldviews
> are
> women
> who lived their whole life
> in archives
> examined and reexamined.
> What is now needed is more
> no.[16]

• • •

15
Helen Fordham, 'The power of the personal: situating Aboriginal memoir in the Indigenous public sphere and as a mode of public intellectual intervention', *Media International Australia*, 168 (1) (2018), pp. 167, 173.

16 Billy-Ray Belcourt, 'Flesh', in *NDN Coping Mechanisms: Notes from the Field*, [House of Anansi Press, 2019], p. 57.

Support Australia's literary culture and become a *Meanjin* subscriber.